Digital futures

Strategies for the information age

Digital futures
Strategies for the information age

Marilyn Deegan and Simon Tanner

NEAL-SCHUMAN PUBLISHERS INC.
NEW YORK
IN ASSOCIATION WITH
LIBRARY ASSOCIATION PUBLISHING, LONDON

Published by
Neal-Schuman Publishers, Inc.
100 Varick Street
New York, NY 10013

© Marilyn Deegan and Simon Tanner 2002

Library of Congress Cataloging-in-Publication Data is available.
LCCN 2001056296

ISBN 1-55570-437-9

Published simultanously with Library Association Publishing, London.
Printed and made in Great Britain.

Contents

Acknowledgements

No work is ever the product of only its author or authors. Rather, it grows out of a mass of influences, professional and personal, written and unwritten. Many people have been important to us in the formulation of the ideas that have gone into this book; this is our opportunity to show our appreciation publicly.

First of all, our greatest thanks are due to Elisa Mason who did a great deal of the primary research for the book. She visited libraries, trawled the internet and hunted down obscure and half-remembered references with tenacity. Her contribution has been invaluable to us: we would never have managed without her.

A number of friends and colleagues gave us very specific help in reading drafts of chapters, discussing ideas and sending us useful references. Others have been important to us in helping to shape our thinking over many years, and in contributing to our professional lives in countless different ways. In particular, our present colleagues at the Universities of Hertfordshire and Oxford have been of enormous help. We would like to acknowledge especially Tim Ayers, Ellen Bahr, Bruce Barker-Benfield, Mike Cave, Stephen Chapman, Gillian Evison, Lee Ellen Friedland, John Garrett, Jessie Hey, Hanne Marie Kværndrup, Alan Lock, Norbert Lossau, Di Martin, Julie Mitchell, Charles Oppenheim, David Price, Kathryn Ray, Oya Reiger, Brian Robinson, Miriam Selzer, Rebecca Sholes, Michael Shoolbred, Harold Short, Joanna Soedring, Joanne Lomax Smith, Mackenzie Smith, Thornton Staples, Kathryn Sutherland and Bill Worthington.

All the partners in the Forced Migration Online team throughout the world and the Malibu hybrid library teams at the Universities of Oxford and Southampton and at King's College, London, have also been influential, as have the METAe Metadata Engine partners, Cimtech, the Pilkington Library and DILS at Loughborough University and Denmark's Electronic Research Library, DEF.

We'd like to thank Helen Carley and her colleagues at Library Association Publishing for their meticulous editing and for their unfailing support and patience. Finally, our most heartfelt thanks are due to Jane Turner and Louise Heinink who have lived with us through the writing of this for many months, and who showed such tolerance and forbearance while we were so abstracted. We dedicate the book to Jane and Louise.

Introduction

This book seeks to examine the strategic issues in realizing a digital future for libraries and librarians. The rapid expansion of the internet and of electronic communications means that the gathering, storage and transmission of information present fresh challenges to those responsible for preserving the cultural memory of society. Given the magnitude of the information explosion, it would be all too easy to view the future of libraries, and of librarians, as purely determined by technology. We prefer to take a holistic view of the digital domain, and try to situate new developments in their social, cultural and historic contexts. We do not advocate technology for its own sake, and we hope this book maps the transition of libraries into the wired world as evolution not revolution.

The authors are conscious that a single work cannot cover in any great depth all the issues facing librarians and other information workers as they engage in digital activities. This book is therefore planned as the first in a series of *Digital Futures* volumes, each of which will deal in more detail with a major topic in digital library research and development. Anyone interested in contributing to such a series is invited to contact the authors at **marilyn.deegan@qeh.ox. ac.uk** and **s.g.tanner@herts.ac.uk**.

We have assumed little prior knowledge in our audience, rather an interest and concern about where cultural institutions are headed in the changing world of information and communication. However, we have included some technical explanation to aid a basic understanding of the fundamental issues. Because this field gives rise to a great deal of new specialist terminology, we have provided a glossary of key terms, acronyms and abbreviations.

The chapters follow a logical progression from creating and collecting digital content through to its delivery and management for the long term. They can, however, be read and understood individually. We look at how librarians and information workers can locate the electronic resources most relevant to the needs of their users, integrate these resources into the infrastructure of their institutions, manage the necessary technology, and anticipate future trends in the digital age. This book is intended to be most useful to librarians, archivists and information managers in libraries and information organizations of all types: educational, public and corporate. We hope that students in a number of disciplines will find the ideas and concepts described here illuminating. The volume will also appeal to others in the information and culture business: museum curators, scholars who are interested in digital culture, the media, technologists and web content providers.

In writing this book we draw upon a combined experience of building, using and managing technology in information and library contexts that amounts to 25 years or more. Over time we have accrued many ideas about this wired world in which we live, and through our friendship and professional relationship with each other we have shared, discussed, implemented and debated our ideas. Our professional roles have led both of us to spend a lot of time in other people's libraries, in the UK and throughout the world. These libraries range across all the sectors: national, academic, public, government, corporate, museum and archive. It has been our privilege to work with rare and fragile materials, unique works of art and literature, and innovative information resources within some of the greatest libraries in the world. It has also been our privilege to work with dedicated and passionate librarians striving to preserve and make accessible the very foundation stones of human civilization.

It is no accident that a lapsed scholar and a lapsed librarian author this book. We continue to contribute to our professions and communities, we still work in these areas and think of ourselves in terms of these backgrounds. The large difference is that what we *do* every day is not constrained by the traditional boundaries of our backgrounds. We increasingly meet people who transcend traditional professional boundaries, and this shift in working practices and career paths is reflected in society as a whole and in the content of this book. We hope our audiences have a similarly inclusive vision and we have written this book for them.

1

Digital futures in current contexts

In the paper-based environment, libraries and information centres have been the central links in the information chain. We are, however, in the midst of a profound transition resulting from the digitization of information, and all components of the information chain are in a state of flux. The parts played by authors, publishers, libraries and other information service providers are changing, and in many instances the boundaries which have demarcated the roles of these players have become blurred.

(Dorner, 2000, 15)

Just as the method of recording human progress shifted from the quill to the printing press 500 years ago, so is it now shifting from print to digital form. The library will continue to provide books and the printed record, but must now also deliver texts, images, and sounds to the personal computers of students, faculty and the public.

(Karin Wittenborg, **www.lib.virginia.edu/dlbackstage/services.html**)

Introduction

The worlds of both communication and the production of information are changing rapidly, and it is the convergence of these, and the consequent huge impact on libraries and library practice, that this book aims to address. In this introductory section, we examine the background changes in communication and information over the last 50 years, and the concomitant changes in libraries, as well as the changes in the publishing industry. We give some basic technical definitions in order to elucidate some of the terms used elsewhere in the book.

This chapter will discuss the following issues:

- the information revolution in a wired world
- information explosion
- the nature of digital data
- storage and transmission of digital data
- developments in digital data creation
- printing and publishing
- changes in libraries
- digital libraries
- automating information retrieval
- the world wide web
- why the world wide web is not a digital library
- changing names for managing content
- unresolved issues.

Information revolution in a wired world

Over the last 50 years, the computer and communications revolution has changed radically the way many organizations do their business. According to Charles Jonscher (2000), we are now living in a wired world. With old-style twisted pair telephone wiring, co-axial cable, and optical fibre there are physical communication networks almost everywhere on the globe, and the places these do not reach can be covered by satellite. Business and military communication needs have promoted most of the telecommunications developments, and the rapid growth in mobile telephony, fax and e-mail have transformed business and financial transactions. But the greatest recent advance in communications technology was initially an academic development: the world wide web was invented by Tim Berners-Lee in the late 1980s in order to improve the storage and currency of electronic documents at CERN, the European particle physics laboratory. The rest, as they say, is history. But history has much to tell us about technological change and its effects on human society, which we would do well to note as a background to the changes affecting libraries that we are considering here. Humanity has always used technology. The wheel is technology, a flint to light a fire is technology, anything that has been developed to do work so that human effort is easier is technology. In recent years, information and communication technologies have generally been referred to as 'new' or 'high' technologies – they are highly visible, and have not yet, despite their pervasiveness, become part of the natural infrastructure of society which, according to Borgman is invisible when it functions adequately and only becomes visible upon breakdown (2000, 19–20). 'Technology', as the computer scientist Bran Ferren memorably defined it, 'is stuff that doesn't work yet' (Adams, 1999). Interestingly, Jonscher sees the development of information and communication technologies as a 'curious turn' that society took four decades ago away from mechanical and engineering developments and into microelectronics, giving birth to the digital age (2000, 4).

The influence of new technologies on future developments is often wildly miscalculated, and human ingenuity is such that tools are often employed for purposes other than those for which they were designed. To give some examples, in 1876 Western Union suggested that the telephone had too many shortcomings to be seriously considered as a means of communication and was inherently of no value to them and in 1943, Thomas Watson, chairman of IBM, opined that there would probably be a world market for around five computers. More recently, Bill Gates, whose life work seems to be aimed at proving Watson wrong, famously stated that he couldn't imagine that anyone would need more than 640K of memory in their computer. The internet was developed in the 1960s for a very restricted and specific purpose: the maintenance of communications in the USA in the event of a Soviet invasion: for Castells, it was 'the electronic equivalent of the Maoist tactics of the dispersal of guerrilla forces around a vast territory to counter an enemy's might with versatility and knowledge of terrain' (1996, 6). Who could have predicted the myriad uses it would be put to within less than three decades?

On the other hand, huge social changes have been predicted, mediated by technologies, which have not come about: supersonic aircraft, for instance, which in the 1970s, when Concorde was first designed, were supposed to revolutionize the speed of global travel, have remained a rare and expensive luxury. The infrastructure cost of supersonic flight has remained very high, while the cost of computing is reducing to that of television ownership owing to the social imperatives driving the technology

cost down. As Castells points out, 'technology does not determine society
. . . technology is society and society cannot be understood or represented
without its technological tools' (1996, 5). Society also has to be ready, both
technically and psychologically, for major technological change to happen.
For instance, all the underlying theories and algorithms for the stored-
program computer were available by the 1850s, but mechanical limitations of the time meant that it could not be built until almost 100 years
later (Swade, 2000). Progress is not a matter of smooth linear change, but
'a series of stable states, punctuated at rare intervals by major events that
occur with great rapidity and help to establish the next stable era' (Gould,
1980, 226), a process characterized by Kuhn as 'paradigm shifts' (1970).
Gleick (2000) suggests that these changes are happening with greater
rapidity than ever before, which is probably why we currently feel change
as a process of constant acceleration.

With the digital revolution, data and information can now be transmitted to all corners of the world, and that is significant for almost all
humanity, and it is significant for libraries. But though many predict that
we are reaching a halcyon period of cheap access for all, there are still
political, cultural and financial issues that prevent this in many strata of
society and many parts of the world. The digital divide exists and could
further disadvantage the poor, the under-educated and those in developing countries as the better-off, the better educated and the economi-
cally developed race ahead into the digital future. Views on the
democratizing nature of electronic networks vary wildly and we need to
be cautious in our evaluation of these: for some we are on the verge of
global utopia, an 'age of optimism' (Negroponte, 1995, 227), for others
the internet 'continues to remain an expensive western toy' in a world
where less than 2% of the population is connected to it (with London
having more internet accounts than the whole of Africa) and where 80%
of the population has never even made a telephone call (Taylor, 2001,
35). In southern Africa, 'for the ordinary citizens, who are in the majority, the financing of bread and butter needs takes a precedence over
information' and the levels of charging 'impose a form of censorship'
(Muswazi, 2000, 78). Indeed, we are more likely to see information equal-
ity being promoted by libraries than by other information organizations,
as libraries, especially public libraries, have been the great information
levellers for centuries, providing more (generally free) information to

their users than the latter could ever have by purchasing it. Libraries need to continue to provide this role in the digital age, even though many users are questioning the need for libraries and librarians in an era of massive free information resources available at the click of a mouse button. However, as we demonstrate in this volume, the information management skills of trained professionals are needed more than ever as we are overwhelmed by data of questionable provenance and unknown value. As Borgman (2000, 194) so cogently points out:

> The claim that the Internet will replace libraries often is based on questionable assumptions. Three common misconceptions are that all useful information exists somewhere on the Internet, that information is available without cost, and that it can be found by anyone willing to spend enough time searching for it.

Implicit throughout this book is a refutation of all three of these misconceptions.

Information explosion

We feel as if there is more information around us and that information overload is a reality, but how much unique information is actually created each year and is it new or are we just being drowned in copies? Studies by Lyman and Varian at the University of California at Berkeley (available at **www.sims.berkeley.edu/research/projects/how-much-info/**) estimate that the world produces about 1.5 billion gigabytes of unique information per year. Apparently this equates to roughly 250 megabytes for every man, woman and child on Earth or the equivalent textual content of 250 books each. The study investigated the amount of *new* information stored in the four storage media (print, optical, film and magnetic), and asked how much storage would be required if it were all presented in digital form. Of course, this study does not tell us whether there is actually more information now than ten or 20 years ago although that seems extremely likely. We have to look to a tightly controlled intellectual community to see in more human terms the actuality of the information explosion as described in this insight into chemistry:

this year chemists will publish a hundred times as many papers than in 1901, when van't Hoff received the first chemistry Nobel prize.

(Schummer, 1999)

In 1961 the doubling period for the total amount of information in science was between 12 and 15 years (Price, 1961), by 1990 it was down to every six years (Braukmann and Pedras, 1990). Now some think it is as short as one to two years or less, although proving this for science is difficult now the internet is a major publishing point. The information explosion can also be measured in economic terms:

America's industrial output weighs about the same as it did 100 years ago, even though real GDP (Gross Domestic Product) is 20 times higher, reflecting the higher knowledge content of contemporary goods and services.

(Cronin, 1998, 3)

This explosion in information, services and resources, whether appropriate to the users' needs or not, consumes attention. Information has to be selected or discarded, read or not read, but it cannot readily be ignored. The actual downside of the information explosion is a deficit of attention, known more popularly as 'information overload'.

The nature of digital data

In order to understand the changes taking place in our information activities, it is vital to understand some of the underlying structures and principles of the digital world. All digital data, from whatever original it derives, has the same underlying structure, that of the 'bit' or the BInary digiT. A bit is an electronic impulse that can be represented by two states, 'on' or 'off', also written as '1' or '0'. A 'byte' consists of eight bits, and one byte represents one alphanumeric character. A ten-letter word, for example, would be ten bytes. Bits and bytes are linked together in chains of millions of electronic impulses; this is known as the 'bit stream'. A 'kilobyte' is 1024 bytes, and a 'megabyte' 1024 kilobytes. Digital images are represented by 'pixels' or picture elements – dots on the computer screen or printed on paper. Pixels can carry a range of values, but at the simplest level, one pixel equals one bit, and is represented in binary form as 'black' (off) or 'white' (on). Images captured at this level are 'bi-tonal' – pure black and white. Images can also be represented as eight-bit images, which have 256 shades of either grey or colour, and 24-bit images, which have millions of colours – more than the eye can distinguish. The number of bits chosen to represent each pixel is known as the 'bit depth', and devices capable of displaying and printing images at high bit depths (36 or 48 bits) are now emerging.

Bit depth is the number of bits per pixel, 'resolution' is the number of pixels (or printed dots) per inch, known as ppi or dpi. The higher the resolution, the finer the texture of a digital image. The resolution of most computer screens is generally in the range of 75 to 150 pixels per inch. This is adequate for display purposes (unless the image needs to be enlarged on-screen to show fine detail), but visual content at this resolution is inadequate for printing (especially in colour), though images of black and white printed text or line art are often acceptable. High-density images of library originals (manuscripts, photographs, etc.) need to be captured in the range 300–600 ppi for print-quality output.

Almost any kind of information can be represented in these seemingly simple structures, as patterns of the most intricate complexity can be built up. Most primary sources held in libraries and other cultural institutions are capable of digital representation (anything that can be photographed can be digitized, though there are issues with the faithful representation of 3-D objects). When digital they are susceptible to manipulation, interrogation, transmission and cross-linking in ways that are beyond the capacity of analogue media. Creating an electronic photocopy of a plain page of text is not a sophisticated process compared with analogue technologies, but being able to then automatically recognize all the alphanumeric characters it contains, plus the structural layout and metadata elements, is sophisticated, and is only achievable in a digital environment. Alphanumeric symbols are the easiest objects to represent in digital form, and digital text has been around for as long as there have been stored-program computers. These symbols are also the most compact to store, an important factor at a time when capacity was limited and expensive. Early computers were good at processing symbols rapidly, but input, output and display of data were difficult. Input was via punched cards or tapes, output through printers or plotters with limited capabilities, and display was limited to ASCII symbols, displayed line by line, often with only upper case available. Special fonts and characters were fearsomely difficult to represent, though some early pioneers made creative use of graph plotters for non-Roman character sets.

The storage and transmission of digital data

Early digital character representations were sparse in their storage needs, and early computer programs economical in their need for processing power. Storage and power have been increasing steadily over the past three decades, with the capacity of the processor chip doubling approximately every 24 months, much to the surprise of many experts (Jonscher, 2000, 111–12), and although this trend cannot continue indefinitely for physical reasons, the immediate future will see further startling increases in computing speed. Increases in network capacity (also known as bandwidth) have also been huge, but rather less linear and predictable than increases in power because there are different factors that come into play here. Bandwidth is delivered through copper wiring (the installed telephone base still in most of the world) which has a relatively low capacity, through optical fibre cables, which have almost infinite capacity (Negroponte, 1995, 23), and through wireless transmission, which has variable capacity, given that portions of the airwaves have to be assigned with care to avoid interference of signals. Adding bandwidth can mean a process of digging up roads and laying cables to replace earlier wiring, a hugely expensive procedure, which must be funded by many different commercial and public bodies in most countries. Storage capabilities for digital data have also been growing exponentially: in the mid-1980s a 20Mb hard drive was regarded as massive storage, and 256Kb of RAM as sufficient memory. Now even laptop computers come supplied with 20Gb hard drives and 256Mb of RAM, which is 1000 times the capacity of machines of less than 20 years ago. But we need all this power and capacity to deal with the data that is coming our way in many media formats, as digital text, digital images, digital video and digital sound. An average page of digital text takes around 20Kb of storage space, which means that there can be 32,500 pages stored on an average 650Mb CD-ROM. High-quality professional digital cameras and scanners can potentially capture digital reproductions of the original in such detail as to require at least 300Mb of storage space, allowing just two images to be stored on an average CD-ROM, and moving images and sound are even more hungry of space and power, though there are advantages in data compression that are helping to reduce the load. Data compression comes in two forms: 'lossless', which means that the compressed file loses no information in the compression and decompression processes, and 'lossy', where there is data loss in the processes. Lossy compression gives more compact results than lossless, resulting in smaller files to store or transport, but the derived images are of a lower quality – which may not matter if the files are for web delivery, but which is unacceptable for high-quality printing or long-term storage.

Increase of capacity and power in any of the component areas of digital processing and transmission are not just linear benefits: the relationship between demand and supply is complex and paradoxical. For example, a desktop computer would probably give excellent service for eight to ten years, but is likely to be replaced in most professional or even personal environments in two to four years (with four years being an average write-off period in many public and private institutions). The resale value is likely to be very low, if there is any value left in the machine at all. This is because new developments render hardware and software obsolete so rapidly. Compare this with other everyday machinery, the car for instance. There are people who change their cars every couple of years, for a variety of reasons to do with reliability, economy or prestige, but rarely because a particular model has become obsolete and will not run on certain roads, and there is certainly considerable resale value left in most cars. In the world of information supply, it is difficult to know whether the advances are driven by user demand or by the commercial imperatives of the suppliers of information and the suppliers of technology. Libraries are caught in the middle, having to purchase and provide ever more expensive and technologically demanding content to a wider range of users across a greater demographic and geographic area.

Developments in digital data creation

Digital text

Despite the difficulties of the early technology, some scholars recognized the value of the computational manipulation of textual materials immediately. Text had to be painstakingly entered on punched cards or tape, but the benefits appeared so great in terms of retrieval and analysis that they persisted. Father Roberto Busa, for instance, formulated the idea of auto-mated linguistic analysis of text in the years 1942–6, and started working with IBM in New York in 1947. He produced more than six million punched cards for his edition of the works of Thomas Aquinas, and in 1992 the first edition of his CD-ROM was published (Busa, 1998). The clas-sical scholar Anthony Kenny wrote a book on statistics in the early 1980s so that other scholars could learn to manipulate electronic text for schol-arly purposes (Kenny, 1982). In the 1980s a new technology appeared in the form of the Kurzweil Data Entry Machine (KDEM), which was devel-oped to provide texts for the blind. It used optical character recognition (OCR) to create electronic text for printing on Braille printers or (eventu-ally) conversion to sound using text-to-speech processing. The KDEM was extremely expensive (in the tens of thousands of dollars), but it could be trained to recognize different typefaces and fonts, and it was relatively accurate – probably as accurate as modern OCR packages. Other text conversion needs could, of course, be satisfied using the KDEM, and large corpora of digital text were created for many purposes. The Oxford Text Archive, for instance, gathered many of the texts that it still supplies as output from the KDEM service operated nationally by Oxford University until the early 1990s, and these have been used all over the world as the basis for digital text collections, at the Universities of Michigan and Virginia in the USA, for instance. Digital text is now everywhere, as output from word-processors, publishers and OCR engines. Interestingly, OCR is faster and cheaper than it was in the 1980s, but it is still not as accurate as it needs to be to replace rekeying and typesetting, especially if the materi-als are pre-20th century. Many library projects use OCR to capture bodies of printed text; others, where the text is too difficult or a higher level of accuracy is needed, use rekeying. However, there are some new develop-ments in the processing of text that greatly improve retrieval from inaccu-rate OCR; these are discussed in Chapter 2 'Why digitize?'.

For maximum usefulness, digital text needs more than representations of alphanumeric symbols on the printed page; it also needs metadata to record other information about the textual object from which it derived. Markup languages such as the Standard Generalized Markup Language (SGML), described in more detail in Chapter 5 'Resource discovery, description and use', define textual metadata and specify complex schemas of standard metadata tags to inform all the processes to which digital text might be subject: description, retrieval, preservation, print output, and so on.

Hypertext, multimedia and digital images

While early document-processing technologies generally operated on strings of linear text, the possibilities of hypertextual linking within documents were recognized too, though this was initially difficult to implement on a computer. Despite the claims of many modern gurus of cybernetic hypertext theory, written text is not linear but can be interlinked, interwoven and annotated on the printed page in highly complex structures not susceptible of computational representation by the first generations of hardware and software. From the mid-1980s, better screen technology, more processing power, the development of the mouse and the advent of the Graphical User Interface (GUI) have transformed the ability of the computer to represent and link documentary objects. In 1996, for example, the first CD-ROM of the Canterbury Tales project appeared: the Wife of Bath's Prologue, published by Cambridge University Press. This presents transcriptions of 58 manuscripts and early printed versions of the work, and generates almost two million hypertext links (Robinson, 1996).

In the last five years, digital camera technology has developed to the extent that digital images can be captured that equal or even exceed large-format analogue photographic reproductions. These have disadvantages, however: the cameras are expensive, and the file sizes huge, which causes problems for storage and delivery. However, from valuable originals, large archive images can be captured and stored for the long term, with lower-quality derivatives being delivered for viewing and printing. This is acceptable for most uses, and means that good-quality images can be integrated with other media for a more complete user experience. As of 2001, the British Library has produced a high-quality digital facsimile of the 15th-century Sherborne Missal that is on display in its galleries on the largest touch screen in the UK. The unique feature of this resource is that the pages can be turned by hand, and it is possible to zoom in at any point on the page at the touch of a finger on the screen. High-quality sound reproduction accompanies the images, allowing users to hear the religious offices that make up the text being sung by a monastic choir. Now documents can be represented by high-quality images, with underlying searchable text, and with annotations in text, sound or video. We give some more examples of the digitization of complex documentary collections in Chapter 2 'Why digitize?'. Cameras are being developed that can capture 3-D images, and there are sophisticated capture devices for digital sound and video, deriving in part from the huge growth in these formats in the entertainment industry.

It is, of course, possible to treat the printed page as an image. Capturing digital images from printed pages has the advantage that the page will appear on the screen exactly as it was in the original. The disadvantage of this presentation is that the search and retrieval functions are lost, but a combination of both image and text representation means that documents can be represented by images, with underlying searchable text and with annotations. We give some more examples in Chapter 2 'Why digitize?'.

Printing and publishing

There is a rhetoric that suggests that we are moving rapidly from print to digital media: this is not borne out by evidence from the publishing industry and from copyright libraries (Leonhardt, 2000, 123). The death of the book has been predicted with every new communication or entertainment technology, the telegraph, recorded speech, film, television and the internet, but the book seems to be thriving. At the beginning of the 21st century, the UK copyright libraries, for instance, are receiving more print material than ever before (in 1999 the figure was around 105,000 items for the British Library alone), and this is without the materials that they purchase. Production of digital data is certainly on the increase, but it does not seem to be accompanied by a concomitant diminution in the printed output, though it is changing both the publishing industry and the world of libraries. In the 15th century, the introduction of the printing press industrialized the production of books, but did not do away with handwriting. What it did do was change book production from a cottage industry carried out in monasteries to a commercial industry, and incidentally resulted in a huge loss of authority on the part of the Christian Church in Europe. The digital revolution is often likened to the print revolution, but it is still rather too early to tell whether the effects will be as far-reaching and transformative.

In the 14th century, monastic production could not keep pace with the demand for the written word, despite large-scale copying throughout Europe. There was a huge potential market for multiple copies of books, and there was also a demand for greater accuracy than copying was supplying. Chaucer's plaintive appeal to his scribe, Adam, exemplifies the problems of careless and inaccurate copying that plagued authors and readers alike:

> So ofte adaye I mot thy werke renewe,
> It to correcte and eke to rubbe and scrape,
> And al is throrough thy negligence and rape.
>
> (Chaucer, 1988, 650)

> Every day I have to redo your work, correcting it and scraping away the errors, all because of your negligence and carelessness.

Johannes Gutenberg, born sometime in the last decade of the 14th century, and trained as a goldsmith, produced the first book in Europe printed from movable cast type, the so-called 42-line Bible. Despite popular misconceptions, Gutenberg did not invent this method of printing, which was known in China and Korea from around the 11th century. What he did was to combine

> the technology of the goldsmith's punch with that of the winepress. The result was the printing press – a machine that combined flexibility, rapidity, and economy to allow the production of books that the increasingly literate, increasingly numerous European city dwellers could afford to buy and read. (Lerner, 1998, 96)

The 42-line Bible was produced in around 1455.

Hand-set movable type not only produced books faster than handwriting, it produced them in multiple copies. While with early printed books it is not quite true to say that every copy is the same, the differences are small compared with the differences between manuscript copies. And printed books can be produced in the hundreds and thousands, even millions, which is the significant advance. Evidence for the instant huge potential market for multiple copies can be found, according to Kilgour, in the estimates of the numbers of books printed in the last third of the 15th century, that is in the 30 years after the death of Gutenberg in 1568. These estimates suggest that there were some 12 to 20 million books printed – more than the number of all manuscripts produced in medieval Europe up to that time (Kilgour, 1998, 82).

More books call for more readers, and so literacy rates rose rapidly in the next three centuries. Paper was made from linen rag during this period, but in the Napoleonic Wars rag was needed to make bandages, so wood-pulp paper processes were developed. Wood was plentiful and the process cheap, which meant that print output could increase. This happened in several ways: more publications were printed, and works were often longer, hence the growth in the multi-volume work of fiction in the 19th century. Periodical publications were produced which appeared monthly, then weekly, then daily and the mass media were born.

Early printing presses were wooden and were hand-operated, and the type was hand-set. This remained the case until the beginning of the 19th century, when things changed rapidly with one of those 'paradigm shifts' discussed at the beginning of this chapter. Printing-press technology moved to iron presses, operated by steam, to mechanical type, to hot-metal type to phototypesetting and then to computer typesetting by the 1970s. Publishing began to become a separate industry from printing in the 18th century, and grew rapidly throughout the 19th century with the increasing mechanization of the processes, and the further growth of literacy rates and the demands of a reading public. 'The total book production of the nineteenth century exceeded that of the eighteenth by 440%' (Kilgour, 1998, 112), and many of the publishing giants that still control the industry (though in very different configurations) came into being during this period.

Computer typesetting brought an unanticipated by-product: electronic text. This was not always kept initially, and when it was, the typesetting codes used for marking up the text rendered it largely unusable for any other process. However, standardization of markup languages (discussed in more detail in Chapter 5 'Resource discovery, description and use') has meant that it is now possible to use electronic text for purposes other than printing, and many publishers have embraced electronic publishing in the last five years, especially in the production of journals. We discuss the implications for libraries of the acquisition of large volumes of published electronic books and journals in Chapter 3 'Developing collections in the digital world', and we also look at some of the models of electronic publication that are changing the face of both the print and the digital worlds.

Changes in libraries

With the revolution in printing and the birth of the publishing industry came new developments in libraries. In the Middle Ages in Europe, libraries were either monastic institutions holding relatively few, very valuable books (and many of them were chained libraries, that is the books were chained to the shelves to prevent theft) or belonged to private individuals. Many of the great libraries of today are based upon some of the collections of these monasteries and individuals. The collections of Archbishop Matthew Parker are vital to the library (named after him) at Corpus Christi College Cambridge; the British Library's founding collections were those of Sir Hans Sloane, Sir Robert Cotton, Edward and Robert Harley, earls of Oxford, and the Royal Collection given by George II in 1757. When the British army invaded the city of Washington in 1814 and burned the Capitol, including the 3000-volume Library of Congress, Thomas Jefferson sold his personal library to the Congress to 'recommence' its library. The purchase of Jefferson's 6487 volumes for $23,940 was approved in 1815. In the 18th century, circulation libraries and subscription libraries started to appear to satisfy the demands of the larger reading public for cheap access to print, and the 19th century saw the rise of the great public libraries.

Mechanization

Librarians have always sought to mechanize routine processes as much as possible, and so were early adopters of computer technologies. Database programs were developed early in the history of computing for use in stock control, payroll systems and other commercial activities.

The adoption of administrative systems for catalogue record creation was an early example of the use of computerized processes in libraries. This started as merely a means of producing, for manual filing, printed catalogue cards or slips, which would be referred to by library staff and users as a means of finding library resources. To extend the duplication of catalogues and thus the number of user access points to the catalogue, microformats were used, 'enabling multiple copies of the catalogue to be distributed for the first time and new sequences, such as title catalogues, to be introduced' (Brophy, 2001, 106). Alongside this new capability to share catalogues, there started co-operative efforts to share the cataloguing load and to benefit from aggregating cataloguing effort across multiple libraries. Because bibliographic description is such a highly structured construct, the computerization of the catalogue was a significant and inevitable next step from these early mechanization initiatives. This was not the computerized catalogue as we know it now in the guise of the OPAC (Online Public Access Catalogue), but a straightforward listing of the library's resources with no links to borrower records or to external resources.

Integrating computerized functions

In tandem with the development of the computerized catalogue came the move to automate circulation functions. Initially, this was no more than associating a borrower number with a book accession number while the full records of each were kept on separate computer database or paper systems. Even these most basic functions were only available to the largest libraries because of the great expense involved. However, this was to change as computing technology became more widespread and software developed the capability to create connections between different parts of databases and to integrate functions in a primitive fashion. As soon as it was possible to get the circulation system to 'talk' to the catalogue, it was possible to automate some library functions, such as overdue notices. As important as the mechanization of routine staff-intensive functions, was the means it gave library managers to measure and assess borrower activity in great detail for the first time through reports generated from the computer logs and databases. This knowledge greatly enhanced acquisitions and stock management strategies and has helped librarians to cope proactively with changes in funding structures, borrower requirements and the user community, and with the accelerating expansion in information resources.

Changes in computing and networking

At the start of the 1980s, automated library functions were generally being achieved through mainframe computers with dumb terminals in large institutions, and it was not until the spread of personal computing that computerization could be seriously afforded by small libraries such as those in schools, smaller businesses, hospitals or other small specialized organizations. The concentration of computer activity in one central processing point also limited those libraries with geographically distant outstations such as public libraries or large universities, and often the computing resources could only be made available in the main library location. It was only with the inception of personal computers, local- and wide-area networks, and the movement from centralized to distributed client–server processing that libraries of all types were able to utilize fully the power of computing technology to automate functions, share information and resources, generate management reports and electronically link libraries together. From the perspective of the library user, they were experiencing computers in the library for the first time not as something which librarians used to facilitate library management, but as a direct point of service to use independently of the library staff.

By the early 1990s, almost all library functions were supported by automation in some way. Functions such as cataloguing, acquisitions, journals, circulation, interlibrary loans, financial control, stock management and user details were all integrated and automated to some extent. This period also saw a large growth in the electronic communication of data from one library to another. Librarians had for many years accessed remote database services for access to reference information and bibliographic data, using a dial-up connection to a local computer which would route information to the host machine, possibly based somewhere else in Europe or America. This was an early form of internetwork access, charging heavy fees not just on connect time, but on a per-item-retrieved basis. In most libraries the end-user could not be given direct access because of the high cost of use (with legal and pharmaceutical-based libraries sometimes the exception) and the librarian was required as a skilled intermediary, and also as a buffer against over-expenditure. As wide-area networks in the USA, UK and elsewhere developed, the emphasis on connect time was relaxed as annual subscriptions with unlimited access were introduced by suppliers. CD-ROM versions of databases for personal computers also relaxed the need to limit end-user access. Wider use of networking enabled libraries to share more data in the form of interlibrary loans, electronic document delivery, electronic mail and also electronic ordering functions, also known as EDI or Electronic Data Interchange.

Electronic Data Interchange

Electronic Data Interchange (EDI) refers to the computer exchange of business information using a standardized data format. Standardized EDI messages are based on common business documents such as purchase orders, invoices and delivery notes, which are interchanged between computer systems without human intervention or interpretation. It has been in use since the 1970s, but it was not until the late 1980s and early 1990s that any attempt was made to move away from proprietary systems to open standards.

> Adopting EDI can eliminate the mailing of paper documentation and the manual processing of quotations, purchase orders, invoices, shipping documents, customs documents, and other business transactions. Because the data is processed and stored automatically, tasks such as re-keying data and printing purchase orders and invoices are eliminated.
>
> (Tallim and Zeeman, 1995)

The use of EDI has been as significant a development for libraries as for the business world. The integration of the cataloguing and ordering process, plus the ability to chase orders that have not arrived on time automatically, speeds up acquisitions and gets resources to the user more quickly on their arrival. Automated financial controls can be pre-set to generate purchase orders and fiscal reports, and also to limit certain types of expenditure to defined budgetary plans. Librarians, as early adopters of EDI, have been among the first to partake in e-commerce and thus understand e-commerce's trials and tribulations but also its great advantages to the management of library services.

Co-operation to mutual advantage

As far back as 1902 we can trace how basic technology was used and the results shared by libraries in a co-operative way. In that year the Library of Congress began selling printed cards that in effect 'made that library the centralized cataloguing agency for thousands of American libraries' (Lerner, 1998, 194). In computing terms we have to wait until 1971 for the same level of resource sharing and economy, when OCLC introduced an online shared cataloguing system for libraries (available at **www.oclc.org/**). Today this co-operative catalogue is available to libraries in 76 countries and territories around the world, with over 46 million cataloguing records available, as well as associated interlibrary loan and reference database services. In the UK, the Birmingham Libraries Co-operative Mechanization Project (BLCMP) was established in 1969 as a joint venture between libraries in Birmingham. BLCMP was created to realize the benefits of a shared approach to library computing and built a large shared database of over 19 million bibliographic records (available at **www.blcmp.org.uk/**). The Research Libraries Group (RLG) also provides extensive shared resources through a set of online catalogues that offer millions of records describing materials created around the world (available at **www.rlg.org/libres.html**).

In many areas, libraries are showing intensive co-operation and sharing of the fruits of computing technology. NORDINFO (the Nordic Council for Scientific Information), which celebrated its 25th anniversary in 2001, was founded as a bridge between Nordic research libraries and the growing information and documentation sector. The general objective set for the coming years is to work towards what has been called 'The Nordic Electronic Research Library'.

Another significant example of sharing for mutual benefit is the important realm of interlibrary loans. No single library holds all published information and most cannot hold even a sizeable sliver of it, but the librarian's role is clearly to provide access to the complete body. The only sensible solution is to share access to the resources through interlibrary loan. All the above co-operatives support this and local co-operatives for interlending exist all over the world at regional and national levels. Most of this is now being managed or documents delivered via electronic means. The British Library Document Supply Centre, for instance, received 34% of requests by postal means in 1993-4 but now receives less than 13% by post and the remainder by electronic means (Maynard, 2000).

Digital libraries

The digital library, the electronic library (generally taken to be synonymous with the digital library), the virtual library, the hybrid library, the library without walls are all concepts that librarians seem to be dealing with all the time. What do they mean? Do they mean the same to everyone who uses the terms? Do they all mean the same thing? Do we all mean the same thing when we talk about a library? From its original etymological meaning of a 'collection of books', a library can mean a collection of almost anything in modern parlance: software routines, for instance. Every library is different, every digital library is different, and different players are advancing many definitions for the digital library. Arms (2000, 2), for instance, defines a digital library as:

> a managed collection of information, with associated services, where the information is stored in digital formats and accessible over a network. A crucial part of this definition is that the information is managed.

For the Digital Library Federation in the USA:

> Digital libraries are organizations that provide the resources, including the specialized staff, to select, structure, offer intellectual access to, interpret, distribute, preserve the integrity of, and ensure the persistence over time of collections of digital works so that they are readily and economically available for use by a defined community or set of communities.
>
> (Greenstein, 2000)

Borgman (2000) devotes a whole chapter to trying to define a digital library (called 'Is it digital or is it a library?') and concludes that (as is to be expected) the term has multiple meanings, and, for her, these cluster around two themes:

> From a research perspective, digital libraries are content collected and organized on behalf of user communities. From a library-practice per-

spective, digital libraries are institutions or organizations that provide information services in digital forms.   (51)

Some prefer to work with the concept of the 'hybrid' library, as they believe that this more closely describes the reality of libraries, which have always been hybrid. The digital is one more (albeit very different) format that librarians have to deal with in a multi-format environment, where for many years non-documentary mixed-media objects, both analogue and digital, have been growing in importance, and where technology for access has had to be provided. Most libraries can supply microfilm and microfiche readers, video players, audio tape and CD players, as well as terminals for access to digital resources. However, there are often strategic reasons for defining activities as coming under a digital libraries heading – the possibility of securing funding, for instance, from programmes which are defined as digital library initiatives.

Hybrid libraries are, according to Rusbridge (1998):

Designed to bring a range of technologies from different sources together in the context of a working library, and also to begin to explore integrated systems and services in both the electronic and print environments.

They exist 'on the continuum between the conventional and digital library, where electronic and paper-based information sources are used alongside each other' (Pinfield et al., 1998, 3). The concepts of virtual libraries or libraries without walls reflect the integrative possibilities inherent in the digital: if significant library collections are digital, then the confines of space no longer define boundaries upon information. Virtual collections from many different sources can be assembled and accessed from anywhere, without the user even knowing where the sources reside, and personal virtual collections can be built to serve many purposes. Hence a virtual library could potentially be enormous, linking huge collections from all around the world together, or it could be very small, being the personal digital collection of one individual.

Digital libraries are, like any so-called revolutionary change, a development of a whole range of underlying theories and technologies that have come together to create a paradigm shift. The speed of recent developments has taken some librarians by surprise, especially the exponential growth of the amount of digital data available, but they are understandable if we look at some of the precursors that have led to the current trends: new developments rarely spring fully formed from the ether.

For the purpose of the present work, our understanding of digital libraries is somewhat eclectic. There are many different kinds of digital libraries creating, delivering and preserving digital objects that derive from many different formats of underlying data, and it is very difficult to formulate a definition that encapsulates all these. We would, however, like to propose some principles that we think perhaps characterize something as a digital library rather than any other kind of digital collection. These derive in part from the definitions above and in part from our own experience. They are:

1   A digital library is a managed collection of digital objects.
2   The digital objects are created or collected according to principles of collection development.
3   The digital objects are made available in a cohesive manner, supported by services necessary to allow users to retrieve and exploit the resources just as they would any other library materials.
4   The digital objects are treated as long-term stable resources and appropriate processes are applied to them to ensure their quality and survivability.

Automating information retrieval

Vannevar Bush, one of Roosevelt's advisers in World War II is generally credited with being the first thinker to suggest mechanical and electronic means of dealing with complex information, and of finding paths through information universes that could be marked for others to follow. Bush was grappling with the problem that has beset humanity since the invention of printing, and possibly before. How, when so much information is available, does one remember what has been read, make connections between facts and ideas, and store and retrieve personal data? Pre-literate humanity was capable of prodigious feats of memory, but the total amount of knowledge it was necessary to absorb was orders of magnitude smaller than it is now. When writing became widespread, personal notebooks and handbooks were used as *aides-mémoires*, but these could handle only a fraction of the data that even one individual had to cope with by the 1940s. In his seminal article, 'As we may think', published in the *Atlantic Monthly* magazine (1945), Bush conceptualized 'thinking machines' that would help the modern world make sense of the information explosion, and he proposed that an automated 'memory extender' be employed, a device he called a 'MemEx' in which an individual could store all his or her books, records and communications. This would be mechanized to enable rapid and flexible consultation. Interestingly, given developments in digital technology at that period, the MemEx was essentially an analogue machine and used microfilm for information storage with a mechanical linking process. The machine was never built by Bush, but drawings of it exist, and a simulation of it was produced some years ago by Nyce and Kahn (1991).

For some reason, Bush's article caught the popular imagination: *Life* magazine published an illustrated version entitled 'A top US scientist foresees a possible future in which man-made machines will start to think', and it was summarized in *Time* with the title 'A machine that thinks', and Bush has even been hailed as a 'Father of Information Science' (Buckland, 1992, 284). He is certainly thought of as the father of hypertext, even though the word itself was not coined until the 1960s. He is, however, rarely examined in relation to the developments he was drawing on, according to Buckland. 'Little attention, in contrast, has been paid to Bush's MemEx in relation to its *own* context: the visions and technological developments of information retrieval in the 1930s' (1992, 284). Buckland (1992) and Rayward (1994) attribute many of the developments underpinning Bush's theoretical achievements to Paul Otlet, the Belgian bibliographer who had helped develop the Universal Decimal Classification, and to Emanuel Goldberg. Indeed, for Buckland 'Bush's understanding of information retrieval was severely incomplete' (1992, 285).

Emanuel Goldberg developed very high-resolution microfilm, and also the technology underlying microdots, in the 1920s. In 1932, he wrote a paper describing the design of a microfilm selector using a photoelectric cell, which Buckland sees as 'the first paper on electronic document retrieval' (1992, 288). In 1934, Paul Otlet published his *Traité de Documentation* which 'is perhaps the first systematic, modern discussion of general problems of organizing information . . . one of the first information science textbooks' (Rayward, 1994, 237-8). Otlet saw huge possibilities in new forms of information recording and transmission: he was aware of the information and communication possibilities of telegraph, telephone, radio, television, cinema and sound recordings. For Otlet, 'the book is only a means to an end. Other means exist and as gradually they become more effective than the book, they are substituted for it' (Otlet, 1934, quoted in Rayward, 1994, 244). Otlet visualized new kinds of work desks where there would be no documents, only a screen and a telephone with access to documents on film which could be called up at will. Otlet also formulated some new organizational principles which would hold all the documents in a linked relationship: a Universal Network for Information and Documentation which would connect centres of production, distribution and use regardless of subject matter or place (Rayward, 1994, 246) – a development that uncannily presages the world wide web.

Though Otlet and Goldberg may have formulated the underlying theories upon which hypertext and information retrieval, and therefore digital library developments, came to be based, it was Bush's legacy that inspired later thinkers and developers. In 1962 Douglas Engelbart (an early follower of Bush) started work on the Augment project, which aimed to produce tools to aid human capabilities and productivity. He also was concerned that the information explosion meant that workers were having problems dealing with all the knowledge they needed to perform even relatively simple tasks, and Augment aimed to increase human capacity by the sharing of knowledge and information. His NLS (oN-Line System) allowed researchers on the project access to all stored working papers in a shared 'journal', which eventually had over 100,000 items in it, and was one of the largest early digital library systems. Engelbart is also credited with the invention of pointing devices, in particular the mouse in 1968.

The mid-1960s saw other pioneers conceiving of grand schemes that at the time seemed so innovative as to be impossible, but now are coming to realization. Ted Nelson designed his Xanadu system in 1965, in which all the books in all the world would be 'deeply intertwingled' (in his words – Nelson incidentally coined the word hypertext). Nelson also tackled the problems of copyrights and payments by proposing that there should be electronic copyright management systems that would keep track of what everyone everywhere was accessing, and charge accordingly through micro-payments (McKnight, Dillon and Richardson, 1991). Impossible to implement at the time (Xanadu was described by Wolf (1995) as 'the longest-running vapourware story in the history of the computer industry'), these ideas are now commonplace, but it took Tim Berners-Lee to put them all together in the late 1980s.

The world wide web

The problem that the world wide web was initially created to solve was document management. Berners-Lee was employed by CERN in the 1980s to devise a system that would allow the organization to keep track of all versions of all the documents that its employees were creating, editing and exchanging constantly. This is the same problem that Engelbart was dealing with 20 years earlier with NLS and Bush 50 years earlier with the MemEx. The web is based upon a relatively simple set of concepts: it relies on there being an underlying network of networks that can connect any computer to any other computer (which do not have to be of the same type) provided connections can be routed to allow them to exchange information. Given this infrastructure, what Berners-Lee did was implement the information management, storage and exchange goals of Goldberg, Otlet, Bush and Engelbart before him, drawing, consciously or unconsciously, upon all their underlying ideas. The key to the development of the web was the complex linking potential of hypertext, and Berners-Lee added to this Hypertext Markup Language (HTML), which allowed all text for the web to be encoded using the same system, the Hypertext Transfer Protocol (HTTP), to specify how information exchange between machines should be handled, and the Uniform Resource Location (URL), which specified addresses for documents. Despite huge developments in web technologies over the last ten years, the underlying principles are relatively unchanged. These developments are discussed further in Chapter 5 'Resource discovery, description and use'.

Why the world wide web is not a digital library

The world wide web has many of the features of a digital library, and if the web did not exist our conception of digital libraries would be very different. The web is undoubtedly the means via which most digital libraries are accessed, but it is not a digital library itself as it lacks those characteristics we suggested would define digital libraries. It is not a managed environment, it has no collection development principles and most significant of all, the digital objects are not perceived as having durable value – though many of them do. Indeed, one of the issues being tackled in the digital library world is the vexing one of how to guarantee a record of the information available on the web for future generations. Much of the web is ephemeral information: advertising, personal web pages, announcements, etc., which come and go with great speed. In the past, this sort of information was available on paper, in handbills, newspapers and many other forms of prints. Much of it survives, albeit haphazardly. Accidental survival of web resources is unlikely. We deal with these issues in more detail in Chapters 5 and 8 'Resource discovery, description and use' and 'Preservation'.

Changing names for managing content

The integration of technology into the natural working practices of many organizations has led to a number of management initiatives that continue to have a distinct impact upon librarians. These are now drawn together under the umbrella term of content management, but have gone by many names before:

> The names may change, but in many ways the story is the same. Over the past several years, we have seen a quick and accelerating shift from one term to another that attempts to name the technology responsible for creating, updating, managing, and distributing material in many forms . . . Call it a 'document', 'knowledge', or 'content', the problem set that was identified years ago is, at its core, the same. There is simply more of everything – more core material, more forms of it, and more ways to distribute it.
>
> (Trippe, 2001, 22)

It is in these corporate environments and management methods that many of the digitization, storage and access solutions were first implemented and developed and then put to wider use. Librarians may be said to have managed containers of knowledge content in the past, but the growth in computing use from the 1960s onwards propelled librarians and other information workers into the management of content. Megill (1997) points out that the information an organization needs to keep for re-use, that which is worth sharing, managing and preserving to function effectively, is the 'corporate memory'. It is the job of 'information managers' to keep, store and release this information in a timely fashion and as Lerner points out, special libraries 'exist solely to make expensive professional workers more effective at what they do' (1998, 182). Technology was introduced to try to resolve some of the difficulties inherent in corporate environments where 80% of corporate information was to be found in documents and e-mail, rather than structured database records (Megill, 1997, 7) and thus was difficult to retrieve. This was termed 'information management' or 'document management' as it drew together people from wide professional backgrounds, including librarians, record managers, archivists and computer scientists. It was the cutting edge for a time, but soon it became noticeable that the ability to find a document, drawing or data was not considered cutting edge enough to fulfil the corporate desire for flexibility, productivity and control. By putting technological solutions foremost it had been forgotten that information is internalized and interpreted by people: the 'knowledge' element, that which we know, was missing. It is interesting to note that the immediate response to this was to implement even more technology under the heading 'knowledge management'.

Knowledge management (KM) is often discarded as nothing more than a buzz term for something that was already in place. Brophy describes it accurately as 'better thought of as the process of engineering conditions under which knowledge transfer and utilization happen' (2001, 37). One would think this would signal a shift from technology towards people (such as the focus of community provided by libraries), but KM is renowned for implementing intranet solutions with complex knowledge databases to allow workers to share their information for the benefit of the whole organization. Of course, to transfer knowledge is more difficult than to record it, and learning (the process of acquiring knowledge) is not inherent to many of the technology-based solutions on offer.

> The importance of people as creators and carriers of knowledge is forcing organizations to realize that knowledge lies less in its databases than in its people. It's been said, for example, that if NASA wanted to go to the moon again, it would have to start from scratch, having lost not the data, but the human expertise that took them there last time.
>
> (Brown and Duguid, 2000, 122)

KM is fast becoming outdated as a concept and so in this new century we are returning to information in the term 'content management'. This is such a wide term, encompassing a broad and complex field, because as Gilbane points out 'everyone needs to manage content, but the similarity ends there' (Trippe, 2001, 22). Undoubtedly, modern libraries are in the business of content management and so how librarians and libraries will fit into this new management 'reality' is discussed in Chapters 3 and 9 'Developing collections in the digital world' and 'Digital librarians: new roles for the Information Age'.

Conclusion

Librarians, as we have shown here, are always at the forefront of the latest technologies in order to find new ways to optimize the management of libraries and resources, and to provide improved services. There are some outstanding problems with which libraries are still struggling that have to some degree been exacerbated rather than resolved by technology. Interoperability has been a significant technical and political problem for libraries ever since computing was first used to share data. (Interoperability is discussed in detail in Chapter 6 'Developing and designing systems for sharing digital resources'.) It is probably fair to say that all attempts at full interoperability between libraries, systems and standards, and between communities have not yet succeeded, and are unlikely to succeed. Even assuming technical hurdles can be overcome, there are also the political issues of control, resourcing, legal frameworks, regional, national and international community differences, and the traditional boundaries of different cultural sectors such as libraries, schools, museums, galleries and archives. The goal of the world-wide global library is probably unreachable while the issue of interoperability still remains as the biggest sticking point of all.

The other unresolved strategic issues revolve around money, infrastructure, scalability and sustainability. Computing in libraries is no longer showing the immediate cost savings in return for investment that were delivered in the 1980s and early 1990s. So far in this chapter we have discussed the way that computerizing routine tasks has saved time and money, while enhancing services and freeing library staff to do more management and less paper chasing. The situation now is that these developments are taken for granted in many organizations and future developments will not necessarily instantly save staff time or reduce costs. The real benefits from technology now for libraries are improving resources and services, not replacing the human factor. This is discussed in more detail in Chapter 4 'The economic factors', where we examine the financing of technology, and in Chapter 9 'Digital librarians: new roles for the Information Age', where we evaluate the changing library profession. Of course, the issues of sustainability and scale become paramount once significant investment has been made and there is an undercurrent of dissatisfaction about the sustainability and scalability of digital technology. Issues of preservation and continuing access to resources are discussed in Chapter 8 'Preservation' in particular.

2

Why digitize?

Cultural institutions are investing in digitization for two reasons. First, they remain convinced of the continuing value of such resources for learning, teaching, research, scholarship, documentation, and public accountability. Second, they recognize that changing user behavior may jeopardize these resources and their stewardship.

(Kenney and Rieger, 2000, 1)

Introduction

Most libraries today are re-evaluating their information delivery services in this new world of digital information, and some are contemplating the digitization of collections within their own holdings for a wide variety of reasons and purposes. Embarking on digitization projects can be onerous and costly, and libraries need to be certain of all the implications of such an endeavour before they begin. While it is relatively easy to obtain funding for discrete projects, recurrent funds for ongoing activities are harder to come by, and the commitment to maintain digital content for the long term needs to be planned and costed alongside the initial costs of conversion. However, libraries can greatly enhance their services, skills and prestige through good digitization projects. In this chapter we examine the benefits of the digitization of collections, outline many of the practical, strategic and institutional issues to be considered, and describe a number of different projects and programmes to illuminate the points made.

This chapter will discuss the following issues:

- practical and strategic issues in the digitization of library collections
- the benefits of digitization
- formats of materials for digitization
- what a digitization project involves
- the digital lifecycle approach
- running a digitization project
- digitization projects and the management of risk
- some example projects, including newspaper, periodical and grey literature examples, plus the Gutenberg Bible, photographic collections and digitization for the print disabled
- digital library programmes.

Practical and strategic issues in the digitization of library collections

Digital collection development is part of a broader perspective on collection development, and generally needs to be assessed using the same criteria. However, there is a difference between reviewing collections already held by the institution with digitization in mind, and choosing to acquire digital materials from elsewhere. We deal with building digital collections in more detail in Chapter 3 'Developing collections in the digital world'. In-house holdings have been initially acquired or retained because they are perceived to have some value to the community served by the library, and thus theoretically they might all be candidates for digitization. In reality, there will be complex factors within both the library and the community it serves that will dictate certain priorities for digital capture and delivery. As Hazen, Horrell and Merrill-Oldham (1998) warn:

> The judgments we must make in defining digital projects involve the following factors: the intellectual and physical nature of the source materials; the number and location of current and potential users; the current and potential nature of use; the format and nature of the proposed digital product and how it will be described, delivered, and archived; how the proposed product relates to other digitization efforts; and projections of costs in relation to benefits.

The amount of material available for potential digitization in any library (however small) is likely to be greater than the resources available and so careful assessments of costs and benefits need to be made before embarking on projects.

The benefits of digitization

We have discussed in Chapter 1 'Digital futures in current contexts' some of the properties and attributes of digital materials that make them fundamentally different from analogue materials, even though they may contain the same content. Some of these properties prove to be disadvantageous to the presentation and survivability of cultural materials – the evanescence and mutability of the digital object, for instance. On the other hand, there are considerable benefits of digital access to library collections. The digitization of resources opens up new modes of use, enables a much wider potential audience and gives a renewed means of viewing our cultural heritage. These advantages may outweigh the difficulties and disadvantages, provided the project is well thought out. Institutions large and small are therefore embarking upon programmes of digital conversion for a whole range of reasons. The advantages of digital surrogates include:

- immediate access to high-demand and frequently used items
- easier access to individual components within items (e.g. articles within journals)
- rapid access to materials held remotely
- the ability to reinstate out-of-print materials
- the potential to display materials that are in inaccessible formats, for instance, large volumes or maps
- 'virtual reunification' – allowing dispersed collections to be brought together
- the ability to enhance digital images in terms of size, sharpness, colour contrast, noise reduction, etc.
- the potential to conserve fragile/precious originals while presenting surrogates in more accessible forms
- the potential for integration into teaching materials
- enhanced searchability, including full text

- integration of different media (images, sounds, video, etc.)
- the ability to satisfy requests for surrogates (photocopies, photographic prints, slides, etc.)
- reducing the burden or cost of delivery
- the potential for presenting a critical mass of materials.

Any library considering digitization of its holdings will need to evaluate potential digitization projects using criteria such as these. They will also need to assess the actual and potential user base, and consider whether this will change when materials are made available in digital form. Fragile originals that are kept under very restricted access conditions may have huge appeal to a wide audience when made available in a form that does not damage the originals. See the Digital Shikshapatri described below for an example of this kind of widened accessibility. It may also be possible to display materials whose original format has made them inaccessible: large maps or older newspapers, for instance. The Women's Library (formerly known as the Fawcett Library) has a unique collection of large-sized women's suffrage banners, many of which are woven from a variety of materials – cotton and velvet for instance, often with appliqué lettering – which are now in a fragile state. The sheer size of the banners and their fragility means that viewing the original is heavily restricted, but digitization of the banners has opened up the potential for much wider access (**http://ahds.ac.uk/suffrage.htm**). Libraries should be warned, however, that making such facsimiles more widely available might result in more requests to see the original, rather than fewer. This has already been the case in some libraries, and dealing with the requests puts an additional load on library staff.

Formats of materials for digitization

Most libraries hold a wide range of formats of manuscript, printed, visual and audio materials from all periods, in a variety of sizes, on diverse substrates and in different conditions, all of which may be candidates for digitization. Digitization is the process of conversion of *any* physical or analogue item into a digital representation or facsimile. The physical items that may be candidates for digitization may include:

- individual documents
- bound volumes, both print and manuscript
- photographs, — both prints and transparencies
- microfilm and microfiche
- video and audio
- maps, drawings and other large-format paper items
- art works
- textiles
- physical three-dimensional (3-D) objects.

These may present many problems of handling, and some may need to be assessed for conservation treatment before any digitization can be contemplated. Each format will almost certainly need to be digitized using different methods, and indeed there may be a range of options for any one object, depending on the potential use of the digital collections and the resources available. As we suggest in Chapter 1 'Digital futures in current contexts', anything that is accessible to photography can be digitized. The digitization processes are numerous, and include:

- image scanning
- microfilming and then scanning the microfilm
- photography followed by scanning of the photographic surrogates
- re-recording video and audio on to digital media
- rekeying of textual content
- OCR of scanned textual content
- tagging text and other digital content to create a marked-up digital resource
- digital photography – especially for 3-D objects or large-format items such as art works.

We are faced with a large variety of potential originals that may be digitized and many means of digitization and presentation of digitized resources.

What does a digitization project involve?

While there is significant variation in the original materials and the methods of digitization, there are some common themes to every digitization project. First, it is essential to assess the original materials to identify the unique characteristics of the collection. These unique characteristics will drive the digitization mechanisms and help define the required access routes to the digital version. Additionally, whether the end product is a handful of data files or thousands, they will have to be organized, given file names and placed in some logical structure. Having a clear vision of the information goals to be achieved from the original materials and the means of delivery are essential to a successful digitization project.

It must also be remembered that digital capture is only one of the many processes involved in the highly complex chain of activities that are attendant upon the creation, management, use and preservation of digital objects for the long term. Capture is likely to incur only a relatively small proportion of the total project costs. Any digitization project is likely to involve some or all of the following activities:

- assessment and selection of originals
- grant applications and fundraising
- feasibility testing, costing and piloting
- copyright clearance and rights management
- preparation of materials
- benchmarking
- digital capture
- quality assessment
- metadata design and creation
- delivery
- workflow processes
- project management
- long-term preservation.

Without careful planning for *all* these elements, projects are unlikely to succeed. Costs will rise, deadlines slip and acceptable quality may not be achieved. Detail about the diverse practical activities involved in carrying out digitization projects is outside the scope of this book, but there are many excellent guides available in both print and on the web. See Hazen, Horrell, and Merrill-Oldham (1998); Kenney and Rieger (2000); Lee

(2000); the Arts and Humanities Data Service (**www.ahds.ac.uk/**); the Higher Education Digitization Service (**http://heds.herts.ac.uk/**). RLG's *DigiNews* (**www.rlg.org/preserv/diginews/**) and *D-Lib Magazine* (**www.dlib.org/**) also present essential reading.

The digital lifecycle approach

When choosing to digitize library collections or to acquire digital materials from elsewhere, it is important to apply a lifecycle approach. Digital collections will need to be managed in a much more active way than documentary collections if they are to give value to their creators and users, and to survive for the long term. As Jones and Beagrie (2001, 18) suggest:

> The major implications for lifecycle management of digital resources, whatever their form or function, is the need to actively manage the resource at each stage of its lifecycle and to recognise the interdependencies between each stage and commence preservation activities as early as practicable. This represents a major difference with traditional preservation, where management is largely passive until detailed conservation work is required, typically many years after creation and rarely, if ever, involving the creator. There is an active and interlinked lifecycle to digital resources which has prompted many to promote the term 'continuum' to distinguish it from the more traditional and linear flow of the lifecycle for traditional analogue materials.

While Jones and Beagrie are referring to the lifecycle approach in terms of digital preservation, the concept, by its very nature, has to be built into all stages of the creation, accessioning and management of digital resources. The UK-based New Opportunities Fund, which in 2001 made available some £50 million for digitization projects (**www.nof.org.uk/tempdigit/index.htm**), suggests in its technical guidelines that the stages of the lifecycle are creation, management (for the long term), collection development (that is, aggregating the digitized materials in cohesive sets), access and repackaging (or ensuring reusability). Digitization and the management of digital resources are costly activities, and it is vital that the value of the resources created can be realized over the longest possible period: creating sustainable resources is the best way to ensure this. It is important also to consider the lifecycle of the object that is being digitized, for the analogue and digital will intertwine as different instantiations of an information object – sometimes it is the analogue version satisfying the user's need, sometimes the digital. Data may be searched and then printed out, the digital being a route to another analogue object. Sometimes digitization is used so that access to the analogue object can be restricted, sometimes materials are digitized so that the originals can be de-accessioned (though this is rarer now than was once predicted). So the relationship between the digital and the analogue remains complex, and both need to be factored into the life-cycle vision.

The most important reason for this lifecycle approach is to create a sustainable resource right from the start. For many analogue originals, there will only be one chance to digitize and so it is crucial that the digital files are 'future-proofed' as far as that is possible. The goal (desirable but not always possible) is one-time capture for all future uses, so planning for the long term is essential. This is no easy matter, as the long-term issues and consequences of creating and managing digital objects cannot be known, and in particular it is difficult to estimate ongoing costs. But the better a digitization project is planned, the more likely it is that the digital materials will have a long and useful life.

Running a digitization project

The decision to embark on a digitization project may be taken at a number of different levels in a library, and for a whole range of reasons. While many of the major considerations may appear to be practical ones, if a project or programme is to be successful then the financial, political and strategic implications need to be carefully thought out before the project even starts, in order to ensure that the overall benefits and costs to the institution are clearly understood, as we have outlined above. Financial factors and constraints are so crucial and complex that we have devoted the whole of Chapter 4 'The economic factors' to them, and at all stages they should be borne in mind.

The disparate processes involved in a successful project require different skills and most need some degree of professional training (this is dealt with in more detail in Chapter 9 'Digital librarians: new roles for the Information Age'). Projects ideally should not be undertaken lightly or as an add-on to an already full-time role for a librarian – though they very often are. And some of these processes can take time well beyond what can ever be factored for them: the clearing of copyright for instance. It is vital that all the component processes listed above are well understood by those managing digitization projects, and that good feasibility studies and pilot projects are undertaken.

Given that the creation, delivery and management of digital content is costly in terms of funds, effort and opportunity, a deep understanding of all the attendant activities is needed. In particular, library managers, while not necessarily being cognizant with every technical detail, must have a sufficient grasp of the complete process in order to understand and allow for the impact upon the institution – which could be considerable. But the advantages are significant, as we will demonstrate in the discussion of a range of projects below.

Digitization projects and the management of risk

For libraries, embarking on digitization projects can be risky and, as we have outlined, there are many issues which have to be considered in the planning of such projects. Without good planning, and some risk management tools, costs can spiral and projects can over-run their schedules dramatically. However, there are some well-understood ways that risk can be minimized. In particular, the use of feasibility studies and pilot projects can identify areas of risk and reward for modest cost (Tanner, 2001).

A feasibility study focused on a detailed implementation or digitization issue is an excellent risk management tool. Measurable results are gained for a low expenditure, and this both helps to inform decision making within a supportive environment and provides good evidence of the full costs. Piloting of processes is the transition from experimentation to action by putting the feasibility study results into practice. It is essential to try to replicate real project conditions as closely as possible, and the outcome must be real products and systems. By measuring every aspect of the pilot, very accurate final costs can be extrapolated. Two useful feasibility studies, carried out for the Refugee Studies Centre Digital Library and the JISC Image Digitization Initiative, are available on the website of the Higher Education Digitization Service (HEDS) at the University of Hertfordshire (**http://heds.herts.ac.uk/**).

Within this testing phase, benchmark samples of the end product should be produced that will provide the point of reference for any quality assurance checks in the future. In any project, it is possible to define a tight set of technical parameters for a task and still find variation in the standard of product created. The benchmarks provide support for the technical specification by defining what is acceptable quality. They are also supportive for the project team as a means of ensuring that the quality goals do not move during the progress of the project through external pressures. Ensuring quality assurance is a pervasive and ongoing process and there is a straightforward cost justification, for it is essential. The cost of reworking an inadequate digital product is far higher than the cost of the initial work, and the costs keep on rising every time any element is reworked. Quality assurance is there to ensure that the final product is correct and that the process to achieve it is efficient.

Some example projects

Within this section we describe a number of projects and programmes that have successfully digitized content. The focus of this section is mainly upon text-based resources, but it includes photographic and visual resources as well. The projects we describe all deliver many of the benefits listed above, plus issues of social inclusion and the way that libraries can address their user community through digitized resources. There are specialist libraries dealing with film or audio that are investing in the digitization of these media, such as the National Sound Archive at the British Library and the British Universities Film and Video Council, and many museums are investigating the scanning of 3-D objects. Detailed discussion of the digitization of time-based media or 3-D objects is, however, outside the scope of this book.

Digitizing Gutenberg

Johannes Gutenberg and the Bibles he printed in the mid-15th century have iconic significance in the worlds of both written and digital culture. As we describe in Chapter 1 'Digital futures in current contexts',

Gutenberg's developments in printing ushered in a revolution in the production and dissemination of knowledge. The significant and far-reaching changes that are being brought about today through new modes of information production and exchange are often likened to those brought about by the widespread adoption of printing technologies. In 2000, when the 600th anniversary of Gutenberg's birth was commemorated, he was named 'Man of the Millennium' and to celebrate this the State and University Library of Lower Saxony in Göttingen, Germany, mounted an exhibition of early European printing, the centrepiece of which was their copy of the Gutenberg Bible. Some 48 copies or part copies of this survive, out of around 180 that were originally printed. Only four of these are printed on vellum, of which the Saxony copy is one.

Given the pivotal cultural significance of Gutenberg's work, it is appropriate that his surviving Bibles should be viewed as candidates for digitization. But there are many other reasons for producing digital facsimiles of this work, not the least being its aesthetic qualities and the possibility of bringing these to a wider audience. In 1996, Keio University in Japan embarked on an ambitious programme to capture digital facsimiles of Gutenberg Bibles, including its own volume acquired that year. The HUMI Project (Humanities Media Interface, and also a Japanese word for books, writing or learning) plans to digitize ten copies in all, and has currently completed six of these: the Keio copy, two copies at the Gutenberg Museum in Mainz, two copies at the British Library and one copy in Cambridge University Library. These can all be accessed via HUMI at **www.humi.keio.ac.jp/**.

In 2000, to accompany the anniversary exhibition, Göttingen produced a digital facsimile of their copy of the Bible, together with the 15th-century Göttingen Model Book which laid out decorative patterns to be used in the Bible, and also Helmasperger's Notarial Instrument, a document that details a legal dispute between Gutenberg and his investor, Fust. This latter document provides the proof that Gutenberg was indeed the inventor of movable type. The Göttingen Gutenberg is available on the internet (**www.sub.uni-goettingen.de/gdz/**) and can also be purchased on CD-ROM for faster loading of the digital files (**www.saur.de/**).

The availability of seven versions of the Gutenberg Bible in digital form that can be compared instantly is of enormous importance to the study of early printing. No two copies of the work are the same, because the illuminations and rubrication were added by hand after printing, and the British Library/Keio team found evidence of changes of plan during the course of the printing process (**http://prodigi.bl.uk/gutenbg/background.asp/**). There is no other way to compare all these fragile and rare Bibles side by side since they are distributed across the whole world. It is also important to disseminate such vital cultural witnesses to the widest possible audience, which these digital products allow.

The Digital Shikshapatri

The Digital Shikshapatri is a joint project of the Indian Institute Library and the Refugee Studies Centre at Oxford University and the Oxford Centre for Vaishnava and Hindu Studies. It has the wide participation of Swaminarayan Hindus from around the world. The main aim of the project is to digitize the Indian Institute's Shikshapatri manuscript, one of the great treasures of British Hinduism, and many different supporting materials, and make these available on the internet and on CD-ROM for use by a wide range of individuals and institutions. The Shikshapatri text contains the essence of Hindu moral codes for everyday life, and is of huge importance for devotees of the Swaminarayan Hindu sect. It has become an object of pilgrimage for Swaminarayan Hindus from all over the UK, and every year some 900 devotees visit the Bodleian Library in Oxford to *Darshan* (venerate) their holy manuscript, making it the most visited single manuscript in Oxford. The manuscript cannot be handled by visitors owing to its fragile state, and digitization allows not only more extensive study, but also contextualization with a range of supporting materials and wider access.

Hindus of the diaspora experience a level of cultural dislocation that increases with the amount of time individuals or families have spent away from the home country. While a degree of cultural assimilation is healthy for both migrants and hosts, cultural identity for the migrants needs to be maintained. This manuscript is a great force of cultural cohesion for British Hindus, whose young people are in danger of losing some of their cultural roots. Digitization of these materials is therefore of great importance for the cultural cohesion of diaspora communities, and will also bring the materials to a wider and more diverse audience (**www.shikshapatri.org/**).

The Digital Shikshapatri has been funded by the UK's New Opportunities Fund, and is one project in the World Cultures consortium of digital projects that are seeking to make the cultural richness of a number of diaspora communities in Britain more widely available (**www.nof.org. uk/tempdigit/index.htm**).

The International Dunhuang Project (IDP)

The world's earliest paper archive and one of the richest resources for medieval Chinese and Central Asian history was a cache of manuscripts, documents, and paintings discovered in 1900 in a hidden cave near the town of Dunhuang, Gansu Province, China, and hidden to human view since the early eleventh century. (Whitfield, 1999)

The International Dunhuang Project (**http://idp.bl.uk/**) is an excellent example of how international co-operation in digitization projects can create a resource to enhance the study of a wide range of valuable materials that are scattered all over the world. The history of the Dunhuang Project has a whiff of Indiana Jones romance about it. The materials in question were discovered in a cave near Dunhuang in China in 1900 by a Daoist monk. The cave had been sealed up since the 11th century, and inside was a library of tens of thousands of Buddhist texts amassed by monks between the fifth and the 11th centuries, including manuscripts, scrolls and wooden tablets, written in many languages and scripts. Besides the written materials were textiles, wood-block prints and other artefacts. In 1907, the archaeologist Sir Aurel Stein was the first foreigner to visit the site, and soon thereafter other scholars from all over the world arrived, and departed with many of the treasures, which were thus dispersed all over the world. What was discovered over the next few years was a whole complex of caves filled with precious artefacts and with walls covered with exquisite paintings. Around 492 decorated caves, large and small, are extant today. Dunhuang, a small 2000-year-old town in northwestern China, was once an important caravan stop on the Silk Road linking Central Asia with China, hence the richness and diversity of the collections. There is an excellent description of the caves and their discovery by Roderick Whitfield (**www.textile-art.com/dun1.html**).

Stein brought thousands of manuscripts and other artefacts back to Britain, where they now reside in the British Library. Other materials are held in Beijing, Paris and St Petersburg, with considerable collections in Japan. Digital technologies offer the potential to reunite these materials virtually, and also to enhance them with images of the cave paintings, as well as editoral materials, annotations, transcriptions, translations, etc. The British Library now has a large searchable database of manuscript catalogue records and digital images online (**http://idp.bl.uk/IDP/ idpdatabase.html**), with information about some 20,000 manuscripts and printed documents. Digitization is of particular benefit to this project as 'many of the manuscripts are split between collections and there are numerous unidentified fragments which may belong together' (Whitfield, 1998, 169). In addition, Northwestern University is carrying out a project to create 3-D images of the cave paintings from high-quality photographs and architectural drawings of the caves: a painstaking process of image enhancement, analysis and modelling which could revolutionize under-standing of these artefacts, and their relation to the written materials housed within the walls of the caves (**http://court.it-services. nwu.edu/dunhuang/Merit/**). This huge, international multimedia project is creating a true virtual library of one of the world's most significant cultural spaces.

The New York Public Library

The New York Public Library (**www.nypl.org**) has made available a number of its collections in digital form, concentrating in particular on materials deriving from local (New York City and State) and wider US sources. These include the famous Lewis Wickes Hine photographs of the construction of the Empire State Building, 1930–1; Berenice Abbott's views of changing New York, 1935–8; the Schomburg Collection of African Americans from the 19th century; the Small Town America Stereoscopic views from the Robert Dennis Collection; and the Hudson River Portfolio. Some of these collections form part of the Library of Congress-led American Memory Project discussed in more detail below.

The Hudson River Portfolio (**www2.nypl.org/home/Hudson/index. html**) is of particular importance here as it shows how one major public library can draw upon a wide range of its own holdings and catalogues to create a digital collection which is both diverse in materials and formats and culturally cohesive. The materials presented as part of the Portfolio are aimed at students, scholars and the general public, and offer a range of 19th century artefacts representative of the art and culture of the Hudson River and the surrounding regions. Included in the digital collection are maps, panoramas, prints, photographs, architectural works, guidebooks, literary works and histories. Images are presented in thumbnail and larger (sometimes full screen) formats; they are all linked to CATNYP, the research catalogue of the Library, and the printed works are made available both as page images and as searchable full-text using Dynaweb full-text searching software. Navigation of the Portfolio is provided through a number of routes: a historical overview is offered which takes the user through the importance of the River for trade and transportation, tourism in the region in the 19th century, and the art and literature of the period. Alternatively, the materials can be accessed visually via a panorama of the River which can be 'travelled' digitally. The original from which the panorama derives was created in 1845 by the New York engraver William Wade. This was ten feet long and illustrated both sides of the Hudson River between Albany and New York City. The user traverses the River along the digital panorama, with 'views' offered at key points along the way, drawn from photographs, prints and engravings. Topics can also be accessed through an alphabetical list, or via a list of the actual collections. The New York Public Library has used great imagination in the construction of the Portfolio, and shows how a corpus of materials can be presented from a number of viewpoints using a variety of metaphors of navigation. These metaphors have been chosen to fit the geographic subject area admirably.

Newspapers

Newspapers are particularly difficult both to preserve and to access: they are large in format, prolific in output. Their creators intend them as essentially ephemeral – important today, discarded tomorrow – and so they print them on paper that is produced with cheapness in mind, rather than survival. There is, however, no other medium in our history that records every aspect of human life over the last 300 years – on a daily basis – in the way that newspapers do. They are also fearsomely difficult to extract information from unless indexed (a monumental task in itself) or unless the researcher knows the exact dates he or she seeks. There has been grave concern for decades about the survival potential of historic newspapers, given that many of them were printed on acid paper. Major libraries such as the Library of Congress in the USA and the British Library in the UK have been microfilming newspapers for many decades in order to preserve the historical record as well as, or instead of, preserving the objects. But there is also concern about the preservation status of microfilm, which itself deteriorates. Microfilm is also not as accessible a medium as the paper originals. The fate of newspapers has leapt into prominence over the last year with the controversies caused by Nicholson Baker and others about selection and retention policies in the UK and the USA. We deal with this in more detail in Chapter 8 'Preservation'.

For users of many kinds, newspapers represent a source of information that is of monumental importance, and they are unparalleled as a primary source medium. However, it takes dedicated researchers to handle broadsheet-sized bound volumes of crumbling paper, or miles of microfilm, especially when most newspapers are minimally indexed. What makes newspapers such a unique resource (their diversity, their multimedia nature) is what also makes them so difficult to manage. Extracting content from the text of newspapers without presenting all the information around it, as well as the layout and typographical arrangement, is an impoverishing exercise, and clippings without context lose much meaning. In historical perspective, too, those aspects of newspapers which are often ignored – such as advertising – become a huge source of social, economic, political and cultural information. But researching these is a mixture of diligence and serendipity.

British Library Online Newspaper Archive

In the first half of 2001, the British Library Newspaper Library (**www.bl.uk/collections/newspaper/**), OCLC Preservation Resources (**www.oclc.org/oclc/presres/**), the Malibu Hybrid Library Project at King's College London (**www.kcl.ac.uk/humanities/cch/malibu/**), and Olive Software (**www.olivesoftware.com/**) produced a prototype system for the digitization, indexing and presentation of historic newspapers. This is available from **www.bl.uk/collections/newspaper/**.

Eighteen reels of microfilm were selected, containing newspaper issues that centred around British 'national' events:

- *1851*: On 1 May the Crystal Palace was opened, which housed the Great Exhibition of the Industry of all Nations.
- *1856*: The Crimean War ended with the Treaty of Paris.
- *1886*: The Irish question in British politics; the defeat of Gladstone's Home Rule Bill, and his resignation.
- *1900*: A centenary year. Also, the events of the Boer War in South Africa featured prominently in the national press, particularly the relief of Mafeking on 17 May 1900.
- *1918*: 11 November, the armistice ending the 'Great War' of 1914–18.

The digital images of the newspaper pages were obtained from microfilm images, a relatively cheap and speedy process. Some 20,000 pages were scanned. One of the main problems with digitized newspapers is that it is difficult to obtain good results with OCR from older texts from microfilm, but even more problematic, most OCR works at the level of the page, which can provide acceptable retrieval from simple documents, but not from compound documents. Here, retrieval needs to be at the level of the individual component. In the case of newspapers, retrieval is only truly meaningful from articles, advertisements or other individual objects, rather than from full pages.

With the British Library Newspaper Project, each individual page was 'zoned' into its component logical objects (articles, adverts, etc.) which are stored as individual images in an XML (Extensible Markup Language) repository. OCR was then carried out on the components, allowing retrieval of these as separate items rather than whole pages, though items can also be retrieved and viewed in their original context on the page. Boolean searches are possible across the whole database, revolutionizing access to this important resource. See Deegan, King and Steinvil (2001) for more details on this project.

Periodicals

Periodical publications are of huge importance in scholarship and cultural history, but many of these, especially earlier publications, are relatively inaccessible. JSTOR (**www.jstor.org/**) and MUSE (**http://muse. jhu.edu/**), described in Chapter 3 'Developing collections in the digital world', are periodical projects which are operating within commercial parameters, but there are a number of collaborative projects funded by public bodies that are rescuing valuable materials and bringing them to new audiences.

DIEPER

The DIEPER (Digitized European Periodicals) Project (**http://gdz. sub.uni-goettingen.de/dieper/home.htm**) is a collaborative endeavour between libraries in Denmark, Germany, Austria, Finland, Belgium, France, Greece, Italy and Estonia to create a virtual library of online journals throughout Europe and to create a central access point to these. The DIEPER partners have scanned some of their own journal holdings, and they have also built a register of the holdings of digital archives of periodical literature throughout the world so that users can locate and search materials rapidly, and institutions planning to scan such literature can check if digital versions already exist. The questions DIEPER has been attempting to answer are:

- Which printed periodicals have been digitized in Europe or anywhere else in the world?
- How can these be accessed from one search point?
- In which journals can full text be searched?
- How can digital periodicals be preserved?
- How can rights of authors, publishers and libraries be preserved?
- What are the likely subscription models?
- How will online licensing and accounting operate?

Of particular value to the wider digital libraries community is the establishment of technical standards for the digitization of periodical literature by the DIEPER project, and the unification of the search options presented to users to enable simultaneous searching across linked repositories. A key goal of DIEPER is a dramatic improvement of access to older periodical literature, as well as the provision of surrogates, which will allow libraries to better protect the originals. The partners believe that availability of these resources through a central register will greatly increase use, which in turn will convince the online hosts that accessibility to them should be maintained for the long term. It may also be possible that the DIEPER strategy will reduce operating costs in libraries and help to fill gaps in existing collections.

Australian Co-operative Digitization Project (ACDP)

The aim of ACDP was to digitize all Australian serials and all Australian fiction monographs first published between 1840 and 1845 and make them available over the web (**www.nla.gov.au/acdp/**). It was a collaborative project between the University of Sydney Library, the State Library of New South Wales, the National Library of Australia and Monash University Library, supported by ten other institutional and industry groups. Digitization was done from microfilm. In some cases new microfilm was produced first, which provided preservation surrogates as well as digital images for access. This project uses both searchable full text and page images, with searchable text for fiction and page images for the periodical publications. Browsing by the catalogue record and by structural navigation has been enabled. One periodical, the *Colonial Literary Journal and Weekly Miscellany of Useful Information*, has both page images and searchable full text created by OCR, with a level of OCR accuracy of 95% claimed (**www.nla.gov.au/ferg/**).

Grey Literature: Forced Migration Digital Library

Since 1997, the Refugee Studies Centre at Oxford University has been planning and implementing a digital library from its unique collection of grey literature on forced migration (the study of refugees and other migrations through conflict, disaster, development or other unforeseen occurrences). The Centre has been collecting key items of grey literature from organizations of many kinds (governmental, non-governmental, intergovernmental, relief agencies, policy groups), and from individuals, for the last 20 years. It now has some 15,000 items in the collection, which is consulted by researchers and practitioners in forced migration from all over the world. However, until now the collection could only be consulted in Oxford. Items in this collection are mostly modern printed or typewritten documents. The Forced Migration Digital Library, part of Forced Migration Online (**www.forcedmigration.org/**), a major information resource on refugee and forced migration issues, is bringing a critical mass of these items to a wider community for searching, consulting and printing.

A feasibility study carried out by the Higher Education Digitization Service (HEDS) at the University of Hertfordshire (available at **http://heds.herts.ac.uk/**), which examined a representative sample in detail, revealed that the documents were mostly in fair to good condition and would respond well to scanning and the use of OCR for indexing purposes. Rekeying was rejected because of the increased costs. All items in this collection are in copyright, so much of the work preparatory to digitization has concentrated on clearing copyright, which has been a demanding, time-consuming and costly process (Cave, Deegan and Heinink, 2000). As of autumn 2001, some 3000 documents have been digitized, around 100,000 pages.

The Forced Migration Digital Library is delivered using Olive Software's Active Paper Archive, described above, which will allow in-depth search and delivery of documents through a web browser. Page images are displayed for browsing or printing, with the search capability of Active Paper Archive using uncorrected OCR as the basis for full-text indexing and text retrieval. Metadata records defined in the Dublin Core metadata standard (see Chapter 5 'Resource discovery, description and use') are also available for searching. The project is working with centres around the world to produce other online collections of grey literature about forced migration, cross-searchable through an integrated interface – a true 'virtual library'.

Photographic collections

By depicting a past world photographs can provide invaluable information about events, people and daily life.

(Klijn and de Lusenet, 2000, 2)

Many libraries and other cultural institutions hold photographic collections large and small, and these collections are increasingly at risk because of inherent instabilities in the photographic process; even relatively recent materials like colour prints of the last ten or so years are fading and losing definition. Many of the holdings are in urgent need of conservation and reformatting, and some of the materials are actually dangerously unstable, such as nitrate film stock, which can ignite or even explode without warning. A survey of photographic materials in Europe carried out by the European Commission on Preservation and Access (**www.knaw.nl/ecpa/**) revealed that the 140 institutions that responded to the survey hold some 120 million photographs, half of which are over 50 years old. This is an astonishing number, and gives some sense of the scale of the world's photographic stock, all of which is at risk. Around four-fifths of the survey respondents had already begun digitization of their photographic holdings or were planning to digitize in the future, with protection of vulnerable originals being a crucial motivation. Digital surrogates are excellent substitutes for photographic originals and can provide almost all the content information that the original can yield, though of course artefactual information cannot be conveyed other than in the metadata.

Many libraries rely heavily on photographic materials, which are in some demand by users, picture researchers and commercial organizations. The availability of digital surrogates can reduce handling of the originals considerably: the Royal Library of Denmark estimated that to find between three and five pictures, a user may handle as many as 300 originals (Klijn and de Lusenet, 2000, 19). Accordingly, many institutions around the world are digitizing photographic collections. The American Memory project at the Library of Congress is rich in digitized photographic materials; Klijn and de Lusenet (2000) discuss many European libraries that are embarking on digitization of the visual heritage, and the European Commission on Preservation and Access (ECPA) has set up the SEPIA project (Safeguarding European Photographic Images for Access) which is funded by the European Union to investigate ways of safeguarding photographic collections, including digitization for access (**www.knaw.nl/ecpa/sepia/**). In the UK, the JISC Image Digitization Initiative (JIDI) has digitized photographic collections from libraries in HE institutions for wider access for educational purposes. These collections include the photographs from the personal collection of Gertrude Bell, held at the University of Newcastle (**www.gerty.ncl.ac. uk/home/index.htm**), and the photographic and slide collections of the Design Council, which are archived in two different institutions, the Design History Research Centre at the University of Brighton (**http://vads.ahds.ac.uk/vads_catalogue/DCA.htm**) and the Department of History of Art and Design, Manchester Metropolitan University (**www. artdes.mmu.ac.uk/had/design.htm**). In Australia, the PictureAustralia service provides access to digitized photographs recording all aspects of the country's history, with images supplied by a number of cultural institutions (**www.pictureaustralia.org/**).

Digitization for the print disabled

One of the great benefits that digitization can bring to libraries is the possibility to extend their reach beyond the traditional user base. In the past, many libraries have had little to offer those who cannot read or hold printed materials – the print disabled – but new developments are creating new possibilities for equalizing access to printed materials and enabling new educational and recreational activities. There is now a set of principles known as 'design-for-all' which suggest

> that library IT systems and interfaces are designed in a way that can be easily read by all users of the library, be they physically visiting the library itself or accessing it remotely and regardless of any disability or access preference they may have. The RNIB describes design for all in relation to websites as 'a single version of the website which is accessible to everyone, however they access the Internet'.
>
> (Brophy and Craven, 2001)

The print disabled have just as much need for information and communication tools as any other section of society, and organizations and libraries specializing in serving this group have been trying to fill this need for many years with 'talking books' read out loud by armies of volunteers and generally recorded on cassettes. The problem with cassettes is that access is linear, so works with a non-linear structure are almost impossible to handle. Some of the commonest forms that most of us take for granted are beyond the reach of the print disabled – cookery books, gardening books, religious works, for instance. Textbooks used in schools or colleges need indexes, tables of content and other modes of structural organization in order that they can be read efficiently. According to the DAISY Consortium, 'the next generation of digital talking books will provide this functionality' (**www.daisy.org/**). DAISY is the Digital Audio-based Information System, which is used to create digital talking books with better access mechanisms for more complex documents. The DAISY consortium is working closely with the Open Ebook Forum (**www.openebook.org/**), which is itself offering some redefinitions of what constitutes publishing. DAISY is based upon open, international mainstream standards, enabling the creation of source files of digital text, which can be used in a variety of publishing modes. These include e-text on the web or on local storage media, Braille printouts, and narrated text which is playback-device independent, giving a number of different listening possibilities.

Realizing the new opportunities that the digital medium offers for the extension of library services to the print disabled, a group of European libraries and organizations for the blind formed a consortium to produce customized workstations and training materials for the use of blind or print-disabled students. The ACCELERATE project was funded by the European Union and ran for two years from 1999 (**www.lib. uom.gr/accelerate/**). While to the rest of the world, the development of GUI interfaces was a great step forward in navigation of complex information spaces, to the print disabled this was a disaster, reliant as they had become on text-to-speech processing technology, which works admirably in a text-only environment. The ACCELERATE project (with partners in Greece, Cyprus, Austria and Holland) has developed adapted workstations for print-disabled students, plus training manuals for librarians who need to understand the special needs, and user manuals to train students in the navigation of the tools of a modern academic library: the library catalogue, databases (online and on CD-ROM), the internet, and the adaptive equipment which provides the access to the tools. What is immediately obvious for the sighted can take significant training for the print disabled. Already, blind students in Greece and Cyprus are reaping benefits from this project, and some interesting issues are arising for debate as a result of ACCELERATE's work. Should institutions, for instance, wait for the print disabled to ask for services, or should services be put in place and then advertised to attract this hitherto under-represented set of library users? To what extent should civilized society be providing library services to other disadvantaged groups, and how can digital library developments assist with this? Could the whole educational experience of the print disabled be transformed by maximizing digital formats?

Also funded by the European Union, the MIRACLE project (Music Information Resources Assisted Computer Library Exchange), which began in 1999, is a two-year endeavour to produce and standardize musical scores in Braille. The project's aims are:

- To develop a system whereby libraries and institutions producing music Braille can share resources of information and documents through electronic access to a standardized catalogue and through the downloading of the digital Braille files;
- To make the system the basis for a world-wide virtual library of Braille music information and documents. . . . By creating such a catalogue and database the amount of Braille music available to clients around the world will be dramatically increased;
- To add spoken music and large letter music files to the database in order to test their delivery and acceptability. Through this distribution to stimulate other libraries to join in this type of production, using common standards. (**www.cordis.lu/libraries/en/projects/miracle.html**)

Digital library programmes

The projects described above are, on a large or small scale, creating digital materials for exploitation in a wide range of ways. There are now many organizations throughout the world going further than this and creating digital library programmes at an institutional, national or international level. These are strategic initiatives that require planning, funding and implementation over a considerable period of time, and draw on a whole range of skills and managerial input.

In the USA, the Library of Congress has been leading a programme to create a National Digital Library, which began in the early 1990s. The

Library worked with the National Science Foundation and a number of institutions funded by the Foundation, as well as publishers, museums and educational bodies in the USA and elsewhere. It now has some seven million digital items from more than 100 historical collections in its American Memory database and this continues to grow rapidly. The Library of Congress has been working with international partners to promote strategic digital library implementations worldwide, and has also been influential in the development and promotion of methodologies, technologies and standards (**http://lcweb2.loc.gov/ammem/ammemhome.html**).

The Bibliothèque nationale de France began planning a major programme of digitization at the same time as plans were drawn up for the new library at the François Mitterrand/Tolbiac site at the end of the 1980s. The Bibliothèque now has around 30 million pages of documentary materials available in digital form (much of which relates to the 19th century). For technical and economic reasons most content is presented just as page images, but there are also works available in full text. Around two million pages are accessible through the internet via the Bibliothèque's *Gallica* web service (**http://gallica.bnf.fr/**) together with collections of visual materials.

Digital technologies are well integrated into all the Bibliothèque's operations, and what is of particular interest is the hybrid reading experience offered to users who work on-site with the collections. Terminals are available in all reading rooms, and readers may ask for items from the analogue collections to be delivered to the research reading rooms. Digital documents can be selected on screen and downloaded from dedicated servers via the high-speed internal network. The workstations in the research reading rooms offer facilities for annotating, highlighting, tagging, creating hypertext links, and word- and image-processing the digital document. The workstations are integrated with other functions of the system, so that users can also access electronic documents via the internet or search external databases (**www.bnf.fr/site_bnf_eng/ bibnumgb/index.htm**).

The British Library also began conceiving of new digital possibilities while planning a new building, and digital technologies are integral to its operations now that the Library has moved to the new site. During the 1990s, the Library undertook a programme of technical innovation under its Initiatives for Access programme, intended to 'assist the library in intelligently appraising the best way to exploit the new opportunities that technology is increasingly offering' (Alexander and Prescott, 1998, 17). The projects have included the digitization and advanced image enhancement of the Anglo-Saxon Beowulf manuscript, the digitization of Gandahran Buddhist scrolls – 2000-year-old artefacts which are the oldest South Asian manuscripts of any type – the digitization of sound archives, of patents and also of microfilm. Now that it is installed in its new St Pancras premises, the Library is embracing digital access to its collections and its new goal is that 'the collections of the British library and other great collections will be accessible on everyone's virtual bookshelf – at work, at school, at college, at home' (**www.bl.uk/**). The Library is currently building an advanced digital library infrastructure to enable it to deliver digital content. This content comes from both the materials it makes available digitally from its own collections, and also from the whole range of born-digital materials that it receives each year on voluntary deposit and needs to preserve for the long term.

In Japan, the Electronic Library Service of the National Center for Science Information Systems (NACSIS-ELS) provides an integrated system of bibliographic databases and electronic document delivery of Japanese academic journals on the internet. Journals are either born digital, or are digitized by NACSIS-ELS, once copyright clearance has been given by the professional societies who own the rights. More than one million pages have been digitized, and are available for full-text searching and downloading (Adachi et al., 1999; **www.nacsis.ac.jp/els/els-e.html**). At the National Institute for Japanese Literature (NIJL), a digital library system for Japanese classical literature is being developed from a number of existing databases, which includes full text, movies, images and catalogues, with linkages between them to form a multimedia database. In addition, NIJL has constructed a Digital Study System to allow users to make full use of the digital materials. This includes an image annotation program to add textual annotations to areas of images that can then be searched along with keywords from catalogues or full text from databases (Adachi et al., 1999).

The New Zealand Digital Library (NZDL) is a research project at the University of Waikato whose aim is to develop the underlying technology for digital libraries and make it available publicly so that others can use it to create their own collections. A number of collections of New Zealand

and Pacific materials are made available through the Waikato website, as well as collections in music, Arabic and women's studies, and a considerable amount of material in human rights. Researchers are developing methods for, among other things, digital collection management; Maori, Arabic and Chinese language systems; internationalizing the library interface; optical music recognition and musical collections; and a whole range of interface and information-mining projects (**www.nzdl.org/cgi-bin/library/**).

Conclusion

The projects and programmes described here cover almost the whole range of materials that it is possible for libraries to digitize, and they exemplify the numerous benefits that can be conveyed through the increased availability of rich library objects in digital form. Everything described here is free, requiring only that the user have access to an internet terminal. There is huge diversity in the methods, techniques, hardware, software, standards and protocols employed and what is presented here is the merest fraction of the digital activity that the libraries of the world are engaged in. This material is available for searching, analysing, some for downloading or printing and all for the enrichment of human knowledge.

We are now reaching a critical mass of digital content that can begin to fulfil some of the promise of the medium claimed over the last ten years. Some say that we are moving too fast:

> technology is still often used unnecessarily, rarely fully exploited, and has brought new problems which are sometimes not acknowledged: it is time-consuming, expensive, and because of incompatibility, in some cases may prove to be of little long-term use. . . . There should be a strong argument for the additional benefits of computerization which will counter the additional costs. (Whitfield, 1998, 166)

Judicious consideration of the issues laid out in the first part of this chapter should help librarians avoid some of the pitfalls and minimize the risks attendant upon these new modes of working. Perhaps the question that needs to be posed here is not 'Why digitize?' but 'Why not digitize?', for it is vital to examine all the alternatives to digitization in any pre-project assessment, including the option to do nothing. Embarking on digitization projects for the wrong reasons and without full consideration of all the issues not only risks failure, but has opportunity costs too. Digitization is right for many libraries and collections, but it might not be the right route for everyone in all circumstances, as we examine in more detail in Chapter 4 'The economic factors'.

3

Developing collections in the digital world

Any library that is actually installed in a specific place and that is made up of real works available for consultation and reading, no matter how rich it might be, gives only a truncated image of all accumulable knowledge.   (Chartier, 1992, 88)

The library of the future seems indeed to be in a sense a library without walls . . . the library of the future is inscribed where all texts can be summoned, assembled, and read – on a screen.   (Chartier, 1992, 89)

Introduction

The universal library, holding all the world's printed artefacts, has been a utopian vision for several centuries, according to Chartier (1992, 62). This vision underpins the amassing of great collections in research and public libraries – the goal being to have all of human knowledge under one roof. When these collections were being put together, long gone were the days when any one individual could have read all of the writings of the world, if indeed they ever existed, but the dream of one space where the reader could wander around and interact with all of human ideas, history and memory was a seductive but elusive one. Now there are new utopian visions of the universal *virtual* library, where the user can surf through cyberspace and find all of human knowledge waiting to be accessed. Most modern libraries have more pragmatic goals: to build collections which satisfy most of the information needs for most of their users. In the digital world, the means of achieving these goals are changing, the costs of doing so are problematic, and the communities of users are fluid. As McPherson suggests, 'A library today has to be part of a global or national network if it is to meet all its users' needs' (McPherson, 1997, 1). In this chapter, we examine the increasing use of digital resources that are obtained from outside the library, and how these relate to the analogue collections that are the traditional province of libraries. Is digital collection development different from collection development of non-digital resources? What are the strategic issues facing library and information professionals charged with the delivery of hybrid information, much of which they may not have direct control of?

This chapter will discuss the following issues:

- why digital?
- advantages of digital data
- the new universal library: the distributed hybrid library
- collection development: just in case, or just in time?
- digital content and its supply
- electronic serials
- scholarly journals
- new modes of journal publishing and republishing
- the future of serials publishing
- reference works
- e-books.

Why digital?

In the previous chapter we discussed the many reasons why individual institutions might choose to convert some of their holdings to digital form and deliver them more widely within and outside the institution. But the great majority of digital (or indeed any) resources that a library will access will come from outside the library, from publishers, from republishers, from other libraries, and from websites of organizations large and small, as well as individuals, who are delivering digital content. Given that these materials derive from a wide variety of sources, professional and non-professional, compose many different data types, each with its own set of formats, and are delivered on a whole range of substrates (disk, tape, CD-ROM, DVD), libraries are facing a management task of unprecedented proportions. However, libraries have coped with great changes in the objects they handle, the means to describe them, and the users of them since libraries began, and are well placed to thrive in the digital library environment.

In a recent article, Robert M. Braude suggests that using the term 'digital' in 'digital library' is a redundancy, and points out the difference between the 'product that we manage in libraries, information, and the familiar container for that product, the codex book' (Braude, 1999, 85). These containers have influenced library architecture, but they do not themselves define what a library is. Braude suggests that as 'we did not bother to qualify our libraries by calling them clay libraries or papyrus roll libraries, why now do we have to call them digital libraries?' (Braude, 1999, 86). While these comments are valid, and in terms of the intellectual management and understanding of data need to be taken seriously, there *is* a distinction to be made between traditional libraries and digital libraries (or digital collections within libraries). The physical containers for information are capable of direct access, and are managed physically – they are stored in environments best suited to their particular needs and delivered physically to the users for access. Digital data is ephemeral and fragile, can be detached from its 'container' with (usually) minimal effort (which works inscribed in codices cannot), can be replicated indefinitely almost to infinity, can be altered without trace. While the differences between analogue and digital data may be more of degree than of substance, they are sufficiently large to need different approaches.

The relationship between container and information is, in fact, a complex one, where form and function intertwine to contribute to meaning. The book allows much more sophisticated organization of information than did the scroll; interestingly, the computer screen owes more to the scroll than to the book, and though hypertextual linking is complex, it has probably not yet achieved the sophistication of the printed page for information presentation. There are, of course, many advantages of digital data, but, interestingly, the terminology of the print world still rules: digital collections are digital libraries, new electronic texts are e-books, and Whitaker's guide to the availability of CD-ROMs is called *CD-ROMs in print.*

Advantages of digital data

The different formats of digital data are discussed in Chapter 1 'Digital futures in current contexts'. There are sufficient advantages to the provision of digital data to make tackling the difficulties that they might pose for libraries worthwhile. Digital data can be accessed from anywhere there is a network connection and a terminal or computer (subject to the necessary authorizations). It can be searched and manipulated in ways impossible to manage in the analogue world, it can be downloaded, printed, annotated, shared, or exchanged. Importantly in a library environment, digital data has permeable boundaries – that is, digital media can be inter-related in ways that make it difficult to tell where one object begins and ends. In a digital version of an article, for instance, the footnotes can be live links to the referents, allowing instant access. If, in turn, that resource has live links to other referents, then the user can pass from article to book to article *ad infinitum*, picking up information along the way. Given the underlying structures of digital data, these links can be made between many different formats – images link to text, text to maps, texts to video or sound, and so on. And the information objects do not need to reside in the same collection, or even in the same country or continent. As long as the network connection can be made, the link can be followed. From virtually anywhere, the user can access resources from virtually everywhere – digital data has the virtues of ubiquity and simultaneity.

The permeability of boundaries in the digital world has some interesting consequences (and disadvantages): if we are unsure where the information objects begin and end, how can we know who owns them? What are the implications for the management of intellectual property rights and for payments to owners or rights holders? How are we to cite sources? How can the user trust that the object is what it purports to be?

The new universal library: the distributed hybrid library

The emerging hybrid library that holds and provides access to a plethora of information in a multiplicity of formats is the reality that all libraries, large and small, specialist and general, are facing. But the rapid proliferation of digital data *does* have serious implications for library management, resources and economics: users are expecting more from their libraries than access to physical materials, and librarians are seeking to provide this through the purchase of electronic datasets, the digitization of parts of their own holdings, and the licensing of electronic journals and other published materials.

Shifting perspectives

The digital world has also caused a shift in the perceptions of users and librarians, and in the underlying paradigms upon which libraries are based, which means that owning and controlling resources on a local basis is no longer the only efficient or effective way of satisfying information needs. Libraries have, of course, always shared resources in the non-digital world. As Rebecca T. Lenzini states: 'It doesn't matter if you have it, it only matters if you can get it' (Lenzini, 1997, 46). Interlibrary loan and document delivery have been valuable services to all users of libraries large and small for many years, and there have been reciprocal reading arrangements and other co-operative efforts. Brophy points out that 'few libraries have more than a small percentage of the materials that users may want. Hence, users need to draw from collections and services provided by many different sources' (Brophy, 2001, 207). There has been co-operation, too, in the sharing of catalogue records through OCLC and other co-operative cataloguing ventures. But the rise of the internet, and the ease with which resources can be accessed and shared, creates new opportunities, as well as posing practical, economic, and strategic problems for library managers.

Guenther sees the digital library as a parallel development alongside traditional collections (Guenther, 2000, 35): tomorrow those collections could be integrated in new, hybrid configurations. The key concept is user perception of information: in the modern world users are increasingly seeking a one-stop shop to satisfy their information needs. Surfing the web might be fun, but it is time consuming and can turn up a great deal of chaff before the grain of wheat is retrieved – and librarians are excellent chaff-sifters. While the one-stop shop goal may be as unattainable as the universal library, perhaps what libraries can offer users is a first-stop shop which moves them on in a seamless fashion to resources outside the physical or virtual bounds of the library, with the guidance and expertise that only librarians can provide. What users want is the resource and the information: they may be less interested in the format of that information. Format is only relevant when it impedes retrieval: if a book is available on a shelf nearby, then that could be as useful as an electronic text, but if the book is unique and is only available in physical form many thousands of miles away, then an electronic text will serve the purpose. The main goal of the hybrid library is to find the shortest path between the expression of an information need and its satisfaction, and also to provide the unexpected to the user: what Lenzini refers to as the 'delighters' – those unexpected discoveries which are 'the strongest satisfiers of all' (Lenzini, 1997, 47).

Collection development: just in case, or just in time?

Just in case

From the time of the great library at Alexandria, founded by Ptolemy I in the 3rd century BC, libraries were established as the holders of collections of writings. Nearly half a million book rolls are thought to have been stored at Alexandria, and the kings were avid collectors, amassing volumes from all over the known world. Collection development, therefore, has been the primary function of libraries from the beginning, and the size and scope of collections is what has defined a library and its importance. This traditional view is expressed by Miksa (1989, 781) thus:

> A library is first and foremost a collection of the graphic records, knowledge records of humankind. A library, if anything, is a collection. If there is no collection, there is no library.

Collection development is carried out by specialists and is aimed to supply the present and future needs of the users of the library. Collections are built in anticipation of these needs, so that when the need is expressed, it can be fulfilled as quickly as possible – this is the just-in-case model of library provision. The collection is an investment, which will pay back in terms of benefits derived by users (Burke and McGuiness, 1997, 3). The extent to which this model succeeds is difficult to estimate. Users are rarely experts in information seeking, and they may select their resources from the set of what is available locally, depending on the type of library and the degree of need. A reader wanting a crime novel from the local public library may be satisfied from a whole range of possibilities presented on open shelf, or may have read a review of one specific work and insist that it is provided. A student at an educational establishment with an essay deadline may choose out-of-date or inappropriate resources because other students got to the library first and borrowed the more relevant books. An academic or writer, on the other hand, will need precise resources, whatever the cost or difficulty; if they are available locally they will be satisfied, if they have to wait they may be frustrated. A lawyer researching a case will not only need precise information, but will need it to be not just up to date, but up to the minute.

Size of library holdings or amount of library circulation are often taken as metrics to estimate the worth of a library (and many universities, for example, will use numbers of books in their library as marketing tools in their student prospectuses), but there can be some salutary corrections to this. For instance, a recent survey at the British Library, which holds millions of items in hundreds of languages, from all periods since the dawn of writing, revealed that the most-used resources are those written in the last ten years and are mostly in English. Mercer (2000) points out that statistics for holdings, user traffic and reference enquiries are used for budgeting and other key decisions, but declares that 'standard statistical observation does not always reflect or define what is "good" or "of value"'. For her, 'understanding what is "of value" becomes even more difficult and complex as an increasing number of our resources become digitized'. Libraries exist to add value to the documentary heritage by aggregation, cataloguing, research and expertise, and it is increasingly difficult, on current funding with the influx of digital data alongside the increasing supply of print materials, to carry out these activities within the bounds of any one institution. Do libraries need to find some new modes of operation to cope with this? In the digital world, the notion of an identifiable collection is questionable. What counts now as part of the collection? And does it matter? A library with modest physical collections but excellent, well-organized, well-described links to a range of quality digital resources might satisfy the needs of its users better than a larger organization with substantial but lesser-used print collections.

Just in time

In the business world, the advent of computerized stock control has meant that suppliers of all kinds of goods – from aircraft parts to food – have moved from holding stock just in case it was requested to obtaining stock just in time for its use. This has resulted in greater precision of supply chains, and reduction in costs of warehousing and storage. In libraries, there is much debate about this changing model and the potential it has for delivering library services. The traditional library holds physical resources, many of which may not be accessed for decades, in order that they may be supplied rapidly at the time of need. Given that digital data can be supplied instantly to anywhere from anywhere, and that digital data often replicates physical data, do the physical versions need to be kept a) locally on-site or b) at all? Even in the print world, libraries have been re-evaluating some of their periodical subscriptions in the last 20 years in the face of declining budgets and increasing costs, and many have opted for cancelling subscriptions and using document delivery instead.

A number of cost–benefit analyses have been carried out which suggest that this approach makes good economic sense – these are assessed by Tammaro (2000). For instance, one study suggests that 'the library could make available double the number of periodicals by changing the acquisition policy from ownership to access, with an additional cost of only 15%' (Tammaro, 2000, 160). The paradox here is that as journal subscriptions are cancelled, publishers raise prices to compensate, eroding the financial benefits of the just-in-time model. The just-in-time model will therefore only succeed if it is not too successful (Blagdon, 1998, 273). If costs to libraries rise too steeply, they may have to be passed on to users. Anecdotal evidence from users suggests that this move does not necessarily satisfy all their needs – they have to be increasingly precise in articulating requests if they are to get what they want. And they lose the benefits of browsing the latest journals, though abstracting services that are increasingly available through databases and the internet can often provide sufficient information for decision-making purposes. There is, too, a desire for instant access by users, who may not want to wait weeks for requested documents to arrive. Electronic document delivery can ease this: document supply services such as the British Library Document Supply Centre can often provide the item within 24 hours.

Though a shift to the just-in-time model of document supply can save money, it can be difficult to predict demand for budget planning purposes. With the just-in-case model, annual subscriptions can be known in advance, but with just-in-time supply, apportioning fair budget shares to all stakeholders can be complex.

Print on demand

The just-in-time model is one being adopted in the production of printed materials, as well as in their supply. Many publishers are experimenting with providing print on demand, which is only made possible when publishers hold large archives of works in digital form that can be output to printing and binding technologies. Bertelsmann, for instance, the world's largest publisher, is building a digital database of out-of-print books which it can deliver rapidly in printed form – a strategy categorized as 'sell first, print later' (Robins, 1999, 13). This has obvious advantages to the publishers in stock control and budgeting, and is also a boon for libraries and readers. Out-of-print titles with low demand can be returned to circulation, something that would have been uneconomic for a publisher producing conventional print runs. netLibrary (see below) also offers a print-on-demand service.

Digital content and its supply

Digital content is being delivered in libraries that derives from many different sources and under a whole range of divergent financial arrangements or controls. The financial implications of the purchase and maintenance of digital data are discussed in Chapter 4 'The economic factors'. Some of the key sources of digital data are:

- a library's own holdings that have been digitized
- purchased datasets on CD-ROM
- purchased datasets that are online
- electronic publications with a paper equivalent
- electronic publications with no paper equivalent
- electronic reference works, which increasingly have no paper equivalent
- e-books.

The resources listed above, though digital, do not necessarily change the delivery paradigm from ownership to access. All of these might be wholly owned by the library and delivered by the library to the same sets of users as the analogue versions, but this is unlikely. Even if this were true, users within the library would have a different experience of using the resources, which most would find beneficial, though there are still reluctant adopters of technology who might feel disadvantaged. There are other sources of digital data that do change the paradigm; these include:

- digital holdings of other libraries and non-profit organizations
- the internet and its myriad resources.

Electronic serials

As discussed in Chapter 1 'Digital futures in current contexts', electronic publishing has moved from a niche activity for major publishers to a mainstream part of the core business, in particular in the area of electronic serials. There are many advantages of electronic serials delivery for publishers, authors and readers. In most academic disciplines, rapid turnaround of articles is a key factor, with science, technology and medicine (STM), and law, being the most demanding of speed. Speed, however, is not the only advantage of electronic serials publication. Leonhardt suggests that journals are 'in a nascent third generation: forward and backward hyperlinking of citations' (Leonhardt, 2000, 122). The first two generations were electronic text supplied by e-mail, and web publication in HTML and PDF, and a fourth generation is on its way using expert systems. These new generations of serial publications have significant advantages over the print versions.

It is outside the academic world that serials publication has exploded into electronic provision. Newspapers, newsletters, and trade and popular magazines are now as ubiquitous on the world wide web as they are in print. AJR Newslink (the *American Journalism Review*) reports that there are (as of spring 2001) 3400 US and 2000 non-US newspapers online, with surprisingly good coverage in the developing world. There are 53 titles listed for Africa, 24 for Central America, six for Nepal, and even one in Mongolia (**http://ajr.newslink.org/news.html/**). It would be impossible to quantify the number of magazines, and more particularly newsletters, available electronically, as they arrive and depart with great speed. But many (perhaps most) print publications have some kind of electronic counterpart – even if it is just a sample website to lure users to subscribe to print. Substantial numbers of newsletters are free on the web, some with no print equivalent. This is a potential nightmare for the preservation of the documentary heritage, which we discuss further in Chapter 8 'Preservation'.

Advantages of electronic serials

The advantages of electronic publication for popular serials are many: timeliness, reach, ability to include mixed media, interactivity. Some publications, for instance have interactive advertising, which allows users to link direct to the sites of the advertisers. For the readers, these are a great boon: the items can be accessed far from home, there is often added value, and some publishers offer 'My Paper' facilities where the user can select a profile and receive only articles that he or she requests. If you are interested only in international news, sport or TV listings, then that is all you need receive. But increased revenue for suppliers seems to be elusive, with many losing money for their online offerings. Some online versions are free, and the service is funded with advertising. So why do publishers engage in something that is likely to lose them money? The possible answers to this question are many, but probably most suppliers feel that they have little choice: if an organization is not visible in the digital world it may as well not exist.

For libraries, the choice to provide popular materials in electronic form is generally less of a financial question, given that many are free, and more of an organizational one. Selection of titles to which to provide links will be guided by the mission and subject base of the library. If the print versions of these are subscribed to, there may be decisions about maintaining the print subscription, but stability of reference, given the interactivity of the online product, and the need to maintain the historical record, might dictate that print subscriptions are maintained. Management of the electronic data – cataloguing, linking, maintaining links etc. – is, however, an unwelcome extra load in periods of eroded library budgets.

Scholarly journals

The numbers of electronic journals being produced have increased exponentially in the last ten years. Fosmire and Yu (2000), in a review of scholarly journals, report 39 electronic journals in 1994, two to three times that number two years later and over 1000 in 1997. The vast majority of STM publishers, and many in the humanities, are now producing electronic journals. The increase in the numbers of electronic journals is accompanied by an increase in the overall volume of journal publishing. With the pressure on scholars to publish more, faster, journal sizes are growing (more issues per year, more pages per issue) and new journals appear regularly in print, online or both.

Currently, most publishers offer electronic journals alongside print versions, with (sometimes) free access to the electronic journal for subscribers to the print. Some charge more for print plus electronic access, and an increasing number of journals are available only electronically. On average, at the beginning of 2001, anecdotal evidence from collections librarians suggests that to take print plus electronic subscriptions is costing libraries a 10% increase in overall journal subscriptions.

The means of supply of scholarly journals is changing rapidly, with many institutions purchasing titles direct from the publishers, rather than through vendors. Many publishers license electronic journals as package deals of subject sets, which can be problematic. In a department-based institution, for instance, with devolved budgeting, reaching agreement with departments about levels of shared financial contribution can be problematic. To give a brief example of how a major science journal publisher is handling the move online, Blackwell Science Journals Online offers a range of purchase options through the *Synergy* online journal system, 'to ease the transition from print to online journals' (**www. blackwell-science.com/online/default.htm**). These are:

- **Option 1:** Combined Subscription (print + online): 110% of the print subscription price
- **Option 2:** Online-Only Subscription: 90% of the print subscription price
- **Option 3:** Collection: one-year deal for consortia wishing to access the complete collection of journal titles while maintaining most of their print subscriptions

- **Option 4:** Choice: online-only journals discounted further for bulk purchase.

It is worth noting that a consortium of Dutch libraries formed in late 1997 recommended that subscription to the print plus electronic version should cost no more than 7.5% more than subscription to print alone, and that subscription to the electronic version should cost no more than 80% of the print rate (Sosteric, 1998). A notable exception to current pricing models is the journal *Nature* for which the licence to the electronic version costs 20 times the print subscription. Many libraries in the UK have boycotted the electronic *Nature* for this reason.

Other purchase or access options are through aggregation services such as Journals@Ovid (**www.ovid.com/products/journals/index.cfm/**) which has over 440 STM journals from 60 different publishers going back to 1993 available as searchable full text. These are linked to each other through their references, and are also integrated with bibliographic databases – a third-generation service. Other aggregating services proliferate, such as EBSCO and Ingenta. One of the largest new players in the domain of journals aggregation is TDNet, a journals service offered by Teldan Information systems. TDNet can provide access to 180,000 periodicals from all over the world and claims it has hundreds of libraries as clients. They also supply filtered, analysed, real-time and customized information services, which are 'adding real value to information used by managers, scientists, consultants, professors, decision makers and information professionals'. This, they suggest, moves information supply from the 'Information Age' to the 'Informed Age' (**www.teldan.com/**). Users accessing journals through TDNet can

- view integrated alphabetical lists of journals
- search journals, publishers and aggregators
- search tables of contents across the collection
- order e-mailed alerts of new issues
- define private profiles.

Long-term access to electronic journals

An issue that has been raised many times in discussions of electronic journals is, what happens to the backfiles if an individual or organization cancels a subscription? With print, the volumes remain on the shelf. Is this still the case with electronic? Many suppliers provide the actual data, rather than a link to it, and the licences include the rights to the back-files as well. But librarians need to be sure when they are negotiating sub-scriptions that these rights are included. Another potential problem is the maintenance of complex links in backfiles of journals when sub-scriptions are cancelled. Is this an added technical load on the library sys-tems team? Will some of the links disappear in time, never to be re-created?

Non-commercial scholarly publishing

There has been a great deal of debate in scholarly circles and the aca-demic library community over the commercial model of scholarly pub-lishing. The argument against using commercial publishers is that academic institutions pay their scholars to produce research output, they give this free to publishers, and then publishers sell this back to academic libraries in monographs and journals. This is something of an over-sim-plification, but it makes the point – and some academic institutions are moving towards cutting out the middleman (though sometimes it is not quite clear who is the middleman). Organizations such as the Interna-tional Consortium for Alternative Academic Publication (ICAAP, **www.icaap.org/**) and the Scholarly Publishing and Academic Resources Coalition (SPARC, **www.arl.org/sparc/**) have been established to create a more competitive marketplace for academic publication throughout the world. Partners in both these endeavours have already produced a number of high-quality, peer-refereed journals that are available free or at significantly lower costs than those charged by commercial publishers.

Problems in non-commercial publishing

For scholars, publishing outside the mainstream, reputable, stable print world has been a difficult move. Fears (well founded) that appointment boards and tenure and promotion committees would not recognize the worth of electronic publication held many back, though scholars were early adopters of electronic communication for the sharing of ideas, and they participate enthusiastically in discussion groups and news groups. A notable exception to this reluctance to publish electronically has been in physics, where an electronic preprints archive was established at the Los Alamos High Energy Physics Laboratory as long ago as 1991. arXiv.org (**http://arXiv.org/**) is a fully automated electronic archive and distribution server for research papers. Areas covered include physics and related disciplines, mathematics, non-linear sciences, computational linguistics and neuroscience. Publishing in physics is time critical, and traditional journals were not moving quickly enough for the scholarly community. The archive is a community-based activity that allows scholars to mount papers awaiting publication on the archive for viewing by other scholars; upon publication the published article replaces the preprint. This has been extremely successful, and there are some new initiatives growing out of it such as the Open Archives Initiative (OAI), which has been established as a 'forum to discuss and solve matters of interoperability between author self-archiving solutions, as a way to promote their global acceptance' (see **www.openarchives.org/**).

There is a recent development in the scholarly community that could revolutionize scientific publishing, the Public Library of Science (**www.publiclibraryofscience.org/**). This is an advocacy group, which has called on scientific publishers to hand over all research articles free six months after publication to public online archives. Large numbers of authors are threatening to boycott publishers who don't agree to this, and over 20,000 scientists in 155 countries support the action. Scientists sign up to the group via an open letter published on the web, and the numbers are growing daily. This is an excellent example of the use of the web to change the power bases in publishing: individual scholars must accept the terms of publishing conglomerates in order to gain academic recognition, but a critical mass of scholars has a combined voice, which is more likely to be heard.

New modes of journal publishing and republishing

Electronic production of publications is not only of huge benefit for those who are publishing new materials, it also offers many opportunities for the re-engineering of valuable content in back issues of journals. There have been several initiatives in the last five to ten years that have republished journal materials in electronic form, to great benefit to the communities of libraries and their users.

JSTOR and Project Muse

JSTOR is the brainchild of William Bowen, president of the Andrew W. Mellon Foundation, and was originally conceived to solve space problems in libraries. The plan was to convert back issues to electronic files, allowing libraries to dispose of the paper version and thus free up shelf space and save capital costs. A collateral benefit is that smaller institutions who have never purchased some of the titles in the first place can now access them at a fraction of the cost of the initial subscriptions. According to its publicity materials, JSTOR 'injects new life into materials that seem moribund'. JSTOR has been extremely successful; it now has the full back runs of 117 journals in a wide range of disciplines. Current journals are not available in JSTOR, which operates a 'moving wall' policy, different for each journal. For some the wall is five years, that is, journals are made available electronically five years after print publication. For others, the wall is only two years (**www.jstor.org** or **www.jstor.ac.uk/**). JSTOR is extremely popular with users: a recent study showed that students used the online JSTOR service 20 times more than they used the equivalent print resources.

Project MUSE has similar aims to JSTOR: it publishes back runs of significant scholarly journals, but it also provides the latest issues as well. MUSE has one of the most elegant designs and efficient searching mechanisms of any academic service. MUSE was founded by Johns Hopkins University Press in 1995, and it now supplies over 100 titles from a number of publishing partners (**http://muse.jhu.edu/**).

The future of serials publishing

In the first two generations of electronic delivery, serials online or on CD-ROM were either replicas of the print format, or were actually less functional and less attractive. Complex page presentations, graphics, symbols, colour, etc. were difficult to replicate electronically. Advances in processing power, storage, bandwidth, screen technology, encoding, presentation and search algorithms mean that more functionality is now possible. What has been lost is the potential for browsing along library shelves, but even this is now being addressed. Abstracting and alerting services can be customized so that users are informed of new tables of contents or individual items in which they have registered their interest. Portals and personalized information environments (see Chapter 7 'Portals and personalization: mechanisms for end-user access') also allow users to control what information they receive and the way it is presented to them.

Serials themselves look set to change formats and delivery modes to a more fragmented and episodic, yet complexly linked, style. When the constraints of preparing an edition of a newspaper, magazine or journal for one-off printing no longer apply, items can be delivered as they are ready for publication. This is likely to be popular with users, but has consequences for libraries in the management, access and preservation of the documentary heritage. In the future, what will constitute a journal or a newspaper? What will constitute an issue, a volume? New modes of storage, access and cataloguing will be needed to reflect the changes.

Reference works

There are some works of reference that are so clearly better suited to electronic supply and access that they will almost certainly never again appear in print. Searchable databases are, of course, tools that have been used in libraries for many years. In the 1970s, when services such as Dialog and MEDLINE were first offered, connection time was so expensive that reference librarians spent a great deal of time with library users refining their information needs prior to connection to databases, and this expert guidance meant that users got the best possible answers to their information queries. In the 1980s, when reference sets on CD-ROM began to appear, these were often still used by librarians on behalf of users. The rise of open-access terminals and PCs meant that increasingly users checked out the CD-ROM from the issue desk and had unmediated interaction with it – with varying degrees of frustration given that most products had different interfaces and search methods. With networked CD-ROMs, access could be from outside the library, and users had to be even more self-reliant.

Dictionaries and encyclopaedias are extremely well suited to structured electronic delivery: they have outgrown the capabilities of the book format and are enriched by digital presentation. Oxford University Press was one of the first publishers to make a dictionary available on CD-ROM, with the first version of the *Oxford English Dictionary on CD-ROM* appearing in 1990. This was a DOS-based product that was difficult for users to access, but already the benefits of the electronic format were clear. *OED2 on CD-ROM* was released in 1992 and was still selling in 2000, when the *OED Online* became obtainable. Indeed, in many ways the CD-ROM is still a preferred product: the online version lost functionality, for internet presentation has not up to now offered the sophistication of data manipulation that complex databases on mainframes, standalone PCs or CD-ROMs allow. Moving from paper to CD-ROM to online in the case of the *OED* brings up a key question inherent in all such developments: version control. The printed book is a stable format: editions can be recorded and are instantly recognizable. The non-rewritable CD-ROM is also stable, but online publication has a lability that is closer to the pre-printing press production of books, where each individual work could be (and probably was) changed with each copying. There is a tension in the production of such resources released online: are currency or stability the most important factors? How are users kept informed about updates? How are earlier versions archived for historical reference? How is the relationship between each version recorded? These questions are key to librarians, for whom the authenticity and reliability of the documentary record are of paramount importance.

Given the suitability of the electronic format for evolving, structured data, web-based dictionaries are now common. The Merriam-Webster site offers free access to the *Collegiate Dictionary and Thesaurus* (**www.m-w.com/home.htm**) and even permits other sites to mount a free dictionary search linked to the Merriam-Webster site. The massive *YourDictionary.com* (**www.yourdictionary.com/index.shtml**) links to an incredible 1800 dictionaries in 230 languages. One imaginatively named resource that is linked to by *YourDictionary* is the *Antonym– Homonym–Meronym–Holonym–Hypernym–Hyponym–Synonym Dictionary of English*. When activated, the link leads to the more prosaically designated *WordNet* dictionary (**http://vancouver-webpages.com/wordnet/**). Clearly, *WordNet* has creative marketing staff.

Encyclopaedias have also been greatly enhanced by their conversion to electronic form. In particular, these works of reference benefit from hypertextual linking and multimedia features. Again initially published on CD-ROM (and with many still available in this format), encyclopaedia publishers took a severe beating financially when Microsoft first produced its *Encarta* encyclopaedia and negotiated deals to have it bundled free with new PCs. Why buy an expensive volume or CD-ROM, or even go to the library, when an encyclopaedia came free? The problem here is that *Encarta* is not always as comprehensive or historical as other more traditional encyclopaedias, so users may not be accessing the most suitable products for their needs. On the other hand, online encyclopaedias are available to such a wide audience that many people who have never before used an encyclopaedia or even thought to use one are finding valuable information. Online encyclopaedias proliferate (a web search on 'encyclopaedia' returned more than 200,000 hits), from the monumental *Encyclopaedia Britannica*, to the free *Encylopaedia.com*, to niche works such as the *Wood Badge Patrol Name Encyclopaedia* (**http://www.kfumscout.dk/ kku/wbpatrols.html**), produced for scouts in Denmark. These offer a whole new world of reference to readers, who may once have visited the library for the information they offer.

E-books

> We may not see the full effect of ebooks, for example, until a generation or two has grown up with them and accepts them as readily as television and video games have been accepted by earlier generations.
>
> (Leonhardt, 2000, 123)

E-books are the latest fashion in the world of digital media. Electronic text has, of course, been around for almost as long as there have been computers (see Chapter 1 'Digital futures in current contexts'), and electronic books have been available on CD-ROM and the internet for some time. Some of these have been experiments in interactive or hypertextual fiction, and have been of interest to a small cadre of enthusiasts but have not made much impact on the reading public or on libraries. Eastgate Systems (**www.eastgate.com/**), the developers of the StorySpace hypertext software, market a number of interactive hypertext books, including

Afternoon, by Michael Joyce, one of the first such works to appear.

E-books are different, as they have been designed for use with specialist readers such as the Gemstar reader (formerly the Rocket eBook Reader) and the Everybook Reader. These readers are dedicated machines, with no functionality other than those associated with the reading process – though they allow annotation and bookmarking, and access to reference tools. The first Rocket eBook Reader appeared in 1999 and held only ten works at a time – the first book to be marketed by Barnes and Noble at that time was *Monica's Story,* by Andrew Morton, signalling that these devices were intended for a popular market. E-books were more expensive than the paper versions. There is now a second generation of Rocket eBook Readers marketed by the eBook company (**www.softbook.com/**), which hold thousands of pages and can link to the internet to download titles. They also have a built-in dictionary. Five thousand titles of recent, popular works are available from the eBook company. The marketing hype claims 'Everything you need for a good read is built right in'. Available from RCA, the Gemstar is the size of a hardcover book, and retails at $299 (there is also a version with a leather cover that retails at $699). The Everybook Reader mimics a regular book even more closely. It has a double, facing-page portrait format that folds open, and costs a hefty $1600. E-book readers are not easily available in the UK, but the Microsoft Reader software available for PDAs allows e-books to be accessed and read on these devices.

There are a number of advantages to e-books, but they are unlikely to take off in the popular market because of the price. The readers are relatively light and have the capacity to store thousands of pages. They offer annotation facilities, bookmarking, linking to dictionaries, and instant access to thousands of titles through built-in modems. There is now experimentation with electronic ink in an attempt to combine the efficiencies of the digital medium with the convenience of paper. In the *Librarian's eBook Newsletter,* Susan Gibbons (2000a) explains:

> Paper is convenient in that it is extremely light and easily portable. However, reusing paper usually requires the lengthy and costly process of recycling. Digital displays, such as an LCD screen, can be easily and instantly reused thousands of times, but the appliance itself is often bulky and awkward to carry around. Two electronic ink products currently in develop-

ment hope to wed the advantages of both mediums and eliminate the drawbacks.

She goes on to explain the new Gyricon electronic ink technologies being experimented with by Xerox. The Anoto company in Sweden is working on developing a digital pen and digital paper that look set to revolutionize writing technologies if they take off. The pen works on the Bluetooth wireless communications protocol, which provides short-range links between mobile PCs, mobile phones and other portable devices (**www.bluetooth.com/**). The paper is regular printer paper overlaid with a proprietary pattern of dots. When the digital pen moves over the paper, snapshots of the dots are taken more than 50 times per second. The Bluetooth connection transmits the data to the nearest internet connection along with the time and the owner's details (**www.anoto.com/**).

Evaluation of e-books in libraries

There have been a number of trials of e-book readers in public libraries, with some surprising results. The Monroe County Library System in New York purchased 20 readers for experimental use in five libraries. Given that the suppliers of readers and e-books did not envisage that libraries would be a significant market, difficulties were encountered in integrating these into library procedures. For instance, e-books available from the SoftBook company could be downloaded only over an analogue phone line, while the libraries used mainly digital phones. Cataloguing proved challenging, and 'each reader was catalogued as if it were a container for multiple items . . . and the titles and authors listed in content notes (505) field. Any time a title was added or deleted from the reader, the cataloguing record had to be adjusted accordingly' (Gibbons, 2001, 73). Users, however, found the experience of using e-books a positive one: 'within only two weeks of their availability, more than six months' worth of patron holds were placed' (Gibbons, 2001, 74) and 35% stated that they would prefer to use e-books to paper.

The Richmond Public Library in British Columbia, Canada, has piloted the delivery of e-books to its users, also with some success. The e-book readers are pre-loaded with 13 popular titles, and reserved by the users. The library plans to provide a service in the future that will allow users to dial into the library's server and download more titles. The librarians do not envisage the replacement of conventional books by e-books; they state:

> The Ebook is just one more way to provide improved service to our customers and offer them access to the world of knowledge, information and entertainment. The important thing for the library is to connect people with books, reading and learning, in whatever format. Traditional books will always be around. The future will likely be a mix of new technology and traditional materials and services. One advantage of having Ebooks is that customers have access to more books than will fit on the actual library shelves. They are also terrific for people who travel and don't want to carry a bunch of books with them.
>
> **(www.rpl.richmond.bc.ca/rplinfo/ebooks.html)**

There are problems with the delivery of e-book titles via libraries: e-book readers are not compatible with one another, so titles purchased for one reader cannot be read on another. E-books do not necessarily change the definition of 'borrowing' either, as if an e-book is 'loaned' to a reader, it cannot be used by another reader. We discuss the commercial implications of these aspects of e-books in Chapter 4 'The economic factors'. But there are increasing numbers of titles, and it is possible to download some public domain works from the internet for perusal via e-book readers. It is also possible now to provide more timely information to the readers: each of the e-book reader manufacturers is partnering with one of various current affairs publishers – the *Washington Post*, the *Wall Street Journal*, the *New York Times*, *Time* magazine or *US News and World Report* – to provide news compilations (Gibbs, 2000). See Cox and Ormes (2001) for an excellent review of e-books and their use. In the long term, Sarah Ormes opines, public libraries will circulate e-books that can be downloaded directly from the library catalogue for users to peruse on their own e-book readers. 'They may choose to do this in the library itself or most probably via the library's Web site. This will mean the library user will no longer have to physically visit a service point to borrow or return library books' (Ormes, 2000). Ormes feels that this could have far-reaching consequences for public libraries, but as these institutions are often used as a low-cost alternative to book purchase, the cost of the readers is likely to be a determining factor.

E-books on the web

The provision of e-books through websites looks likely to have the largest influence of any electronic development on how libraries do their business. Project Gutenberg, which has been in existence for more than ten years, has had a team of volunteers rekeying texts, and now offers more than 3000 public domain titles free. But now new kinds of businesses are emerging on a new scale, which promise hundreds of thousands of titles from the world's major publishers to be made available at relatively low cost for the library market. Three of the main companies that have recently emerged in this new market are Questia, ebrary and netLibrary. All offer the full text of books, journal articles and encyclopaedia articles, and also added value in terms of reference and discussion services.

Questia

Questia (**www.questia.com/**) is the most potentially threatening to the traditional role of libraries. The company plans to deliver 250,000 books – a collection that will be larger than those of many small libraries. Users are targeted directly, and pay reasonable subscriptions for access. Many of the world's major publishers have signed up to provide content for Questia.

> There has been huge controversy in academic libraries in the USA, as Questia largely bypasses libraries in its marketing, but has librarians on its collection development teams. Licenses with publishers preclude marketing directly to libraries, as the publishers do not want to erode their established markets within libraries. Wilfred Drew of SUNY Morrisville College Library on a discussion list asked 'Are people from our own profession stabbing us in the back? Do these people hope to outsource their library services? What do they hope to accomplish by being involved with Questia?'
>
> (Drew, 2001)

Questia's marketing materials promote their e-books as an addition to library resources, suggesting that the reference librarian can interact with both Questia and local collections, using a free Questia search function to mine their own collections: a hybrid library, in fact.

ebrary

ebrary (**www.ebrary.com/**) markets its services directly to libraries in order to 'augment the library services and provide its patrons with access to complete text contained within published, authoritative content' (**www.ebrary.com/libraries/index.html**) – libraries are partners rather than customers. It too has negotiated arrangements with major publishers, enticing them with the opportunity to reach 260 million internet users worldwide, maximize sales by allowing browsing, and (interestingly) recoup revenues lost to the photocopy industry. ebrary is not yet launched, but an article in the *New York Times* in June 2000 reports:

> Ebrary.com already has more than 130,000 volumes in its demonstration database and says that it may include as many as 600,000 by the time it opens in the fall. (Guernsey, 2000)

Searching and browsing will be free; users will pay for downloading and printing. Reference tools, maps and archival works will also be available. Revenues are collected by micropayments, which give a share to the publishers – as they make nothing from photocopying, this is attractive, for if traffic is heavy, profits could be substantial. Unlike other publishers of e-books, ebrary do not digitize volumes; rather they obtain the files direct from the publishers in PDF.

netLibrary

netLibrary (**www.netlibrary.com/**) is the e-book publisher that many feel has the most to offer libraries. It targets academic, public and corporate libraries, and has published collection development policies for these main areas. The company declares in its publicity that its core business is creating and distributing electronic versions of books to libraries, and that it is the only e-book system that understands the challenges librarians face. netLibrary values librarians, and its guidelines are based on ALA standards. It has also negotiated with OCLC to maintain an archive of titles, should netLibrary no longer be available, and MARC cataloguing records for the netLibrary titles are available from OCLC. Access to the titles within netLibrary accords with traditional library circulation models: only one user at a time can view an in-copyright text within the collection, and browsing is allowed for up to 15 minutes (Gibbons, 2000b).

netLibrary has been evaluated by a number of institutions, including the University of Texas at Austin, an early-adopter site. The University currently links to 17,500 netLibrary titles, and statistics show that the books are well used and the experience of adopting the service has been positive.

Conclusion

The changes brought about by digital data affect all aspects of collection development and delivery in libraries. In the wired world, many users, given the choice between digital and physical delivery of data will opt for the convenience of digital data, which they can access from their pre-ferred location. As data is detached from the notion of boundness to a physical container, the traditional book format, so too is the supply of information detached from the bounds of the physical library. But libraries still hold many resources that are not, and never will be, digital. Physical collections amassed over centuries are vast witnesses to the wis-dom and cultural heritage of the world. These must not be allowed to fall into disuse, overwhelmed by the digital onslaught.

Libraries exist to extend knowledge and information beyond what individuals could locate or purchase for themselves. They are integral to the notion of civil society: holders, preservers and interpreters of the cul-tural memory. Without libraries, the cultural memory is lost, without cultural memory, society cannot continue to function. What we know is based on the foundations of what was known. We are pygmies standing on the shoulders of giants.

The development of digital collections should be guided by the same principles as the development of any other library collection, those of meeting the needs of the perceived user base and of acquiring materials that might be valuable to the users of the future. The fear is that with the increased costs of purchasing and managing digital data, resources are being diverted from analogue data. Chartier's vision of the library without walls quoted at the start of this chapter is probably unrealizable, for new methods of information and communication do not necessarily replace their predecessors. E-mail and text messaging have not replaced the telephone, digital data is unlikely to replace books. The hybrid library of the future will require changes in the physical layout of libraries, but the library *with* walls is likely to be the nerve centre of the library without walls. As Wilson reminds us, 'the digital or hybrid library is a white elephant if it exists only because it is digital. People must want what libraries deliver, or libraries will become irrelevant' (Wilson, 2000, 81).

4
The economic factors

Information is more useful than money. (Dyson, 1997)

Introduction

The effective utilization of resources is one of the most important management activities in developing digital content and establishing digital libraries. The history of library development has many examples of great libraries being created through the largess of benefactors or the tax-paying public without necessarily having much consideration to the cost-effectiveness of the development: between 1881 and 1917 Andrew Carnegie contributed $56 million to build 2509 libraries (**www.carnegie.org/**). The new market economies faced by today's manager mean that, even in those few scenarios of generous funding, every last drop of value must be squeezed from the available resources to maintain that funding now and in the future. Senior managers are confronting ever more difficult decisions on resource allocation, with the significant issue of opportunity costs to contend with, as described in this chapter. There are several aspects to the effective utilization of resources in relation to digital information. There are the immediate start-up costs of either creating or purchasing digital content; the further implementation costs for establishing a digital library or even just basic access to bought resources; which are followed by the costs implicit in managing and maintaining a digital resource in the longer term. Hand in hand with resource expenditure go the value and benefit derived from the resource itself, how these are measured and offset against costs – can going digital ever become cost-effective? Whether there are intentions to recover costs in their use or to seek profit in the future is a key strategic question that every library manager will have to address in developing digital information resources or digital libraries.

Markets are based upon perceived value and this also has a distinct effect upon digital library development: we cannot afford that which we do not value. Value is a concept based upon individual perceptions, sometimes directed by marketing and other promotional activities, but in actuality it has always had an element of personal choice. The majority of markets are based around the differentials in perceived value rather than actual assets, and these market forces can be seen to be at play in digital library development. Digital libraries being developed now have to demonstrate that their value is greater than the actual assets being delivered or investment in their initiation will be hard to acquire. The intersection between what the user is shown to need, what they actually want and what they are prepared to pay for, is what will constitute value. Without demonstrating 'apparent' values the digital library will be undervalued and thus unaffordable.

In this chapter we seek to describe the strategic influences and implications of these issues in the creation, purchasing and managing of content, and in measuring its cost-effectiveness. Will it be possible to divert to digitization resources saved in other areas of operation or is the only viable option to pass costs on to the users of digital products?

This chapter will discuss the following issues:

- the cost and benefit relationship of digital content
- digital libraries: are they cost-effective?
- breaking even in the digital library
- opportunity costs
- optimizing spending in digital content creation
- purchasing digital content
- the cost of managing digital content
- reaping the rewards
- reaping the future.

The cost and benefit relationship of digital content

The debate continues to rage over whether digital content creation and management can ever be considered cost-effective. The cost of creation and initiation appears so high that doubts are raised that this investment will ever be recouped in financial terms or even in added value, productivity or enhanced organizational prestige and access. This begs a query as to why libraries are actually embarking upon large-scale digitization projects and digital library programmes? The examples are varied and encompass all aspects of library, education and business development as discussed in Chapter 2 'Why digitize?'. Many corporate organizations are installing knowledge management systems or document management installations and obviously believe that these are cost-effective solutions to their business process. Universities and colleges are developing the digital library concept, often with commercial software solutions and at great expense, because the belief is that this will convey educational advantages to their students and researchers, while enhancing the image of the institution. Public libraries that have a civic duty to provide maximum access to publicly available information are embarking with greater confidence than ever before on digital projects and developing high-quality resources for free or low-cost access. Governments are gearing up to provide public services and information through electronic means, both as a way to disseminate more widely and as a means of reaping perceived benefits in efficiency. National libraries such as the Bibliothèque National de France and the US Library of Congress are investing heavily in content creation as a means of preserving and promoting national and cultural imperatives.

Digital libraries: are they cost-effective?

All of this activity and yet it is hard to find real evidence of how cost-effective these developments are in real terms. Kenney states that 'cost-recovery solutions have been advanced, but to date there is little hard evidence that they will succeed' (Kenney and Rieger, 2000, 171). Further studies show that digitization is becoming a commercialized activity for libraries, as found in an IFLA/UNESCO survey, with 7% returning commercial exploitation as a selection criterion for digitization (Gould and Ebdon, 1999, Section 8) while the remainder cited preservation of the original, and improving access. Commercial entities like Questia (**www.questia.com/**) have secured $130 million in venture capital and promise at least 50,000 digitized books on start-up, and 250,000 volumes within three years (Dolphin, 2001, 104). There is some evidence that the costs may in some cases be well balanced by the intangible or indirect benefits, especially so in national libraries where the purpose is not to reap returns on investment in terms of money but in cultural benefits.

In business, the drive to efficiency has often returned the initial investment in real cash terms. Rolls-Royce and Associates Limited (RRA), an engineering R&D company, identified cost benefits as early as the 1970s in electronically storing drawings and worked towards this ideal during the 1980s and early 1990s (Tanner, 1995, 11). Assessment of time efficiency in the 1970s demonstrated that drawing engineers spent less than 40% of their time actually drafting drawings, with the remainder of their time spent trying to find the right information or master drawing. Clearly, for industrial processes the investment against return equation is easier to measure and returns may be more quickly achieved than in other sectors. Larry Ellison, the chairman and CEO of Oracle, estimates that the USA spends about $500 billion on recordkeeping to support healthcare and could save 80% of this through rationalizing the deeply fragmented healthcare databases into a more unified system (Caterinicchia, 2001).

Finding the benefits of digital implementation

These examples both show that perceiving benefits in digital implementation and the actual realization of these benefits may require a long gestation period and a radical strategy not easily supported by all stakeholders. It may also include some false starts (RRA replacing at least one major implemented system before finding success) before the return on investment and benefits are achieved. Even in educational library services the benefits can be tangible. The digitization of examination papers has demonstrated efficiencies and benefits (Rumsey, 2001). In previous manual systems, examination papers were held in the library short-loan collection. Students, wary of the fines associated with overdue short-loan borrowing, would immediately photocopy the papers borrowed and return them to the short-loan desk to be checked back in. An immediate benefit of the digital version is that the short-loan desk does not need so many staff to facilitate a frequently repeated loan transaction of no more than a few minutes' duration. If by implementing this technology for examination papers (or student reading list materials) the library can release staff time for other duties, then tangible, measurable benefits are obvious both to the library and also to the student who no longer queues for an increasingly tatty original. There are issues always to be balanced in terms of the initiation, infrastructure and integration costs before benefits are achieved and so being able to define what constitutes 'profit', or even the break-even point, is essential as a means of justifying expenditure and then quantifying success.

Breaking even in the digital library

Measuring this relationship between benefits and costs remains a difficult issue and with digital services still developing and the benefits often not yet fully achieved, the point of breaking even seems elusive. For managers looking to inform their planning and investment decisions, there would be obvious advantages in being able to predict when or whether a digitization or digital library project will make the transition from loss into profit. The terms 'loss' and 'profit' here are equated not only in straightforward cash terms, but will include other more elusive factors such as actual service enhancement, improved user access and organizational prestige, for instance. Loss is thus the area where investment outstrips benefits and profit is the area where benefits are greater than the cost of maintaining the service provision. While this is a generalization, it is useful to enable an overall unifying hypothesis of breaking even to be described for all potential sectors of digital library development. Each library will have its own measure of costs and benefits and should attempt wherever possible to transfer these into measurable terms that become comparable, whether through weighted ratings or direct cost comparisons. Without these sorts of quantifiable measures, managers leave themselves open to the criticism of not achieving profit or project goals, without having satisfactory proof to the contrary.

A model for the break-even point in digital library development is illustrated in Figure 4.1.

The illustration is founded on real project information but remains a hypothesis, as actual development is not yet mature enough to provide firm numeric evidence for the whole model. We can see that the investment in infrastructure is high as evidenced by Harvard University's investment of $12 million over five years in the Library Digital Initiative (see **http://hul.harvard.edu/ldi/html/ldi_origins.html**) or the start-up costs of £1 million in digital library systems and service implementation at the University of Central England, UK (see **http://diglib.uce.ac.uk/ webgate/dlib/templates/about.asp**). In all projects and services so far viewed by the authors, the benefits have been initially slow to arrive but once achieved in part they grow steeply, as evidenced by the Refugee Studies Centre developments at Oxford University. Looking to the future it seems clear that the increase in benefits will eventually plateau and with prudent management grow steadily into the future – there are very few scenarios of constant exponential growth in any sector of activity. Costs and investment to achieve goals will be reduced over time after the

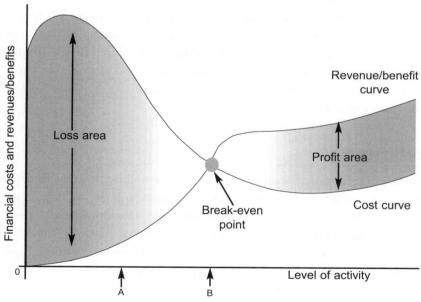

Fig. 4.1   *The break-even point for digital library development*

initial hump of large-scale start-up investment in infrastructure, staffing, training and other implementation costs. The point where the two curves cross (marked as B on the level of activity axis) is defined as the break-even point, where costs and revenue/benefit are perfectly balanced for a short time. The costs of running the service will not plateau at a relatively low maintenance level, but will eventually start to grow again as technology, equipment and infrastructure need to be renewed and the costs of digital data preservation become evident (see Chapter 8 'Preservation').

The area of loss where investment outstrips benefits seems very much larger than the area of profit and begs the question: is digital library development ever likely to be equitable? But it should be remembered that this is nothing new. Libraries have always been expensive to start but have conveyed benefits of many kinds over very long periods that repay the initial investment. The differentials between the cost and revenue/benefit curves after the break-even point might be small but they are not limited; they extend into the future and thus have the potential to repay investment in the medium term. Also, this illustration assumes a zero point starting position, which is unlikely in modern, technically developed organizations. As more technical infrastructure, staff and experience become available then the starting position will slowly move to the right along the level of activity axis until it reaches the point marked A. This means that the initial cost of developing a digital library or digital resource is high at present, but as activity and available experience increase the initial costs will be lower and the benefits will be achieved more quickly.

Opportunity costs

Within any consideration for implementing new technology for libraries in particular, considerations of opportunity costs will be an important factor in decision making and risk management. The opportunity costs are the strategic costs implicit in directing resources to an activity (X), therefore reducing finite resources that might have been expended upon some other strategic activity (Y). The forgone benefits of the strategy Y constitute the opportunity cost of strategy X – there is no direct cash outlay corresponding to the opportunity cost, but there are larger strategic costs in potentially misdirecting resources to a weaker strategy, for both the individual and the organization. In the digital world, these opportunity costs are extremely difficult to perceive in advance, but the results of resource misallocation are soon apparent, and have long-term consequences. For libraries these may be loss or alienation of their user base by not meeting the actual user desires but instead supplying collections that are not suitable for or accessible to their users. The opportunity cost of implementing technology could be very costly to the organization as a whole, where the library is an integral part of the organization knowledge chain.

Optimizing spending in digital content creation

The creation of a digital version generally gives new life to a valued resource. It opens up new avenues of research and use, while enabling wider potential access. However, digitization must be viewed as a goal-oriented tool, and not a purpose all in itself, if expenditure is to be efficiently focused. It is also not solely about applied technology, but more importantly it is about successfully achieving information goals and needs. Having a clear idea of what goals are to be achieved from the resources, and understanding that the limits are mainly the nature of the original materials and the cost–benefit ratios of the conversion are vital. The costing of digitization is a subject that has been the subject of many studies and papers often used to gain a comparative idea of costs when planning projects. The work of Puglia (1999), Tanner and Lomax (1999), plus that of Hendley (1998) is frequently referenced. An up-to-date and accurate point of information for comparative digitization costs is provided by the HEDS Matrix of Potential Cost Factors, which brings together weighted factors to provide sample costs for various digitization scenarios (**http://heds.herts.ac.uk/resources/matrix.html**). However, it is worth noting the following from Kevin Guthrie (2000), president of JSTOR:

> I'd really like you to forget those figures for how much it costs JSTOR to do digitization. They might be helpful, but in reality what matters is not how much it costs JSTOR, HEDS, GDF or any other organization. What matters is how much it is going to cost you.

Identifying cost factors

Within most digital content creation frameworks, the actual conversion/scanning work will usually be a relatively minor part of a wider, more complex, person-driven scheme, as we point out in Chapter 2, 'Why digitize?'. The cost of scanning is relatively low compared with that of copyright clearance, metadata creation or managing the data. Here the first and most important cost factor is identified: people. However obvious, it is worth restating that the more person hours required to complete any task the higher the cost is likely to be. As many aspects of digitization may potentially be automated, some of the conversion costs may be mitigated, but almost no other aspect can be made any cheaper because they will be people intensive. However, the staff costs are often hidden, absorbed by the institution and rarely fully funded by the project budget. Cost cannot always be defined purely as a budget bottom line: the figure put into a budget may not cover the full cost of the time and effort that actually goes into a digitization project. Between institutions and between countries, the cost of staff will vary greatly and in some areas the cost of people will be considerably less than that of acquiring technology and installing infrastructure. While this means that no simple generalization works for everywhere, it is also clear that finding experienced able staff, investing in training and skills and retaining good staff will be key cost factors for all digitization programmes.

There are some other indicators of basic costs, those that are likely to be incurred by every project. These are staff costs for project planning, preparation of materials, some level of quality assurance and checking, and the return of originals to their place in the collection. By far the greatest of these basic costs is preparation, which might include:

- the movement of materials
- inventories and packaging for movement
- time taken to assign unique identifiers to originals
- the cost of clearing copyright or other rights to use materials.

HEDS have estimated that preparation alone can account for up to 30% of total project costs for complex digitization projects (**http://heds. herts.ac.uk/resources/resources.html**). Other indicators will arise from the basic technical specification. For scanning projects in particular there are many different possible combinations of resolution and bit-depth alone, even ignoring other technical treatments, the handling of the original, and metadata and image quality issues. It is thus important to price each project based on the goals of that project. However similar to other projects the proposed work may be, the project goals and originals will always be unique and therefore so should the specification. A feasibility study and pilot are usually recommended to enable a closer definition of prices based upon a small sample at pre-defined specifications.

A feasibility study focused on a detailed digitization issue is the ultimate risk-management tool. For a low expenditure it enables measurable results to be gained. It helps to force decision making within a supportive environment and provides good evidence of the full project costs. Piloting of processes is the transition from experimentation to action by putting the feasibility study results into practice. It is essential to try to replicate as closely as possible real project conditions and the outcomes must be real products and systems. This provides the final evidence that the plan will work, that the quality thresholds are correct and that the end-user and other interested parties will be satisfied. By measuring every aspect of the pilot, final digitization costs can be gained that are very accurate; for any large-scale digitization project this process of study and piloting is highly recommended as a risk-management tool.

Clear goals

To create content cost-effectively requires the information goals to be clear so that the process of creation can be optimized to achieve the required outputs. If the goals remain vague, or are constantly moving, then either the costs will rise dramatically or the project will be deemed not to have achieved its objectives. Investment in selecting the most appropriate resources to digitize, taking into account the information content and physical nature of the original item, will ensure the maximum value from the least costly process.

Purchasing digital content

While the creation of content for the digital library seems both desirable and viable, it will not be the sole form of digital resource held and managed by the digital library. Bought resources from owners of copyrighted materials will be likely to make up the majority of the materials held in most digital libraries. These materials may be 'born-digital' resources, like database products such as OCLC Firstsearch (**www.oclc.org/firstsearch/databases/**), or may be digital re-creations from original materials, like the journals available from JSTOR (**www.jstor.org/**). From the recipient library perspective, they may as well both be regarded as 'born-digital' as that library will only have to deal with the resource in its digital format. This factor is viewed as so strategically important to some libraries that they have taken the approach of designing their initiatives around the future supply of born-digital resources. In particular, Harvard Library Digital Initiative has a philosophy of managing digital resources within the library context and infrastructure, rather than focusing on the digital to the detriment of the core library goals. Managing the costs and materials involved, the methods of access, and the integration process while balancing the resources against the needs of the rest of the library is a key strategic management issue.

There are several models of charging for these digital materials. These interact and interlock as the publishing world attempts to balance the delivery of technical advances with retaining profitability. Getz (1997) suggests that information resources may be offered to a library in one of three main marketing modes:

- the site licence
- the individual subscription
- the pay-per-view option.

Getz also predicts that larger publishers will generally prefer the site licence model whilst the pay-per-view option will mainly be championed by the not-for-profit publishers and smaller institutions pursuing a more active market. In general this distinction appears to have been followed, but the actual market is highly complex and the nuances are intriguing and instructive for future development. The future of charging will be a hybrid of all three main marketing modes.

Site licensing

The site licence model is offered to the organization as a whole, through the library or sometimes directly to the division most likely to use. The costs of use are borne by the purchaser on behalf of the organization, and use of the resource is free at the point of use by approved users. The organization pays one fee for all this use for a limited period. These rates may vary according to the amount of digital resource being purchased (such as number of journal titles), the size of the organization and the level of expected or measured usage. This model remains popular but there are some drawbacks to the implementation that have been unpopular, especially when purchasing from the major journal publishers. Some of these require libraries to continue to subscribe to the paper version of the journal, with the electronic version as an add-on cost on top of the journal subscription. This makes the journals more expensive and reflects the desire of the publisher to maximize revenues from added-value services.

> Other providers find the site licence mode supports the focused content of their resources. A resource like JSTOR, whilst large, is unlikely to gather much individual or pay per view usage because the content is so focused upon academic journals and a specific community. From both the subscribing organization's perspective and the publisher point of view this mode of use has the large advantage of predictability with expenditure and thus revenue being clear at the start of each year to enable planning to proceed based upon known values. There are also many examples of national and international arrangements to make this model cheaper for each of the partner institutions, such as the work of LIBER and its working group on a pan-European approach to digitising journals.
>
> **(www.sub.uni-goettingen.de/liber-wg/)**

Such services may potentially be offered to the individual as an annual subscription or on a pay-per-view basis. Personal subscriptions are directly analogous with print subscriptions but the individual loses out on two counts: they miss the technical and subject guidance of the library plus they have access to the materials but not any ownership in the longer term (see Chapter 3 'Developing collections in the digital world'). In the pay-per-view model, the individual may access the resource to a certain level at zero fee or low-cost subscription for the purposes of identifying the required resource. Once resource discovery has occurred the user then pays a fee for full use of the item, such as the printing and viewing of the full text of an article, the viewing of a streaming video or the licensed use or printing of a higher-resolution picture. RosettaBooks (**www. rosettabooks.com/**) for instance, offer a time-limited product, a self-destructing e-book, which is electronically available at low cost for up to ten hours before the content disappears and has to be renewed (Bowman, 2001a). The concern for librarians is that 'as more and more published content goes digital, they'll have to constantly pay for the work via a licensing model – or risk losing it' (Bowman, 2001a).

Interacting models

What becomes clear is that these models will all interact, and will have consequential impacts upon the purchasing organization. The site licence model seems to protect the interests of the larger publishers, while conferring benefits to the purchaser in terms of organization-wide access at low unit-value costs with predictable (if ever increasing) budgeting. The pay-per-view model is more unpredictable for the organization, as individuals choose the level of use but the organization pays the bill. Historically, this has been an expensive way to use such resources, as demonstrated by the relatively small number of organizations that could afford unlimited end-user access to online databases suppliers such as Dialog in the 1980s and 1990s whose charging was based upon usage and time spent connected. During this period an intermediary, usually the librarian, was the actual pay-per-view user as proxy for the person with the reference enquiry. They not only provided a valued service of producing focused relevant results from the databases, they also ensured the organization did not spend too much money on the process. The growth of local-area networks in larger organizations and the impetus of internet connection made site licensing affordable and made it possible to reach every individual at their work desk without having to police usage closely. Even now if offering unlimited usage of pay-per-view resources, the organization either has to monitor usage/expenditure or confer all the cost on to the individual and act as nothing more than a conduit for the passage of the information resource. As we discuss later in this chapter, the pay-per-view option also has inherent start-up risks for the publisher, as described by Yoder (2000, 173), in that the calculation of initial returns on investment requires a knowledge of likely end-user behaviour that is generally not available at the beginning of such endeavours.

Acquisition dilemmas

For the acquisitions function of the library, the purchase of digital resources remains a difficult balancing act of apparently conflicting interests. The publishers want to retain and enhance profitability, and thus the costs of print journals are rising rapidly every year. Journal prices in the humanities, medicine, science and technology rose by 55% between 1994 and 1999 (Maynard, 2000). But electronic journal provision is not relieving the burden of costs for the library, given that this is often treated as a value-added service, rather than a replacement technology, especially by Reed Elsevier with their large share of the market (**www.reedelsevier.com/**). Thus the library budget appears to be shrinking for the same amount of information resource and the user demand for more digital content direct to their desktops continues to grow. Purchase of a digital product is likely to mean less money for a paper-based one, and thus the balancing of costs against opportunity has arguably never been harder for the library manager. Some institutions have gone down the road of direct charging for the use of digital products. This is surely short termism that may help balance the books today, but library managers may find that the library itself becomes under-funded and even non-existent in the future. If traditional library users transfer their sense of value from the library as a service provider to the few digital resources that they are individually paying for directly, then the further diminishing of the library's role could accelerate.

Acquisitions will not get any simpler and the chances of buying the same information in different guises several times are more likely now than ever before. This makes librarians with tight budgets uncomfortable. In this market, however, Lenzini feels that 'if you buy the same information three times in three different ways, but you meet user needs each time, then that's probably okay' (1997, 46). The cost of trying to de-duplicate the products on offer is probably not worth the amount of effort involved, and user needs must come first if the library is to retain its central purpose. The future remains complex, with a hybrid approach most likely to succeed so long as the information professional takes a central role in promoting the best products for the most appropriate information, and acts as a valued guide through the myriad of resources.

The cost of managing digital content

In the light of the expenditure already made on creating or purchasing digital content there is yet another shock in store – the cost of managing that content and keeping it accessible over time. Digital preservation is dealt with in Chapter 8, but the basic issues of how much it will cost to 'keep and show' is imperative to planning and budget-bidding efforts. Unfortunately the answers are either too vague or too frighteningly high cost to be much comfort – as found by Hendley (1998), and as entertainingly put in a slightly different context by Baker: 'like missile defense, leading-edge library automation is a money pit' (2000).

The actual management of the content has several facets with many layers. The NPO/JISC have produced a useful model that takes into account overlying central functions such as strategy, policy, planning, reporting, management and administration (Feeney, 1999, 72–3) while concentrating on the underlying backbone activities of:

- capture
- preservation engineering
- storage management
- environment engineering
- access/retrieval.

The advice of Kenney and Rieger (2000) to treat digital material as critical assets and invest wisely in the selection and creation of digital resources that are likely to be used and reused over time is welcome, especially in the context of managing content. Without this basic first step of good selection, the rest of the process will never appear valuable or affordable. The NPO/JISC model also addresses how to ensure continued access and reuse over time. Preservation engineering is the process of testing and quality assurance of the actual delivery methodology to ensure that it will work.

Once in active service, there is the continued process of storage management such as back-up and recovery of resources, and any media transfers and data refreshment cycles required to ensure continued access in a form acceptable to the user. In addition to all of the above is environment engineering – the engineering of the technical infrastructure such as the network, operating systems, cabling, configuration management and the continual process of upgrading software and hardware. At the end-user point, basic services are needed, and most importantly from the user's perspective, access and retrieval. This is the top of the backbone, which justifies the rest of the expenditure and is supported by the other layers of the model. This covers issues such as analysing user requirements, guidance and assistance, testing of functionality, provision of tools and interface design. These basic layers, together with strategy, policy, planning, reporting, management and administration are the building blocks needed for managing digital content. In many ways they are analogous to the building blocks always needed for developing traditional paper-based libraries. Consider the cost and effort involved in developing adequate guidance signs, or the everyday cost of returning books to their rightful place on the shelf. The needs of managing the digital content are so great as to be similar to developing a whole new mini-library from scratch. The cost of this new digital activity will be heavy, and in strategic thinking it may be an advantage to contemplate these developments in this way, as a whole new library within a library. The Cervantes Virtual Library, at the University of Alicante in Spain, took this one step further by being created as a new library entirely separate from the already existing University Library (see **http://cervantesvirtual.com/**).

Sustainable development and funding

Sustainable development and funding are needed to manage digital content effectively into the future. Without these two factors, relevant technology cannot be renewed, skilled staff cannot be retained and the intellectual, cultural and educational rewards cannot be reaped. To develop in a sustainable way will require support at the highest levels of the organization to enable it to move from project-by-project funding into a more secure programme base. Any materials that are created will need to be managed into the future, and resources for their perpetual care should be established to address the complete lifecycle of the digital objects, including their long-term management for access. Further, there needs to be continued and extended co-operation between institutions, including further extensions of the commercial–academic co-ordinated effort, as seen in the relationship between Chadwyck-Healey and the University of Virginia to produce a large product: *Early American Fiction 1789-1850* (Seaman, 1999). This sharing of skills, resources and responsibilities allows for greater development and long-term management than would be possible by focusing on purely internal agendas. Beagrie argues that such developments are 'quite probably beyond the means of any single educational or cultural institution' (2000).

Reaping the rewards

To achieve sustainable development and future funding, digital content and services need to be embraced by their audience for their added value. Digital resources will be slowly substituted as the main point of access to some traditional resources, and services will be developed based upon the existence of the digital version. The hope of many is that as the services become used and valued, then the user will be willing to pay at least part of the cost for this added value or the convenience offered. This seems acceptable. The researcher who no longer has to cross an ocean or continent to view the ancient manuscript central to his or her work has saved considerable money, so logic suggests that they should pay for some of the cost of providing the service. The genealogist who no longer has to wade through reams of papers and microfilm to find their distant relative, but can do complex and comprehensive searches of a specific resource, might be willing to pay something towards the service.

The assumption that users will pay for added value is predicated upon that value being visible to them and upon their ability to compare it favourably with past methods. Content is the critical factor according to Seaman and 'nothing brings people back like a well-selected, reliable, integrated and catalogued set of data' (1999, 15). However, the genealogist may not value the increased searching facility if they trust their research skills more than they trust the electronic resource or if they perceive the cost as being too high in relation to the cost of going to the physical resource for themselves. Also, in both scenarios above the suggestion was that the user would pay something or a part of the cost of the service and resource provision, not that they would pay it all. Models for complete cost recovery are few and generally based upon a resource of such intrinsic value to such a wide audience (for instance, great works of art) or on massive content aggregation that the commercial imperative actually subsumes other information goals. It is thus unlikely that many organizations will be able to make convincing revenue-only justifications for their digital services, but this should not dissuade them from seeking contributions from their user base. The key question then becomes how should these be sought and what mechanism best suits the organization and the intended audience.

Digital commerce models

Several models have been offered for digital commerce. Beagrie (2000) offers a range in his paper on sustaining innovative content-based services, Frey (1997) and Houston and Chen (2000) also offer others. In synthesis these are as follows:

Free website

Where the content is free and the advantage gained by the host organization is the prestige of providing such a valuable resource.

Controlled circulation subscription model

Where a registration is required in order to gain access to the resource. Professional bodies sometimes use this for access to their materials and the membership fees defray the costs of provision. Other examples are newspapers that may be using the data for market analysis and thus gaining advantage from controlled access to a proportion of the resource.

Subscription model

Where the user or organization pays directly for access to a specific resource or to an aggregated set of resources. Frey points out that working out the charging level is critical and not a trivial consideration using the example of 'the Wall Street Journal Online where over 750,000 subscribers used the site when it was free, but only 70,000 users subscribed to the site once a licensing fee was implemented' (1997, 31). A disadvantage of this model is how visible it is, with the user/organization paying a lump sum in advance of any benefit received, making start-up risks high. If the users do not value the service enough to risk advance payment then it will fail financially in a very short period of time without other sources of income. Subscription-based services must be supplying a critical mass of content in a key area to become viable.

Advertising subsidized models

In this model, advertising revenue is raised from user access to the resource, with adverts being displayed in banners or frames around the content. This model assumes a very high level of traffic by commercially desirable users for it to be viable, and thus may not be suitable for some content-based sites. Also, some organizations may find that advertising contradicts their charter or their users' perception of them and is thus counter-productive. The advantage of this model is that the user pays quite indirectly for the service and thus may feel they are getting an excellent deal, while the host institution has fewer problems chasing payment for use. Portals can leverage high levels of usage to gain revenue, not just through direct advertising, but through sale of limited proprietary products or services and through-sale, although this drifts into the domain of the transactional model.

Transactional models or pay per view

The premise here is that the user pays for just what they use. This usually means that a certain level of information is free and may convey satisfactory use to a wide number of users, but that charges start when the added-value aspects are invoked such as higher-resolution images, full-text output, quality prints or viewing streaming video. The main difficulty with this model is gathering the payments in as painless a way as possible for both the user and the host. The new popular payment modes, such as micropayments, may make this possible but the cost of gathering the money must always be factored heavily into both the marketing of the service and the amount to be charged for it. Anecdotal evidence suggests that some early implementers of the transactional model actually found they were charging less for the product than it cost them to administer the payment process.

Broadcast models

In this model, information based upon a user profile is 'pushed' directly to the desktop without the user having to constantly interact with a resource or the internet environment. This model is still based upon advertising revenues with Infogate, the 'antidote to information over-load', as a prime example (see **www.infogate.com/**) or the Eudora e-mail system offering their full product if you allow them to advertise within the application space (see **www.eudora. com/**). It is unlikely that this model will suit any but the most commercial of digital library developments.

These models are predicated upon the assumption that the digital library has something to offer for which users will be prepared to pay. It is likely that this will be content-based at first and mostly of low market value to a global economy, but as more teaching, learning, cultural and presentational services are added to enhance the content, then it will increase in marketability. The inclusion of teaching packs and lesson plans in the Atomic Archive (**www.atomicarchive.com/main.shtml**), a site which explores the complex history of atomic bomb development, greatly enhances the other historical, scientific, photographic and video content presented. First and foremost, though, is the need for content and accessibility, and from that foundation value can be added.

Conclusion

The route to sustainability in the future is not going to be down a single path, nor will it be a simple process, and a hybrid approach, both for the future of the library service and for the models of sustainable development, seems the most viable. Beagrie argues that 'digitized cultural information, no matter how worthy, is not in and of itself commercially viable' (2000) and that the investment in its development, maintenance and delivery can only be achieved through initial non-commercial development funding or sustained by the supply of value-added services. This is certainly true of the 'worthy' end of the cultural tableau. But dot.com e-libraries like Questia (**www.questia.com/**), XanEdu (**www.xanedu.com/**) and ebrary (**www. ebrary.com/**) have jointly received in excess of $150 million of venture capital for the digital provision of pragmatic learning resources, aimed at a paying audience, with promises of offering 'the ultimate learning destination' (Dolphin, 2001, 104). This is serious competition to the modern library and will stretch the already pressured library manager's justifications for digital library development in their own institution and their need for sustainable funding for all information services, whether e-based or traditional. The key remains the unique value of the content that could be presented and preserved and the unique modes of access that may be designed for the future. The justifications for investment are not going to only be financial, and strategists need to seek other tangible advantages for their organization to help justify the initial costs of development.

To develop in a sustainable way will require support at the highest levels of each organization and should be based upon long-term goals and returns rather than short-term gain. It is imperative that short-term technical solutions for short-term gain are avoided and that internet-based systems do not risk the underlying valued digital assets by focusing on the immediate problems of funding or technical infrastructure. What appears impossible today might be tractable in the near future. It may be more strategically sensible to wait until the task can be done correctly than to jump in too early, wasting resources and potentially having to rework the project because it is in advance of current possibilities. Library managers will need to bear in mind the opportunity costs inherent in chasing new technology, and ensure they focus on core information goals.

The future is ripe with possibilities for new fund-raising and charging models, with a constantly expanding potential audience. The rise of micropayment, especially in mobile telecommunications technologies enabling internet access such as i-Mode and WAP, has been meteoric. Under this scheme the user pays a tiny amount per transaction direct to their phone connection supplier, which appears in their overall connection bill, rather than constantly referencing a credit card number or other comparatively cumbersome payment method. Particularly in Japan, where ten million phones had internet access utilizing micropayment modes by May 2000, the future for information provision will shift from how much it costs the user to be connected (telecomms or ISP charges) to how much does the unit of data/information costs. With the further rise of WebTV, the sheer penetration into the general global population of access at potentially low cost to electronic information resources and services makes the future look both increasingly competitive for finance and for an audience in a truly global economy.

5

Resource discovery, description and use

At some point the Internet has to stop looking like the world's largest rummage sale. For taming this particular frontier the right people are librarians, not cowboys. The Internet is made of information and nobody knows more about how to order information than librarians.

(Rennie, 1997, 6)

Doing research on the Web is like using a library assembled piecemeal by packrats and vandalized nightly. (Ebert, 1998, 66)

Introduction

In Chapters 2 and 3 'Why digitize?' and 'Developing collections in the digital world' we looked at how decisions might be made in libraries about digitizing local holdings, and how libraries are dealing with the plethora of digital information that they are buying or licensing from major information providers. There are new formats, new resources and new players in the traditional venues of information supply, and the changes are rapid and bewildering. In this chapter, we consider the complexity of the new information spaces within which libraries are operating. We show how the limitations of search engines create confusion and effort for users, and discuss alternative models of resource construction and description, and of metadata creation. We examine the crucial roles played by the library and librarians in bringing some order into the chaos.

This chapter will discuss the following issues:

- the world wide web: structure
- the world wide web: content
- libraries and the web
- search engines and their limitations
- resource description
- metadata
- types of metadata
- metadata schemas
- other metadata systems
- collection-level description
- metadata creation
- collaborative projects in resource description and discovery.

The world wide web: structure

In Chapter 1 'Digital futures in current contexts', we describe briefly the origins and structure of the internet and the world wide web, which are interdependent concepts, given that the structure grew out of the origins. The web is now the largest information space that the world has ever known, and it continues to grow exponentially. Any estimate of how large and complex the web is will always be inaccurate and out of date the instant it is computed. Nevertheless, the scale is frightening: recent analyses report that there are currently around 100 billion hypertext links on the web, and projects which are attempting to map these links suggest that the complexity is on a level with that of the human genome (Denison, 2001; Jackson, 2001; Nuttall, 2001). A British company, Link-Guard (**www.linkguard.com/**), has just completed an ambitious project to map every link on the web. It takes 40 servers around the world, each of which collects and stores a terabyte of information, 12 days to create an updated map of the whole web. What is worrying is that at any one time 10% of the links are broken, the equivalent of ten billion inaccessible hyperlinks. Estimates put the average life of a link at 44 days, suggesting a huge level of instability of information sources. Imagine the chaos in libraries if books disappeared every 44 days, and then sometimes mysteriously reappeared on another shelf with different content – that is the situation we are currently working with. Librarians are used to dealing with 'fixity' in information objects (Brown and Duguid, 2000), but the web is inherently fluid in nature. How will fixity of any significance be achieved by librarians?

The world wide web: content

The web, of course, has not only structure, it has content – a very large quantity of content. It has information about anything and everything that anyone could ever want to know about. And the web grows organically and haphazardly. Anyone can have access to the information on the web if they have a computer, a modem, a phone line, and a small amount of knowledge. And with very little more knowledge, anyone can be a content producer. In many ways, this is no different from the pre-web world, where anyone could produce a newsletter or a document, print it and circulate to whomsoever they wanted. But the properties of digital data and the massive scale of the networks mean that small, local publications, for instance, that were once circulated to perhaps 20 people in the local chess club, or family Christmas letters, are now out there alongside the mass media and all the other internet resources, and they can show up on your screen through a search engine, whether you want them to or not. The web is levelling, and what is problematic is that there is often no way of knowing how valid that content is, given that it is sometimes impossible to ascertain its provenance and pedigree, and given that the information changes constantly. Above all, it is difficult to know how to create knowledge and meaning out of the content. So, in this complex landscape of information, where are libraries and what can librarians do to help users make sense of all this?

Libraries and the web

Libraries themselves are, and always have been, hybrid and complex information spaces, and librarians are trained and experienced navigators of those spaces. With the advent of the web, there are orders of magnitude more information than has ever been held in any library in the world, but libraries and librarians are still best placed to organize that information, using the long established principles arising from traditional librarianship. There are new tools, standards and techniques emerging for the design, description, discovery and presentation of digital information, many of which are being developed in library environments. There are no better information seekers than librarians:

> . . . librarians are not just good at Internet searching because we understand how to play word games. We're good because we know where we need to go and the quickest routes for getting there; we are equipped not just with compasses but with mental maps of the information landscape.
>
> (Block, 2001)

As discussed in previous chapters, libraries are increasingly producers of digital information, as well as consumers and organizers. Well-formed descriptions of digital data are what will ensure its value and survival, and so librarians need to be aware of how to adapt their well-honed skills in description to the newer data formats.

Creating catalogue records for purchased digital resources, adding metadata to locally digitized resources, and cataloguing remote resources are some of the new activities that librarians are having to engage in. Some do this less than willingly, not because they are Luddites, but because, as Shaughnessy has pointed out 'libraries exist in two worlds – the world of Gutenberg and the world of Gates' (1997, 10). Many bibliographic records have not yet been retrospectively converted to electronic formats, and there are collections of primary source materials that have never been catalogued at all, or were catalogued in the 18th or 19th centuries and badly need upgrading. If a resource is not catalogued, it is invisible to users in the print or the digital world, and librarians may find themselves cataloguing the ephemeral popular at the expense of the durable neglected. For the development of well-formed hybrid libraries, it is crucially important that *all* library resources are catalogued online, and that the catalogues can interoperate: a Herculean task. As Arms states, 'helping users find information is among the core services provided by digital libraries' (2000, 187).

Search engines and their limitations

For most users, search engines are one of the prime information-seeking tools for use on the web, ranking second after following links from web pages. Despite the many limitations of the tools, most users become surprisingly adept at information retrieval, but at some expense of time and effort.

Search engines generally consist of three components: a crawler, an index and searching software. The popular Yahoo search engine (**www.yahoo.com/**) is an exception, as it derives from a classification system. The crawler component follows hyperlinks and creates lists of the pages it visits (a process known as 'harvesting') and notes whether they have been indexed or not. The indexing is the key to many of the problems inherent in web searching. Given that many websites are created by people who have only rudimentary notions of information architecture and design, only the most basic level of detail can often be extracted. The information may also be misleading. Some website developers fill the site with key terms to ensure that they are returned with high relevance rankings, and others deliberately use populist terms to attract users to the site, a process known as 'index spamming'. There are a number of popular search engines, which have different features and ranking systems, and different strengths and weaknesses. They all lack both precision and recall – that is, they over-retrieve and they find much irrelevant information alongside the relevant. The Google (**www.google.com/**) search engine performs rather better than most, as it has a different ranking method – pages are ranked by analysing the links in cycles, looking at not just a web page *per se*, but also at the other pages it links to. It can therefore cover more pages than other engines in the same number of crawls. There are companies that offer to ensure high rankings on the Google search engine via dummy 'invisible' sites which link back to the main site and each other, therefore creating a mathematically high linkage rate that lifts the ranking.

In order to improve precision and recall, search engines have been developed that operate in more limited domains – see for instance the Meta Search Engine for Searching Multiple Human Rights Sites at the University of Minnesota Human Rights Library (**www1.umn.edu/ humanrts/lawform.html** or **http://heiwww.unige.ch/humanrts/ lawform.html** (European mirror)). This simultaneously searches up to 15 different human rights websites. The form available allows users to select which sites they wish to search, then displays results consecutively.

Problems with search engines

Several studies have outlined some of the problems with the use of search engines on the web, categorized by Hill et al. as the 'brute force method of searching the Internet' (1999, 9). The first one is coverage. Lawrence and Giles (1999) surveyed 11 search engines, and found that the best of them, Northern Light (**www.northernlight.com/**), indexed around 16% of the pages checked, and the worst, EuroSeek (**www.euroseek.com/**) only 2.2%. Together, however, these engines indexed around 42%, making metacrawlers (which link together several search engines) a promising development, though the increased number of hits can be a problem. See for instance MetaCrawler (**www. metacrawler.com/**), which searches across 13 other popular search engines, including AltaVista and Google. The second problem is user expertise: search engines can perform relatively well when applied by a user who understands search strategies, but in the hands of the inexperienced they may be less useful. Many users will search on only a single term, returning millions of hits. They often do not understand boolean searching or the use of wild cards, or they may enter text with errors and retrieve no results at all. This causes a high degree of user frustration. As Prime (2000) says:

> What I really dislike about the web is that it has a way of making you feel stupid. I really don't feel comfortable with anything that makes me feel stupid because, deep down, I know that I am not stupid, regardless of what the web would have me believe.

Another problem is hidden links: search engines cannot index pages that they cannot access directly. If there is password protection on a website, or the data is generated dynamically from a database (a method of website design that is becoming more widely used), then the search engine may be unable to reach relevant resources.

Resource description

The purpose of creating tools for resource discovery is to allow users to locate the items they seek, whether they know of their existence or not. This is the essence of librarianship. Finding a known object is always going to be easier than finding a range of previously unknown objects pertinent to the topic being researched. In the known case, searches can be constructed by even inexperienced users that will almost certainly result in satisfactory retrieval. Search engines, despite their limitations, perform this task well. It is when the user knows only the field of enquiry, and not the precise resources, that search engines are less useful.

The main reason that information retrieval on the web is so fuzzy is that web page construction and description is imprecise. There are few standard information architectures adhered to by web developers, and the language within which structures are expressed (Hypertext Markup Language or HTML) is overly simple and underspecified. The simplicity of HTML is a major factor in the rapid growth and ubiquity of web-based information, given that it is straightforward to learn and rapid to implement, but it is not scalable for the further long-term development of networked information. Rigorous description and construction will provide better management of digital objects, and more accurate retrieval – the key to this is metadata.

Metadata

For anyone who might wish to design an open and universal library, the possession of such catalogues was a necessity. The sum of their titles defined an ideal library freed from the constraints imposed by any one collection. (Chartier, 1992, 70)

Metadata is one of the principal concepts for the description, organization, exchange and retrieval of information in a networked environment. Metadata is a fashionable term, and subtly different definitions of it are given. 'Meta-' is a prefix meaning 'of a higher or second-order kind', and 'data' is (broadly) 'known facts or things' and (more narrowly) 'quantities or characters operated on by a computer'. The simplest definition that is often given for metadata is that it is 'data about data', that is metadata is data that describes another data object. But 'all metadata is, in fact, data. Whether or not particular information functions as data or metadata is a matter of context or perspective, and what is metadata to one person or application can be data to another' (**http://hul.harvard.edu/ldi/**

html/metadata.html). So a review of a book published in a newspaper is metadata and the book itself is data. In another context the review may itself be data, and have metadata attached to it. The review might be catalogued, for instance, producing a structured metadata object. So in the chain book->review->catalogue record, review can be either data or metadata. (There are other definitions for metadata in the computer science realm that we will ignore for the purposes of this discussion).

Definitions

The following three definitions probably encapsulate all the meanings of metadata of immediate relevance to this chapter. First of all, Gill's elegant statement (2000, 2), which relates data and metadata:

> The term 'metadata' . . . refers to structured descriptions, stored as computer data, that attempt to describe the essential properties of other discrete computer data objects.

Then Dempsey and Heery's (1997), which is about the user dimension:

> Metadata is data associated with objects which relieves their potential users of having to have full advance knowledge of their existence or characteristics.

which means that users can find what they are looking for, even if they don't know that it exists, and finally Lagoze and Payette (2000, 84):

> metadata is structured information about data – information that facilitates the management and use of other information.

Metadata has two main functions, according to Dillon (2000) quoting the world wide web consortium definitions:

- to provide a means to discover that the data set exists and how it might be obtained or accessed
- to document the content, quality, and features of a data set, indicating its fitness for use.

Lucas (2000) suggests three functions for metadata. It is needed to:

- render each item in the collection uniquely identifiable
- provide multiple pathways for finding each item; and
- place the information contained in each item into context with other documents, items, information and knowledge.

How does metadata relate to traditional library cataloguing? According to Gorman, 'metadata [is] a fancy name for an inferior form of cataloguing' (Gorman, 2000), though some might not agree. If we take the broader definitions, then a catalogue record is, of course, metadata. It may be analogue metadata about an analogue object: a catalogue card describing a book, a digital record about an analogue object: a MARC record of a book; or increasingly, a digital record about a digital object: a MARC record of an electronic journal. In the digital library world, the term, as Gill suggests, refers to digital descriptions of digital objects, and these descriptions are constructed to allow the management of these objects over the long term so that they can be accessed and understood by users. As Dempsey and Heery point out, quoting Caplan, there are advantages 'of using a "new" term that does not have the traditional connotations of cataloguing' (Dempsey and Heery, 1997, 2). For Gill:

> One of the most interesting consequences of the metadata research taking place around the globe is that effective cataloguing, historically perceived as an arcane art practised only by librarians, museum curators and archivists, is now becoming an issue for a much wider community.
>
> (Gill, 2000, 8)

Metadata is one of the critical components of digital resource development and use, and is needed at all stages in the creation and management of the resource. Any creator of digital objects should take as much care in the creation of the metadata as they do in the creation of the data itself – time and effort expended at the creation stage recording quality metadata is likely to save users much grief, and to result in a well-formed digital object that will survive for the long term. Well-formed metadata is the most efficient and effective tool for managing and finding objects in the complex information spaces with which libraries are now dealing.

However, it is expensive to create if it needs human processing rather than machine processing. It has been estimated that it costs around $50–70 to create a MARC record for a bibliographic object, and metadata for digital objects can be even more complex and expensive than that for analogue.

Granularity

Before discussing the types of metadata currently in use for the description and location of digital objects, it is important to address the question of granularity. Granularity is the *level* at which metadata is applied to an object or set of objects. The expense of creating metadata rises in proportion to the degree of granularity. The more detailed a level at which the object is described, the more effort (and therefore resource) needs to be expended. In a library catalogue, for instance, a serial publication might have one entry for an entire run, even if this contains hundreds of volumes. The user is given the shelfmark, and then peruses the physical objects for the precise volume, issue or article needed. This is providing metadata at a coarse level of granularity. At the other end of the scale, another library catalogue might provide links to an electronic serial where all volumes, indexes and even individual articles are described. The user can point, click and be taken straight to the individual item. This is metadata at a fine level of granularity.

In resource discovery, it is often difficult to know the level of granularity of metadata. One record may be used to describe a complex, multipart entity: a large website, a library catalogue. Or a record may describe an individual item: a one-page document, a single image. In lists of retrieved resources, these might be delivered side by side, with the user left to make sense of them.

Types of metadata

Cataloguing and metadata creation are processes of substitution, the record stands for the object so that the user has economical information about that object in order to ascertain whether it is indeed what they want. Metadata generally contains a pointer to the location of the object: a classification scheme such as Dewey Decimal indicates a place on a library shelf, a URL the location of a digital object. Many information objects carry their metadata with them so that cataloguing is partly a process of extracting the metadata. The title page of a printed book is a good example of this; the metadata must be processed by a human cataloguer to create an external record. With digital objects, the metadata can be embedded and then automatically extracted, with greater or lesser success depending on the quality of the metadata. Web search engines (discussed above) operate by automatically finding and extracting embedded metadata.

Different organizations creating metadata for different purposes propound different typologies of metadata, and there are probably as many typologies as there are definitions. Here we plan to discuss:

- descriptive metadata
- structural metadata
- administrative metadata.

Descriptive metadata

Descriptive metadata refers to the attributes of the object being described and can be extensive: attributes such as: 'title', 'creator', 'subject', 'date', 'keywords'. 'abstract', etc. In fact, many of the things that would be catalogued in a traditional cataloguing system. Metadata is generally expressed as text, but of course it can be used to describe non-textual objects: maps, images, sound, video. The JISC Image Digitization Initiative (JIDI), a UK-wide project to capture digital images from a range of subject areas including social history, art and design, and geology, produced an extensive set of metadata guidelines (**www.ilrt.bris.ac.uk/jidi/metadata.html**) based on the Visual Resources Association Core Categories (**www.vraweb.org**).

The description of non-textual data in text is problematic as there is more room for subjectivity of perception on the part of the cataloguer than with textual materials. Textual materials are often 'self-describing': they contain textual information about subjects or keywords that can be extracted from the resource itself. With non-textual data, the metadata is created by individuals who, with the help of a range of reference works, make the most objective assessment possible about the object, but subjective bias is unconscious and cannot entirely be ruled out. When describing complex visual objects, the target audience will sometimes determine what is included. A fashion historian, for instance, might look at a photograph of political leaders in the 1920s and be more interested in their hats than in their politics. It is difficult to know all the possible intended uses for metadata, and detailed description is likely to be very expensive, relying as it does on skilled creators. However, using text for all kinds of descriptive metadata means that a single catalogue can combine records for many different kinds of resources, which lets the user search for information without needing to know its format until it is retrieved. There is work in progress on the retrieval of image data by analysis of the image content, but this is fraught with difficulties given that the construction of meaning from image data is a complex and poorly understood intellectual process. However, some useful systems are being developed for the identification of watermarks and trademarks, both of which have well-defined physical characteristics (**www.unn.ac.uk/iidr/**). Other content analysis programs have complex algorithms defining shape, colour, texture, etc. Venters and Cooper review these extensively (1999).

Descriptive metadata can be applied at a fine level of granularity, with descriptions of even one image running into hundreds of words. As in any cataloguing, the application of metadata to digital objects needs to be rigorously controlled, with use of thesauri, name authority files, standard subject headings (Library of Congress Subject Headings, Medical Subject Headings). Good use has also been made in digital imaging of standardized iconographic descriptions, such as ICONCLASS. The Bodleian Broadside Ballads project at Oxford University has applied rich metadata to a collection of 30,000 ballad sheets, using the web version of ICONCLASS for iconographic description (**www.bodley.ox.ac.uk/ballads/**).

Structural metadata

Structural metadata describes the structure and relationships of a set of digital objects. If digital surrogates are derived from complex analogue objects (books, journals, etc.) then the relationship of the components one to another has to be captured in the metadata if a true representation of that object is to be preserved in the digital format. For instance, metadata for a digital surrogate of a book needs to record the page arrangements, the table of contents, and perhaps relationships between sections and chapters. Metadata for digital images of a 3-D object such as a sculpture needs to preserve the relationship of images of different views so that composite views can be created automatically. Structure can be maintained through the use of file management techniques such as a file directory hierarchy or through the encoding of the structure using markup languages such as HTML.

Structural metadata is important because the structure of an information object, whether it is digital or not, is an important indicator of that object's meaning. We can recognize the difference between a letter, a scholarly article and a children's book even if they are written in an unfamiliar language or script by the conventional structures they use. Structure is also vital for user navigation of an information object: a dictionary, an encyclopaedia, a reference book with a table of contents are all navigated through well-understood structures. This is even more important in the digital world as structural clues are less easy to follow. One knows, for instance, when one has read three-quarters of a physical book just by looking at it. With a digital file more explicit markers are required. Indeed, it is probably true to say that without good structural metadata it is impossible to manage digital objects in a repository, or to guide user interaction with these. If good digital library implementations are to be built, a great deal of care and attention needs to be given to structural metadata as this defines the shortest path between the user and the object. It is also vital for the provision of digital materials to the print disabled, who interact with explicit structures through, for instance', voice commands for navigation: 'reread last paragraph', 'go to chapter three', etc. See Chapter 2 'Why digitize?' for some projects that are producing digital materials for the print disabled. The Encoded Archival Description (EAD) metadata scheme described below is particularly strong in structural descriptions, given that mapping structural relationships is a key function of archiving. Work has also been done on describing the structure of documents using the Ebind system which 'records the bibliographic information associated with the document in an ebindheader, the structural hierarchy of the document (e.g., parts, chapters, sections), its native pagination, textual transcriptions of the pages themselves, as well as optional meta-information such as controlled access points (subjects, personal, corporate, and geographic names) and abstracts which can be provided all the way down to the level of the individual page' (**http://sunsite.berkeley.edu/Ebind/**).

As with descriptive metadata, rich structural metadata is expensive to create if this is done manually. However, there are a number of new initiatives that are experimenting successfully with the automatic creation of structural metadata. The European Union-funded METAe Project (The Metadata Engine Project) is developing automatic processes for the recognition of complex textual structures, and predicts that

> The greatest progress will be made by introducing layout and document analysis as key technologies for structural and partly descriptive metadata capturing. A high amount of the typical 'keying work', e.g. the ordering of text divisions such as chapters, sub-chapters or the linking of articles within a periodical will be taken over by the METAe engine. Page numbers, headlines, footnotes, graphs and caption lines are promising candidates for automatic processing as well.
>
> (**http://meta-e.uibk.ac.at/workflow.html**)

The project has 14 partners from seven European countries and the USA. It is co-ordinated by the University of Innsbruck. It is planning to develop application software focusing on:

- the automatic recognition and extraction of metadata from printed material, especially books and journals
- creation of an omnifont OCR engine for the recognition of 'Fraktur' (a German style of black-letter text type) and other typefaces seldom used in modern European printing
- the development of five historical dictionaries supporting the OCR engine
- production of an XML/SGML search engine
- provision of an open source library for a simple web application for presenting digitized printed material.

Olive Software's Active Paper Archive, described in Chapter 2 'Why digitize?', has the capacity to create structural metadata automatically from complex newspaper pages using newly developed zoning and segmentation techniques. Page images of text are analysed, using font sizes, horizontal and vertical lines, text lines and pictures as clues to the structure. A segmentation engine builds a complex map of the pages and the relationships between all the objects, which is output to XML and stored in an XML repository. Users can then search newspapers using the structures, for instance searching only in advertisements, or only in picture captions (Deegan, King and Steinvil, 2001).

Administrative metadata

Administrative metadata is all the information needed to manage a digital object throughout the whole of its lifecycle (see Chapter 1 'Digital futures in current contexts'), and will include all the information needed for preservation (see Chapter 8 'Preservation'). Administrative metadata records information about the creation of the digital object:

- initial capture settings
- scanner parameters
- file formats
- compression
- date of capture.

Much of the administrative metadata that describes the capture process can be generated automatically by the hardware and software.

Administrative metadata also records the information about what is needed to use the object, such as file format, programme used to create it, etc., and also about the legal and financial aspects of access to the object:

- rights management
- payments
- costs
- authentication.

It encompasses any information that might be of use to future caretakers of that object, and it records all the events that happen to it during the entire lifecycle: every time the object has any maintenance functions carried out on it, these need to be faithfully recorded in the accompanying metadata.

For the librarian, good administrative metadata is vital to the provision of services and systems to library users, as it will allow the efficient and effective management and supply of data through the system. However, digital materials coming from outside the library have divergent metadata schemes applied to them, and sometimes scanty applications of the schemas. Administrative metadata is vital for the long-term preservation of digital objects (see Chapter 8 'Preservation').

Metadata schemas

A schema is a formal theoretic description or outline used to define various systems of categorization. This is where things begin to get complicated, for there are many kinds of metadata schemas. First of all there are markup languages, which allow metadata structures to be embedded within electronic text, and can also be used to create metadata records for the description of both textual and non-textual resources – these are analytical frameworks for data description and can be highly complex. Other metadata schemas have record structures more like conventional databases or library catalogues. The power, complexity and flexibility of markup languages mean, however, that the boundaries between text encoding formats and record structures are blurred: record-structure type schemas such as Dublin Core can be expressed using a markup language such as XML. Dempsey and Heery (1997) create a typology of metadata formats that has three bands:

- 'Simple' formats define relatively unstructured data such as that created by web crawlers.
- 'Structured' formats have somewhat richer, structured descriptions.
- 'Rich' formats offer fuller descriptive formats used for the large-scale management of resources.

Both Dempsey and Heery (1997) and Arms (2000, 214) highlight the costs associated with creating rich metadata, which are considerably higher than those associated with the extraction of poor but usable information automatically. The world of networked information will need to accept that different degrees of metadata creation, and varying qualities of metadata, are going to be with us for many years to come. It will be a long time before the digital world arrives at a metadata system that is as widely accepted as MARC is by the international library community.

Markup languages

Markup languages derive their name and their characteristics from the publishing industry, growing out of codes and symbols scribbled by editors into the margins of books or newspapers as indications to typesetters as to how particular features should be rendered. The codes were terse, and referred to a limited set of possibilities in the 'house style' of a particular publishing house or printer. With the advent of computerized typesetting, these codes mutated into electronic typesetting symbols, which were generally proprietary and differed between publishers. The markup in these programs was 'presentational' – it defined how a particular textual feature should look. Early word-processors also operated in a presentational mode: a main heading might be defined as 'Times Roman, Bold, 24 point', and this would be what was printed. If a writer decided that the heading should be 'Arial, 18 point', then all the main headings would have to be changed manually.

Standard Generalized Markup Language (SGML)

In the 1960s and 1970s, a group of researchers at IBM began to explore the possibility of generalizing the markup of documents, so that instead of defining a heading as 'Times Roman, Bold, 24 point', it was defined as a 'heading' of a particular level, 'heading level 1', say. That immediately removed the presentational features of a document from its structure: instead of saying how something should look, the markup defines what it is. Modern word-processors now use this feature in their stylesheets, so that headings, body text, quotes, bulleted lists, etc. are defined as those objects. To change the appearance of the objects, one command is changed in the style definition, which is then automatically applied to all objects of that type throughout the document. The system developed by the IBM researchers was called Generalized Markup Language, or GML. This concept was soon adopted by the publishing industry, and by the mid-1980s Standard Generalized Markup Language (SGML) had been developed.

The key point about SGML is that it is efficient, enabling global processes to be applied throughout a document, however long or complex that document is, or even across a whole group of similar documents – the entire run of a journal, for instance. It is also efficient in that the standard is managed on a worldwide basis, so individual creators of documents, be they large publishers or individual writers, do not need to invent their own markup processes, and it offers a reference point for validity and consistency in document creation.

How do markup languages work?

Markup languages work by describing the features of a text in tags which surround those features. So for instance,

```
<novel>
<noveltitle>Crime and Punishment</noveltitle>
<author>Fyodor Dostoevsky</author>
<part>
<parttitle>Part I</parttitle>
<chapter>
<chptitle>Chapter I</chptitle>
<para> On an exceptionally hot evening . . .</para>
<para>He had been lucky enough to escape . . .</para> . . .

</chapter>
</part>
</novel>
```

This is very simple markup for the first chapter of Dostoevsky's *Crime and Punishment* with the elements: 'novel', 'author', 'part', 'chapter' and 'paragraph' expressed as what they are, not how they are formatted. If a formatting program is applied to the tags, it could state that `<noveltitle>` appear as bold 24 point, `<author>` as italic 18 point, etc. Compare this with tagging for Michael Drayton's poem, *Phoebe on Latmus*:

```
<poem>
<poemtitle>Phoebe on Latmus</poemtitle>
<author>Michael Drayton</author>
<line><line1>In Ionia whence sprang old poets'
fame,</line1>
<line><line2>From whom that sea did first derive her
name</line2> . . .

</poem>
```

Even these two simple examples demonstrate that there are many different kinds of documents, and a tagging scheme would have to be extremely complex to be able to provide all the tags needed for all kinds of documents. Markup languages handle this by providing a Document Type Definition (DTD) feature, which allows users to define tag sets for types of documents which are recorded in the appropriate DTD. So there would be a DTD for novels, one for poems, one for academic articles, one for newspapers, and so on.

One of the most significant advantages of markup languages in general and SGML in particular is that they do not need to use any special character sets other than ASCII, the American Standard Code for Information Interchange, otherwise known as 'plain text format'. Special and ambiguous characters are captured using unique strings of ASCII characters, called 'entity references', which are enclosed, like the tags, in angle brackets and are defined in the DTD. The advantage here lies in the fact that ASCII can be transmitted through networks in e-mails and exchanged with any program that exists that can read ASCII text. SGML is 'system independent', it does not have to be accessed via any particular hardware or operating system. SGML is therefore a powerful interchange format for any kind of text. It has transformed the publishing industry and has made electronic publishing as pervasive as it is today. A survey of publishers carried out in 2000 by the NEDLIB project found that of 14 publishers contacted, ten held repositories of SGML-encoded text (Bide & Associates, 2000, 17).

Hypertext Markup Language (HTML)

In order to be inclusive and permissive, SGML soon became extremely complicated, and when Tim Berners-Lee invented the world wide web he wanted to use the generality and non-proprietary nature of SGML, without its complexity. He therefore defined a much simpler markup language, HTML, a 'common, basic lingua franca that any computer would be required to understand' (Berners-Lee, 1999, 44). Where the specification of SGML runs into hundreds of pages, and many of the tags are obscure and little used, HTML as Berners-Lee defined it had a very limited set of tags. Tags were structural, as in SGML, and encoded elements of documents. SGML is a language that allows users to write their own tag sets, as long as these are declared in the DTD. HTML *is* a DTD of SGML, and so the tags are predefined. Browsers such as Mosaic and Netscape interpret the tags, and render them into particular formats for viewing.

The simplicity of HTML is what has made it popular and has enabled the web to grow at a breakneck pace. However, the simplicity soon proved limiting, so developers began to add features to give designers more control over how web pages would appear when displayed on the screen. HTML has departed from its lean, clean origins and now mixes presentational information with the structural.

As Arms warns us, 'the tension between structural markup in HTML and formatting to control appearance has now become serious' (2000, 175). There are many varieties of HTML, and it is in danger of becoming a series of proprietary formats. This is partly due to the competition between the two main browser manufacturers, Netscape and Microsoft, who add embellishments to HTML in order to maintain marginal advantage over each other, and partly due to attempts by web developers to make HTML do things for which it was never intended – it is a format for *presenting* information, not for *processing* it. Some of the complex tasks routinely carried out, for instance the ordering of goods, have pushed it to its limits and beyond. Auxiliary programs like JAVA and PERL have been designed to work with HTML for information processing on the web, but different browsers do not always respond to these in a uniform manner. This causes problems for the delivery of library materials, as there is no consistency in what the user sees and it is hard to manage materials encoded in this fashion over the long term. HTML was not designed for the preservation of digital objects, but for interchange and display, and so the formatting instructions may impede long-term survival of the digital objects.

eXtensible Markup Language (XML)

> Since HTML is the most successful document format in history, why would anyone want to go beyond it? (Bray, 1997)

XML has been designed specifically for use on the web under the auspices of the world wide web consortium (W3C) led by Tim Berners-Lee (**www.w3c.org/**). Like HTML, it belongs to the SGML family, but the main difference from HTML is that XML is *extensible*. That is, rather than being in itself a markup language with a predefined tag set, it is a framework within which specialized markup languages can be written. XML has no formatting instructions contained within it, it is purely descriptive. Presentational features of a document or website are applied using stylesheets defined by the related standard, XSL (eXtensible Stylesheet language). XML is more rigorous than HTML, and as Brophy states, 'The fundamental point . . . is that because XML tags are meaningful in terms of data content, XML documents are ideally suited to machine processing' (2001, 119).

XML was designed with the goal that it should be straightforward to write programs to process it, and that HTML could be migrated to it without causing chaos. There is so much material written in HTML that a new standard incompatible with it would never be accepted. Another important feature of XML is that it supports Unicode character encoding, thereby allowing a wide range of character sets to be specified, ideographic as well as alphabetic. Unicode is described in more detail in Chapter 6 'Developing and designing systems for sharing digital resources'.

There are many up-to-date sources of information about SGML, HTML and XML available on the web. The best places to start looking for information are the W3C website, and the XML Cover Pages (**www.oasis-open.org/cover/sgml-xml.html**).

The benefits of XML over HTML are only just being felt by libraries, but they are likely to be significant. Better search engines are being written exploiting XML's more sophisticated handling of structures, and global management of large sets of data will be facilitated by the rigour of the specification. The stylesheets, too, offer more sophisticated and attractive presentation of complex materials to the user, which will enhance the user experience.

The Text Encoding Initiative (TEI)

The TEI was established in 1987 to create frameworks for the representation of electronic text, especially in the humanities. It was initially concerned with the interchange of textual information, but has now developed SGML DTDs for application in the conversion of existing texts, and for the creation of new texts in electronic form. The TEI was closely involved in the development of the XML standard, and TEI DTDs are now being implemented in XML. While the TEI Guidelines have tag sets for all aspects of texts, of particular interest to libraries is the TEI Header, which contains bibliographic information to support both resource discovery and resource management, i.e. descriptive, structural and administrative metadata. The Header has four major parts: a file description, an encoding description, a profile description and a revision description. Some of the descriptive metadata fields in a TEI Header can be mapped to MARC records, but much of the administrative information cannot. Given that there is so much bibliographic information already available in MARC records, there are many attempts in the library community to make MARC and TEI Headers interoperable. At the University of Michigan, TEI Headers are generated from MARC records, and Caplan suggests 'it may be that the TEI header will evolve to carry only minimal bibliographic description, with the bulk . . . being replaced by an external MARC record' (2000). See the TEI Consortium home page for full details about the TEI (**www.tei-c.org/index.html**).

Encoded Archival Description (EAD)

EAD is also based on SGML (and XML) and was established to encode archival finding aids and descriptions of archival resources. Though not specifically designed for the description of digital resources, EAD has been successfully used for the metadata of digital as well as analogue collections. Archives collect sets of papers which are often unique and which are the records of individuals, families or organizations. The features of archival collections that have to be recorded with the data objects themselves are the provenance, the original order and the context of the materials. Descriptions of archival collections are complex, hierarchical and analytical; they do not always go down to the item level in collections of large numbers of single items such as letters. As Caplan suggests, 'the distinction of practical importance is that bibliographic description is typically brief, stylized and flat. Archival description is typically lengthy, narrative and deeply hierarchical, making SGML, and later XML, a more suitable transport syntax than MARC' (Caplan, 2000).

Archive descriptions generally conform to a number of related standards: ISAD(G) is the International Council of Archivists standard for describing archival structures, and EAD is based on this. EAD was originally developed at the University of California at Berkeley and has now been widely accepted throughout the archival community. See Pitti (1999) and the EAD website at the Library of Congress (**http://lcweb. loc.gov/ead/tglib/tlhome.html**).

EAD is being used successfully in a number of libraries and archives because of the benefits it conveys for the description and navigation of complex hierarchical information spaces. The Making of America II Project (**www.clir.org/pubs/reports/pub87/contents.html**) and the Bodleian Library in Oxford (**www.bodley.ox.ac.uk/hef-proj/**), for instance, have created complex finding aids for digital and analogue materials using EAD.

Other metadata systems

MARC

The MARC (Machine-Readable Cataloguing) standard has been in existence for almost 30 years. It was originally developed as a standard for exchanging catalogue records, but is now used by most libraries for the online cataloguing of all kinds of library materials. There are a number of different 'dialects' of MARC, of which USMARC is the most widely used. It uses a structure of tagged fields and sub-fields, and allows for rich description of documentary resources. MARC is the longest-established metadata standard used in libraries, but it is not particularly good at describing electronic resources, despite the fact that it has a tag (856) for recording URLs. However, there are many millions of MARC records in catalogues around the world, and sophisticated networks in place for their creation and distribution. Using MARC for metadata of digital objects is therefore attractive to libraries with a significant investment in this format, as it makes the integration of digital and analogue objects at a catalogue level more straightforward. A number of projects exist to provide crosswalks from MARC to other formats (see Chapter 6 'Developing and designing systems for sharing digital resources').

Closely related to MARC is AACR2 (the Anglo-American Cataloguing Rules), which defines standard ways of describing the elements of a bibliographic record and their order in the record. While developed for use in the analogue world, rule sets such as AACR2 provide rigorous approaches to content elements that the digital world would do well to follow. AACR2 'represents the main, coherent body of work that has established how variants, for example in names, should be handled so as to ensure that all records referring to the same entity use the same form' (Brophy, 2001, 122).

Dublin Core

Dublin Core is a metadata standard developed for describing resources on the web. It takes its name from Dublin, Ohio, home of OCLC, where the first Dublin Core workshop was held in 1995. The initial aim of the Dublin Core group was to define a standard that untrained people could learn and apply easily: traditional cataloguing is a complex process and requires professional training. The main characteristics of Dublin Core are:

- simplicity
- semantic interoperability
- international consensus
- extensibility
- modularity.

The Dublin Core element set has only 15 elements; all can be repeated and none are mandatory. The elements are:

- title
- identifier
- creator
- contributor
- publisher

- description
- language
- subject
- coverage
- date
- type
- relation
- format
- source
- rights.

The definitions of these elements can be found on the website of the Dublin Core Metadata Initiative (DCMI) (**http://uk.dublincore.org/ documents/dcmi-type-vocabulary/**). This is an extremely minimalist standard, but it can be enriched by the use of 'qualifiers', and the DCMI is producing sets of 'exemplary qualifiers' which can be applied in particular domains or by well-established agencies. The subject field, for instance, can be qualified by Library of Congress Subject Headings (LCSH), Medical Subject Headings (MeSH) or Dewey Decimal Classification (DDC) (**http://uk.dublincore.org/documents/dcmes-qualifiers/**). In other domains, agencies are collaborating to create qualifier sets for particular projects or resource types. For instance, the Forced Migration Online Project, which is delivering digital materials in many formats to the worldwide refugee studies and forced migration community, has produced a set of metadata guidelines based on Dublin Core and the HURIDOCS (Human Rights Information and Documentation Systems International) recommendations (**www.forcedmigration.org/**; **www.huridocs.org/**) and many other projects use Dublin Core or can be mapped to Dublin Core.

The DCMI is working closely with other standards bodies (such as the W3C) to enable the exchange and organization of metadata. Complex frameworks are being developed such as the Resource Description Framework (RDF) which is 'an infrastructure that enables the encoding, exchange and reuse of structured metadata' (Miller, 1998). It 'integrates a variety of web-based metadata activities . . . using XML as an interchange syntax' (**www.w3c.org/RDF/**). The Warwick Framework has also been defined for the organization of metadata: it might not be possible to describe complex objects using just one metadata schema, so the

Warwick Framework proposes the separation of metadata into 'packages'. Several packages of metadata could point to one object, one for structural metadata, one for descriptive, etc. (Dempsey and Weibel, 1996). Work is also being carried out on collection level descriptions, where metadata is constructed to describe collections rather than individual items (Powell, 1999).

Collection-level description

Describing resources in detail at the level of individual items is a costly and time-consuming process, as we have shown throughout this chapter, and it creates a great deal of data that the user has to negotiate for the discovery and use of valuable resources. Collection-level description is a valuable alternative or adjunct to item-level description. Miller (2000b) suggests that:

> In this content-rich online environment, collection level descriptions fulfill important purposes. Firstly, they serve to provide relatively superficial overviews for large bodies of otherwise uncatalogued material. Secondly, they play an important role in reducing the quantity of material returned in the initial response to a broadcast query across multiple services.

The notion of the collection as an information-structuring principle has been more significant in archives than in libraries in the past (though of course libraries work with many kinds of collections), but in the digital world we can create many kinds of 'collections', even from the same underlying materials, and so descriptions of collections of resources are of great importance. As Powell, Heaney and Dempsey (2000) point out:

> The description of collections is becoming increasingly important in the context of networked information services and is an important underpinning for developing a collective resource.

Descriptions at the level of the collection can reveal much that is valuable to the user, and if such descriptions are created in open, standard, machine-readable formats they can, according to Powell, Heaney and Dempsey (2000), enable:

- users to discover and locate collections of interest
- users to perform searches across multiple collections in a controlled way
- refinement of distributed searching approaches based on the characteristics of candidate collections
- software to perform such tasks on behalf of users, based on known user preferences.

Collection-level descriptions are used for describing all kinds of resources (physical, born digital and digitized) and exposing the descriptions to the user in electronic form. Collections so described are usually structured in a hierarchical fashion, and indeed may themselves be composed of nested collections. The description frameworks need to be rich enough to support this.

There has been a great deal of work on collection-level description carried out in the UK as part of the Electronic Libraries Programme (eLib) and the Research Support Libraries Programme (RSLP), much of this drawing upon the MODELS (MOving to Distributed Environments for Library Services) framework. This work has been of great importance in defining the requirements of complex hybrid information environments, and the UK Office of Library and Information Networking has been a leader in many activities in this area (**www.ukoln.ac.uk/**).

Metadata creation

It is clear from the discussions of types of metadata above that the creation of metadata for digital objects can be a costly business, especially if the metadata is applied at a fine level of granularity. For most organizations and individuals creating and managing digital materials, it is not going to be possible to create new, rich descriptions of individual items. Existing records must be exploited wherever they exist, collection-level descriptions used where appropriate, and the reality that descriptive metadata might need to be sparsely applied initially faced. It is possible to return to descriptions and enrich them at a later stage.

Collaborative projects in resource description and discovery

To address some of the issues we have raised in this chapter, there are a number of national and international projects setting standards for resource description and discovery, and actually cataloguing internet resources. These include Renardus (**www.renardus.org/**), funded by the European Union's Information Society Technologies Programme (IST) (**www.cordis.lu/ist/home.html**), which aims to:

> improve access to existing Internet-accessible collections of cultural and scientific resources across Europe. The approach being taken is to develop a 'broker' service – a single interface for searching and browsing across existing distributed resource collections produced at a national level.
>
> (**www.renardus.org/about/**)

Renardus is composed of 12 partners from across Europe who are working together to 'devise models for sharing metadata, agree on technical solutions, foster standardisation activities, and develop business models to move from the pilot implementation to a fully-functional service'. The earlier DESIRE project (**www.desire.org/**), which ran from July 1998 until June 2000, provided much of the initial impetus for Renardus, and produced a set of useful tools for resource discovery, including the Internet Detective, an interactive tutorial on evaluating the quality of internet resources (**www.sosig.ac.uk/desire/internet-detective.html**) and the useful Information Gateways Handbook (**www.desire.org/handbook/**).

The Imesh Toolkit project grew out of the Internet Scout Directory at the University of Wisconsin. It is an international collaboration funded under the NSF/JISC International Digital Libraries Initiative to produce tools for the building of subject gateways. Its activities include the development of standards for resource collection, cataloguing, management and discovery, e.g. academic guides, virtual libraries and subject gateways. It shares technical, marketing, standards and cataloguing effort, and is investigating cross-searching, cross-browsing and the development of standards for related software and information issues.

The UK Resource Discovery Network (**www.rdn.ac.uk/**) was established in 1999 as a free internet service for providing effective access to high-quality internet resources for the learning, teaching and research community, especially in further and higher education. It is composed of a series of subject-based hubs that collaborate to offer users the ability to search for resources across several hubs at the same time.

In Australia, the Australian Subject Gateways Forum (**www.nla.gov. au/initiatives/sg/gateways.html**) co-ordinates a number of gateways including PADI (Preserving Access to Digital Information), Education Network Australia (EdNA) and PictureAustralia, with a number of new gateways under development.

Conclusion

Digital data creation and care is not in its infancy, but is probably only in its adolescence, and has certainly not reached full maturity. Stakeholders are on a steep learning curve, and the methods and techniques for the management of all stages of a digital resource have not yet reached universal acceptance. There will never be only one way to manage digital resources: local needs will generally require local implementations. What is vital is not a standard monolithic solution, but a range of solutions that preserve interoperability and long-term accessibility, which implies documentation and exchange of information about local implementations. A useful analogy might be with linguistic communities who all understand and speak a particular language, but where dialectal variation can be tolerated, albeit with some degree of translation and explanation. Dialects do develop into languages in their own right, which makes full communication more problematic. Variation of metadata systems is well known in the library and information world through cataloguing practice, both online and in the world of card catalogues. Many iterations of ALA, AACR and MARC standards have been used in libraries, and even when a common version is adopted, local variations soon appear. Dillon argues forcefully that 'libraries would better serve their constituencies if they universally abandoned local variations in records in favour of record creation to serve a broader community' (2000) but, while this is no doubt true, it is unlikely to happen.

In the world of digital metadata, dialectal variation can be accepted and even welcomed, but full linguistic division cannot. Humanity thrives and progresses by adaptation of rules, not by following them slavishly, but having no rules at all leads to anarchy and chaos. As Jones and

Beagrie point out, referring to a Cornell study, 'successful migration programs were significantly hampered by the disparity between openly published file format specifications and the increasing use of modifications to the basic standard, the latter being rarely, if ever, publicly available' (Jones and Beagrie, 2001, 135, referring to Lawrence et al., 2000).

Strong standards, communication, international collaboration and good documentation are the crucial issues in ensuring that resource description and discovery systems are both rich and usable.

6

Developing and designing systems for sharing digital resources

> The purpose of the information architecture is to represent the riches and variety of library information, using the building blocks of the digital library system. From a computing view, the digital library is built up from simple components.
>
> (Arms, 1997)

> To build a successful digital library, there have to be standard methods to interact with archives and digital objects.
>
> (Maly, Nelson and Zubair, 1999)

Introduction

This chapter will describe the essential underlying components in digital library systems. Building upon the previous chapters' descriptions of the information elements and intellectual foundations, we suggest approaches to the development of interoperability of systems and resources, infrastructures and a model for sustainable design. Digital library development is a complex process, involving many different components, technical, informational and human. We do not propose to examine technical architectures and infrastructures in any depth, although we do discuss some high-level heuristic models of digital library design and implementation for the sake of completeness. We focus this chapter more on the fundamental principles upon which these infrastructures should be built, and offer some pointers to more detailed treatments of these issues elsewhere. In this chapter we will discuss the following issues:

- digital libraries and communication
- functionality overlap in digital library environments
- interoperability
- crosswalks
- digital library structures
- the Open Archival Information System model
- digital library architectures in overview
- protocols and standards, including unique information identifiers
- designing digital library systems for sustainable technical development.

Digital libraries and communication

As described in Chapter 1 'Digital futures in current contexts', once computers were able to exchange information with each other, the idea of the digital library could become a realistic concept. The ability to communicate from computer to computer across networks and from one database table to another, both within a computer system and across systems, allowed for sophisticated integration of functions and sharing of data. It is this sharing and integration that enables the library catalogue and circulation systems to work together to deliver book reservations, overdue notices, quick check-in and check-out of materials, plus further integration with other elements of a library automation system. This sort of integration enables EDI to speed acquisitions and simplify budget control, while detailed management reports can be created to measure and assess the performance of many aspects of the library. Extend that integration across networks and include access to systems from other institutions and the digital library has a communications foundation upon which to build structured digital content and end-user services. However, there are intrinsic difficulties with integrating and sharing data from disparate computer systems. There are differences in interface design, data structure and organization, metadata usage and computer system architecture that can make using someone else's system feel as comfortable and natural as trying to speak several foreign languages fluently – it can be done, but not without effort and training. The ultimate goals of all digital library design are to enable local systems to reflect local priorities while not feeling foreign to external users, and the ability to interchange data freely with other systems without human intervention.

In Chapter 1 we proposed some principles that seem to us to characterize something as a digital library rather than any other kind of digital collection. These are:

1 A digital library is a managed collection of digital objects.
2 The digital objects are created or collected according to principles of collection development.
3 The digital objects are made available in a cohesive manner, supported by services necessary to allow users to retrieve and exploit the resources just as they would any other library materials.
4 The digital objects are treated as long-term stable resources and appropriate processes are applied to them to ensure their quality and survivability.

These characteristics are supported by the underlying computer systems and protocols, which enable the management of the digital objects and the sharing of resources in a cohesive and sustainable fashion. As we will discuss further in Chapter 9 'Digital librarians: new roles for the Information Age', the digital librarian does not necessarily have to understand the technical detail of every component of the digital library system, but should understand the basic system functions, and be able to see how the components fit together into a cohesive system for managing and delivering digital content.

The functionality overlap in digital library environments

One of the key problems to be confronted by digital library developers and designers of metadata systems is that libraries, archives, museums, galleries and other organizations concerned with the management of information have divergent traditions that have developed over years, decades or even centuries. Cohesive digital programmes are therefore difficult to implement, as recognized by Bogen et al. in their assessment of over 70 digital library products, where they stated, 'no system will cover all features' (2001). Their research found 30 library information systems, 35 museum management systems and nine digital library systems (some products covered several of their categories). This functionality overlap issue has had to be addressed by institutions like the Royal Academy of Arts in London, where the systems procured and developed have to be responsive to their archival needs and their gallery and museum management needs, and must also allow the management of an extensive art library.

In this environment, the functions offered by various categories and traditions for data management are not distinct or separable, but overlapping and intertwined as shown in Figure 6.1. There are not just overlaps between library, archive and museum management systems but also overlaps with document management, knowledge management and e-commerce systems, especially if corporate environments are included.

Complex cultural and knowledge environments will have most or even all of the components shown in Figure 6.1 at any one time. This is a serious strategic issue. Because of the functional overlaps and the need for systems to talk with each other to interact, we need interoperability not only across disparate systems but also within local architectures and technical structures.

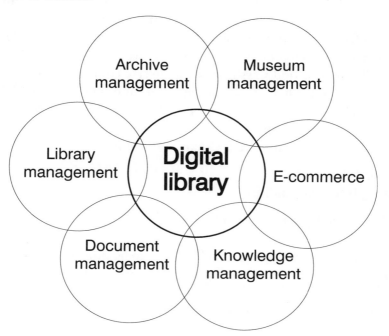

Fig. 6.1   *Functional overlap of management systems*

Interoperability . . .

. . . or 'Why are there so many catalogues and what can we do about it?'
(Wendler, 2000).

Digital information is inherently a sharable resource, but standards and formats change frequently as research in the commercial and non-commercial worlds promotes new developments in the creation, supply and manipulation of digital objects. This is welcome progress, but it creates a diversity that is often at odds with that very sharability that we value. Different information communities, too, have divergent needs and established practices for dealing with their own domains, which it would be impractical to change. Legacy data is a reality, and the costs of conversion to new formats are often unacceptable. Any single library, however small, is likely to have a number of catalogues describing different resources, some machine-readable, some not, and the catalogues may not all be accessible from one single point. On the other hand, global digital library developments mean that it is possible to interact with many catalogues in different languages, with different structures describing billions of data objects (physical and digital) in heterogeneous formats. This has caused serious compatibility problems. As Fox and Marchionini suggest, the challenge is to find ways to link the diverse content and perspectives provided by individual digital libraries around the world (1998, 30). Interoperability is the key to this, as it allows organizations and communities to retain their specialist practices, while putting high-level standards and protocols in place for sharing of information.

What is interoperability?

As Miller (2000a) defines it, to be interoperable:

> One should be actively engaged in the on-going process of ensuring that the systems, procedures and culture of an organization are managed in such a way as to maximize opportunities for exchange and reuse of information, whether internally or externally.

Achieving interoperability is difficult, as it requires resource creators, users, funding bodies, systems and resource managers to agree on the development of standards and formats for information interchange that may not map exactly on to their established practices. Putting in place the requirement to be interoperable is therefore an extra process with attendant extra effort. Miller suggests that there are six aspects to interoperability to be considered:

- technical
- semantic
- intercommunity
- political
- legal
- international.

Technical interoperability is, in many ways, the easiest to achieve, given that there are many bodies working on standards and technologies, and some structural issues are being resolved. The widespread adoption of XML and Dublin Core, discussed in Chapter 5 'Resource discovery, description and use', are good examples of these. Semantic and intercommunity interoperability are related. On the one hand, communities wish to share information more widely than ever before, given the ease of electronic information interchange, but the differences in the semantic spaces within which they operate can be difficult to resolve. Cross-domain information access has always been a problem, as differences in terminology can create real barriers to understanding. While these differences can usually be resolved in the world of face-to-face human communication, machine communication requires more precision to enable information interchange. Even if resources in a particular community are created with internal semantic consistency, when these are exposed to interrogation alongside other resources, confusion may result. There may also be legal or political barriers to information access, and when all the above is seen in a global context, with different languages and cultural practices coming to the fore, the scale of the problem is clear.

There has been a great deal of work in the international digital library community in recent years to resolve the problems of interoperability, while respecting the divergent needs of different communities. Protocols, resource-naming conventions and the development of methods of 'cross-walking' between resources have played a vital part in enabling more meaningful access to resources, rather than just access to more resources. The development of the Unicode standard, too, has meant that one of the largest problems that has faced developers of electronic textual materials for many years, that of representing the character sets of the world, has now been resolved. Unicode is described in more detail later in this chapter, alongside other useful protocols and standards.

Crosswalks

The summary of metadata issues given in Chapter 5 demonstrates the scale and complexity of the creation and management of metadata for resource description, discovery and use. Different communities have different needs, and descriptive metadata in particular is likely to be domain-specific and to use terminology both for metadata tags and for content that might not be easily understood outside that domain. Cross-domain resource discovery is therefore problematic and can seriously impede interoperability. One solution to this is the use of crosswalks. A crosswalk is 'a specification for mapping one metadata standard to another' (St Pierre and LaPlant Jr, 1998). Crosswalk specifications have two main functions: mapping allows search engines to query fields with the same or similar content in different databases, that is, it supports semantic interoperability. Mapping also provides structures for converting one data format to another that may be more widely accessible (Woodley, 2000, 1).

Creating crosswalks is a complex process for many reasons. Older data may not have been well formed in the first place and might require human intervention to make it sensible to another system. Also the standards used in each of the different systems, and that are being mapped between, may be so different that it is difficult to find points of correspondence. Dublin Core is being used extensively as a 'filter' for crosswalks, with a number of specifications defined to map Dublin Core to other metadata schemas: MARC21 to Dublin Core, Dublin Core to EAD, Dublin Core to MARC, etc. Note that when mapping a rich standard to a less rich one, there will be loss of information. MARC21 has many more fields than Dublin Core can handle, for instance. However, this mapping is still useful for cross-domain resource discovery. Another problem with crosswalking between domains is that of terminology. There is no universal thesaurus or authorized terminology that operates across all possible subject areas, and so while structure may translate satisfactorily, content may not. As Woodley suggests 'integrated authority control would significantly improve both retrieval and interoperability in searching disparate resources' (2000, 7) and she opines that 'as the number and size of online resources increases, the ability to refine searches and to use the controlled vocabularies and thesauri will become increasingly important' (2000, 8). A good introduction to crosswalks is available from the Getty Research Institute (**www.getty.edu/ research/institute/standards/intrometadata/index. html**).

Digital library structures

As discussed in Chapter 1 'Digital futures in current contexts', there are many definitions of a digital library and thus defining a single system to manage all the diverse possible requirements is impossible. However, there are some high-level views that incorporate the various interoperability issues already discussed with the collection management, legal, resourcing, preservation and user-centred issues dealt with elsewhere in this book. The following eight principles expounded by Arms in 1995, are a useful starting point. These have been highly influential in the development of conceptual frameworks and thinking in relation to digital library design, structure and function, and remain valid today. They are:

1 The technical framework exists within a legal and social framework.
2 Understanding of digital library concepts is hampered by terminology.
3 The underlying architecture should be separate from the content stored in the library.
4 Names and identifiers are the basic building blocks for the digital library.
5 Digital library objects are more than collections of bits.
6 The digital library object that is used is different from the stored object.
7 Repositories must look after the information they hold.
8 Users want intellectual works, not digital objects.

Any digital library model that is developed without *all* of these principles having been addressed and thought through could be missing something fundamental, and would therefore risk failure. From such principles, a number of developments into actual digital library architectures have been made, with the OAIS reference model dominating the field. The Open Archival Information System (OAIS) model has been adopted by digital-preservation-oriented projects in particular, such as CEDARS in the UK, PANDORA in Australia, NEDLIB in the European Union and others (van der Werf-Davelaar, 1999, 1). We offer here an overview of this, along with some other models of digital library architecture.

The Open Archival Information System (OAIS) model

The OAIS is a relatively simple reference model currently under review (as an ISO Draft International Standard) that contains within itself the means to expand and adapt to most potential design requirements for long-term digital information holding and access (**http://ssdoo.gsfc. nasa.gov/nost/isoas/us/overview.html**). Digital library architectures are very complex and designers tend to use their own terminology within the design process. This makes it difficult to compare designs and also to share ideas if different terms are used. In the digital preservation arena, better harmonization of the terminology used has been one of the major achievements in recent years, ensuring that everyone involved understands more clearly what the other stakeholders mean. However, this new clarity has not yet permeated the whole digital library community. Without even this basic level of understanding, planning in complex fields like preservation and digital library design is very difficult. The OAIS model tries to address Arms' second principle: that our understanding is hampered by the terminology. The OAIS is especially useful in the way it has brought together the terminology and concepts used to describe and compare digital library architectures within an understandable, commonly agreed and overall less complex framework. The OAIS overview shown in Figure 6.2 shows the six functional entities and related interfaces as described by the draft recommendations (CCSDS, 2001, 4-1).

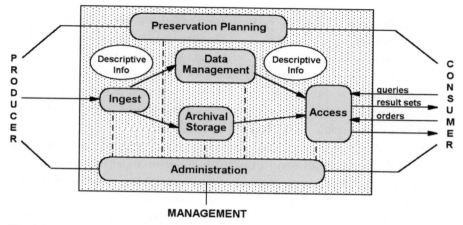

Fig. 6.2   *The OAIS Functional Model*

The six main functions and modules are:

- Ingest
- Archival Storage
- Data Management
- Administration
- Preservation Planning
- Access.

This may not at first glance give the impression of having greatly simplified either the architecture or the terminology, but in fact this is a high-level overview of what is in detail an extremely complex set of processes and technical interactions. Digital libraries are not simple, and the OAIS shows that even a relatively simple model reveals aspects that need to be fitted into the design. Working through the processes described by the functional model, we can see that the OAIS addresses many of Arms' eight principles of digital library development.

Receiving and storing data

The Ingest module provides those services and functions that allow digital content to be submitted to the system for storage and management. Its purpose is to offer a means of collecting, receiving, generating, verifying, authenticating and then re-distributing data to the other processes within the system. It is analogous to the acquisitions module of any library automation system, although the functionality of a digital library will be more extensive than this (see Chapters 3 and 4, 'Developing collections in the digital world' and 'The economic factors').

The Archival Storage module is the area concerned with the storage, maintenance and retrieval of data once it has been accepted from Ingest. It is also in Archival Storage that data is gathered together in collections (known as logical containers) to optimize end-user retrieval from the system. Arranging materials into logical containers to ease retrieval addresses the Arms principles that data is more than just a collection of bits and that the user wants intellectual works not digital objects. This is the store of content that the user will be dipping into via the Access module. In a physical library this might be analogous to the bookshelves and stock.

Data is managed from within the Data Management module. This entity mainly stores and retrieves metadata and administers the database functions, such as maintaining the metadata schema. The cataloguing function, access control information, authenticity and integrity control information are all to be found within Data Management. By using separate modules to store content, the OAIS resolves the Arms principle of keeping content and the underlying architecture separate. The analogies with the traditional library OPAC and circulation module are clear. The resource-discovery issues raised by this module have already been discussed in Chapter 5.

Managing the system and providing access

The overall operation of the system is managed from within the Administration function. It provides essential management information through monitoring, quality control and auditing of the other components, and also looks after agreements and licences with producers. As Arms states, digital libraries exist within legal and social frameworks, and this module addresses these.

The Preservation Planning module evaluates the contents of the archive and provides regular reports and recommendations for updates or data migration, and it monitors changes in the technical environment. Arms' principles state that 'repositories must look after the information they hold' and so putting the preservation planning into the design as an integral function makes this more likely to be achieved. Digital preservation is the focus of Chapter 8.

Finally the Access module supports the end-user (known as the Consumer in this model) access to the content in the system. The keys here are to enable the user to identify a resource's existence, and to have descriptions, locations and availability information easily to hand. The user must be able to request and receive information (which may be a single digital object or a combination of many discrete parts) within a controlled access environment. This addresses Arms' concern that the way the data is accessed and used may be different from the way it is stored and should not be limited by the archive. Chapter 7 'Portals and personalization: mechanisms for end-user access' considers access modes in more detail.

The OAIS model is not a blueprint for implementation, but a heuristic for understanding, and what we offer here is a high-level overview of the model. There are many further levels of granularity within each entity to be explored, expanded and used in digital library system design. These core features in the OAIS model are essential to any digital library scheme, but the way they may be applied in real world development might not seem quite so clear to any but the highly technically literate. Within the hybrid environment of libraries and other cultural institutions, the overlap between various technologies may need some further visualization to aid decision making.

Overview of digital library architectures

The OAIS model shows digital library functions as they appear to the system developer. But how do the various parts of this model appear to the users and librarians who will be working with digital libraries? Figure 6.3 shows many of the actual components that might be found in real working systems, with the user firmly located at the centre, accessing resources within the controlled environment of the surrounding system components. This access is controlled and enabled by:

- interoperability and communication protocols such as Z39.50
- applications (such as middleware, see Chapter 7) providing interface and integration tools

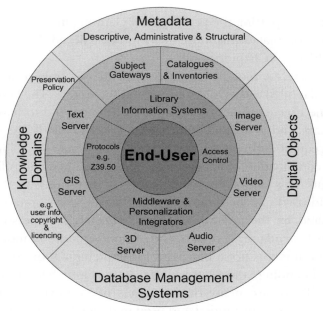

Fig. 6.3   *Overview of digital library architectures*

- information systems for delivering documents and directing users to hybrid resources
- personalization and access control systems to authenticate users and content (see Chapter 7).

The next ring handles all requests for data objects through the data servers for the various media and information types, with supporting systems delivering subject gateways, portals and online catalogues. The outer ring contains the knowledge domain – the information partnerships that define the dynamics of the information space, including such aspects as user information, copyright and licensing agreements and strategic policy frameworks, for instance all the issues that need to be defined for preservation. The metadata and digital objects also sit in this outer ring, distinct from the means of delivery, and are managed by database management systems.

In summary, the outer ring provides structure and controlling mechanisms, the second ring serves content within a context defining system behaviour, while the inner ring provides access and interface mechanisms to present content to the user.

Protocols and standards

Protocols and standards are the bedrock of information interchange and of system functionality. The most relevant are discussed here, although this is by no means an exhaustive list. When considering the digital library structures described above, it is the underlying protocols and data standards that are essential to their operation. The digital librarian will rarely have to understand these in great detail but must be aware of their existence and know how they are applied in their own environments.

A protocol is a set of rules enabling computers to exchange information across networks. The Internet Protocol (IP), for instance, uniquely identifies network points through their IP addresses, enabling any computer in the world connected to the network to send messages to any other. As the Internet Protocol enables one computer to find another on the internet, the Hypertext Transfer Protocol (HTTP) helps ensure that the computers have something intelligible to say to each other when they are linked. HTTP defines the rules for interaction between web clients (browsers such as Internet Explorer or Netscape) and web servers. It specifies how the clients request information and how the servers return the information to the clients.

Z39.50 is another important protocol, which was specifically defined for the exchange of bibliographic data, and is now one of the main communications standards between libraries. It permits searches on remote databases via client applications. In theory, if both client and server are Z39.50 compliant, it should be possible for any client to interrogate any server and retrieve a usable set of results. In practice, vendors have implemented the standard differently, and there are often incompatibilities of record structure at the server end, so interaction is not necessarily straightforward. However, a number of bodies are working to address this. For instance, the Bath Profile is an international Z39.50 specification for library applications and resource description that has been developed to enable interoperability between libraries and cross-domain applications. It is widely supported throughout the international digital library community (**www.ukoln.ac.uk/interop-focus/bath/**).

Unique information identifiers

One of the most common (and frustrating) problems of networked information retrieval is broken links. As we reported in Chapter 5 'Resource discovery, description and use', mechanisms for checking links suggest that at any one time, some 10% of links on the web are broken. This is clearly a huge barrier to information access and use, and is the result of the underlying original structure of the web where an object is identified by its location. The Uniform Resource Locator (URL) names the machine on which a resource can be found, not the resource itself. When a resource is moved, website managers sometimes, but not always, provide a link to the new location, but clearly this is an unstable system, which has proved problematic with the massive increase in the scale and mobility of networked information.

As Heery, Powell and Day suggest, 'unique identifiers are an essential part of the technology that enables electronic trading, copyright management, electronic tables of content, production tracking and resource discovery' (1997, 14). Organizations are working on the solutions to this problem, and there are several systems being developed. OCLC has developed the PURL or Persistent Uniform Resource Locator which, while still naming the location of an object, uses an intermediate location resolution service rather than pointing directly. The object can be moved, and the resolution service will maintain the link to it. Uniform Resource Names (URNs) are intended to provide a unique and persistent name for the object through its lifecycle, and again access is managed by a resolution service, which looks up the location of the object. Juha Hakala (1999) defines the practical uses for URNs in libraries:

> There are two practical reasons why it is important for libraries to start using URNs without delay in cataloguing. First, if [a] library puts e.g. ISBN and ISBN-based URN into a MARC record, it may be possible to locate the document via an URN resolution service even when the URL in the record is not valid any more . . . The other reason is more prosaic: MARC format has a place for URN, and therefore any identifier, including for instance SICI and BICI which do not have a tag in all MARC formats for the time being, can be accommodated immediately.

SICI and BICI

The terms SICI and BICI used by Hakala stand respectively for Serial

Item and Contribution Indentifier Standard (SICI) and Book Item and Component Identifier (BICI). These unique identifier standards are very important for journals or books created or stored in digital format. These materials can be highly complex in the components that make up the content, such as multiple articles or chapters from multiple contributors within one logical container (the book or journal). It is therefore more complex to maintain unique identifiers for the components while retaining the logical structure without using the SICI or BICI standards. The standards define a variable length code that provides a unique identification of an item (e.g. a book or serial issue) and the contributions or components thereof (e.g. chapters or articles). For the SICI there is a standard, Z39.56-1996, which defines the requirements for constructing a compact SICI code that has a unique value for each unique bibliographic item. There is also an automated SICI generator created by Steve Proberts of the Electronic Publishing Research Group at the University of Nottingham (**www.ep.cs.nott.ac.uk/~sgp/sicisend.html**). The National Information Standards Organization (NISO) is currently working on a full standard for BICI (see **www.niso.org/commitap.html**).

Digital Object Identifier

The Digital Object Identifier system has been developed by the publishing industry. This system assigns a unique identifier to a digital object, along with a 'handle' to translate the identifier into a location. The International DOI Foundation has been established to maintain the standard, to approve naming conventions throughout communities, and to appoint agencies to resolve locations. A Digital Object Identifier is defined by the DOI Foundation as a 'persistent identifier of intellectual property entities'. Although a DOI may look like a URL, it functions more like an ISBN or ISSN in persistently identifying a content object rather than a location. The DOI system 'has been designed to be able to interoperate with past, present and future technologies', which means that it can utilize ISBNs and URLs as part of its naming system, thus preserving identification of legacy data. It can also include the SICI and BICI naming systems. The 'handle' component of the system has been designed to use open architecture so that it can develop as the web develops. The handle system is unique in that it can resolve the DOI in different ways. If, for instance, the DOI names identical copies or instances of a content object, then metadata may be attached to the handle that will allow it to retrieve, say, the copy nearest to the user on the network or the copy for which the user's institution has a licence. Resolution might be done automatically, with the user pointed to only one instance of the object, or the user might be pointed to a list of all the DOI matches and allowed to choose which version to access (**www.doi.org**).

The Preserving Access to Digital Information (PADI) subject gateway has an excellent list of resources and explanations of unique and persistent information identifiers (**www.nla.gov.au/padi/topics/36.html**).

Unicode

Character sets are represented computationally by numbers, and characters are displayed through look-up tables, which assign characters to the underlying numbers for display or printing. In the past, there were many different systems for encoding characters. Even a relatively straightforward and popular language like English had a number of possible representations, and different representations sometimes conflicted with one another, with different encoding used to represent the same characters in different systems. Non-Roman and non-Western character sets caused enormous problems, especially for web display. Unicode has changed all that, for it 'provides a unique number for every character, no matter what the platform, no matter what the program, no matter what the language' (**www.unicode.org/unicode/standard/WhatIsUnicode. html**). Unicode is now an internationally agreed standard which can represent more than one million characters: this is sufficient for all known modern and historic languages, as well as all diacritics, breathings (marks in some languages, such as Greek, which aid pronunciation), composite characters, mathematical symbols, etc. Not all possible character sets have been defined, but Unicode offers a standardized method of definition, and new characters are being added regularly. Unicode has been adopted widely throughout the hardware, software and publishing industries. It is one of the most important developments for libraries that have to deal with multilingual content – most libraries, that is. The emergence of the Unicode standard, and the availability of tools supporting it, are among the most significant recent global software technology trends.

Designing for sustainable development

So far in this chapter we have described the various components of the digital library, the issues for interoperability and the various protocols and standards that are emerging in the digital library field. But how does all this apply to the practical development of working digital libraries? As we have pointed out repeatedly, all libraries are different and all digital libraries are different, meaning that there is no simple answer. However, we can suggest some underlying principles that may inform the process of development. This will allow the library manager to think strategically and be able to rationalize a specification of requirements in relation to design. There is a natural tension between the innovative digital library system built today and the sustainability of the data and information in the long term. The value added by services such as portals (see Chapter 7 'Portals and personalization: mechanisms for end-user access') are a thin layer compared with the value of the information itself, or the tools built to access and manipulate the information. It is thus worthwhile planning for the inevitable system obsolescence at the design stage, to ensure that it will be possible to replace the system in the future without damaging the underlying data. This strategic approach allows the technology behind the digital library (or any delivery system for that matter) to be separated from the information content in terms of development options.

Keeping information separate

In designing systems it is a useful strategy to keep information presentation and applications separate from the information resource content, as the various models shown here suggest. A classic problem in migrating between technologies is that often part of the interpretation of the information, its context, becomes embedded in the logic of the application and presentation functions. The growth in XML and stylesheets offers greater opportunities to keep information and presentation separate. For example, where new copyright or licensing arrangements are made, these may be automatically reflected in the distribution of information through the system design, layout and delivery (by changing the stylesheet for the site) while leaving the underlying information resource effectively the same. In this scenario, it makes sense to arrange for the presentational entities to be defined once and applied automatically wherever required across the digital library. It is worth trying to keep all contextual and value-adding elements as close to the actual information content as possible. These can then be contained as an information component in the following layered architecture.

Layered architecture

In designing delivery mechanisms, implementing a layered architecture should be the most effective way to withstand future technology changes. By using such a broad overview model, it is possible to simplify the design and arrangement of the many complex components that will make up the complete system and its various interactions. Most librarians and content providers should be able to model their information using the following layered architecture, which encompasses Veen's model of Structure, Presentation and Behaviour (2001) and layers proposed by Parapadakis (2000).

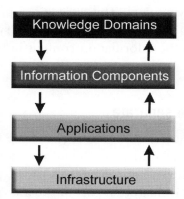

Fig. 6.4   *Layered architecture for delivery mechanism design*

Knowledge domains

The knowledge domains segment provides the structure for the organizational elements of the underlying information resources. It describes the information partnerships and other logical and physical relationships that define the dynamics between the relevent stakeholding parties. For instance, this layer might include user information, copyright clearance information, licensing agreements for content aggregators or subscription information. This layer defines policy, strategy and management of the underlying resources and should include the preservation policy.

Information components

This layer maps the knowledge domains on to the actual information components that the system will display. These need to be carefully managed, with their interdependencies with other layers and data objects defined. These may include catalogues, complete digital collections, documents, images, other data objects and links to other resources. This layer of the system is the most visible to the user and should be designed for maximum ease of use and transparency of access. There will need to be multiple views of the data and multiple paths to finding the data held. Every user should be able to personalize their access and the way they interact with the data. The mapping between the knowledge domain and the application layer will control, manage and direct the way that the user is able to interact with the content.

Applications

The applications layer defines any software applications that will be used to manage the information defined above. This might include library, museum and document management systems, databases, search engines, internet browsers, copyright management systems and other applications. For personalized information environments, this is where the system functionality would be provided to manipulate the information layer to give the user their own personalized view of the content. More information on this layer in contained in Chapter 7.

Infrastructure

The infrastructure layer describes the technical infrastructure that has to be in place to support the applications. This might include servers, networks, telecommunications, workstations, scanners, systems support, maintenance, cabling, physical space required, etc. Once this foundation layer of technical requirements is described, the application and information components layers can be defined with reference to what is possible within the infrastructure. For instance, if the infrastructure layer does not support broadband access for high-data-volume traffic, such as digital video, then it would be a mistake to implement large-scale video content in the information component layer without first addressing the infrastructure layer's capabilities.

The advantages to this layered approach are manifest. It allows a logical distinction to be maintained between the layers, which permits any part to be changed or re-designed without affecting the fundamental design of the whole. This is especially important as it allows for changes in organizational structures and relationships without loss of the information structures. It is then possible to replace an existing application technology without a fundamental redesign of the infrastructure or the information components being managed. Thus elements within the lower layers can be swapped and changed as technologies develop and emerge. The upper layers grow in a more organic sense as new relationships and information resources become available and are developed. By designing and thinking about the structure of digital libraries in this layered way, using Figure 6.4 and also referring back to Figure 6.3, it is possible to simplify the relationships between the various elements and to slot them into their respective places within the overall structure.

Conclusion

The essential underlying components in digital library systems having been described, in the next chapter (7) we will move on to the way these are implemented to enable access to the content. We have suggested approaches to the development of interoperability, infrastructures and a model for sustainable design. However, digital library development remains a very complex process, which involves many different components, and we hope that the focus of this chapter on the fundamental principles upon which these infrastructures should be built will serve as a useful introduction. Librarians should have confidence that these highly technical issues are not beyond their capabilities to manage, or to make decisions about and define requirements for. Effort to understand the overall underlying principles and structures should enable the librarian to discuss with technologists their core information and resource management goals, in order to achieve an end design and a product that will be satisfying to both parties and also highly functional.

7

Portals and personalization: mechanisms for end-user access

The digital library provides convenience, customization, community, accessibility, and quality.   (Guenther, 2000, 39)

The user, having entered the portal, never leaves – the portal goes out into the information universe on his or her behalf.   (Brophy, 2001)

Introduction

The focus of this chapter is on the portal as a means of disseminating and providing information in the digital world. Portals are points of focus where people plan and begin voyages on the internet. Portal content and design is often about developing a desire in the user for information of a type that will ensure they will return, and frequently, to the portal. Thus, concepts of marketing and brand loyalty will be discussed here, along with the synergy of the information resources accessible, the various products offered, the delivery of what the user wants, and the price they are prepared to pay. Many service providers will need to consider their ability to personalize and customize access to portal and digital library resources. The portal and personalized information environment (PIE) may be the answer to satisfying the core objective of easing the information glut that prevents users finding the most appropriate and relevant information. Will the portal be an answer to information overload, or is the portal maybe a Trojan horse of e-commerce companies aiming to reduce our individual choices and decrease the role of the library?

This chapter will discuss the following issues:

- defining the users' digital content dilemma
- delivering content with portals
- the portal as a community tool
- the importance of content
- branding and marketing in the portal arena
- delivering information and delighting the user
- personalization.

Defining the users' digital content dilemma

The delivery of well-designed and developed digital library resources is only one aspect of the solution needed from the user's perspective. The other aspects revolve around finding and using information as quickly as possible in this digital era. As described in Chapter 1 'Digital futures in current contexts', information growth is exponential, and selecting the most relevent materials has become a distinct challenge. The Search Rage study (Sullivan, 2001) suggests that almost one-third of Americans do more than one internet search every day and 80% at least once a week, with 60% accruing more than one hour of searching per week. When asked, nearly three-quarters reported frustration to some significant degree and 86% felt web searching could be more efficient. As described by James Gleick (2000, 88), the information overload is a dystopian disaster:

> All the stuff pouring in causes congestion, takes up space, reduces productivity, floods the basement, and hyperventilates the attic. That is the sensation, anyway, almost universally shared. More than twenty thousand distinct sites on the World Wide Web address the issue of information overload and, inevitably, contribute to the problem.

We discuss some of the limitations of the search engine approach in Chapter 5 'Resource discovery, description and use'.

The users' dilemma is that they have a distinct desire for information, but the digital environment does not seem to actually make life simpler or information more accessible. In this environment the librarian should be the user's hero and digital library services a safe haven. The information profession is probably the only group intent on simplifying access to and retrieval of information from this glut of resources.

The digital library community is becoming increasingly aware that valuable digital resources are often hidden away and not available to the widest community. As so aptly put by Maly, Nelson and Zubair (1999):

> Currently, there exist a large number of superb digital libraries (DLs), all of which are, unfortunately, vertically integrated and all presenting a monolithic interface to their users. Ideally, a user would want to locate resources from a variety of digital libraries dealing with one interface.

The web portal is now the most standard interface aggregating diverse library resources and services through a single access and management point for users. The problem of there being 'too much stuff' is an age old one for libraries and in the digital world portals are one way, among many, to address the issue.

Delivering content with portals

Portals are more than a means of getting from information point A to information point B via the shortest and easiest route: they are also about delivering an array of value-added services. Portals are not based solely on internet technology; there are examples of resources portaling across multiple media. The *Wall Street Journal Interactive Edition,* for instance, reuses financial and business news articles 'for a variety of web sites, for display on personal handheld devices and for infotainment video' (Anderson, 1999) and demonstrates that resource use is hybrid and that the portal may have to cross these virtual boundaries.

Definitions

A couple of broad definitions of a portal are:

- a website that provides an entry point to the internet, and offers value-added services such as directories, searching, information news, and links to related websites (Rowley, 2000)

- an interface providing access to a multitude of disparate information sources which can be internal, external or both, the favoured interface for a portal being the 'ubiquitous browser' (Elion, 1999).

There are various other definitions of a portal, many of which seek to distinguish between a portal and an information gateway:

> A subject gateway facilitates access to networked resources for anyone who is looking for resources on that subject. A portal . . . in addition offers a variety of additional services aimed largely, though not exclusively at the relevant subject community . . . portals tend to 'deep mine' selected resources in their subject areas by providing searching and sometimes other discovery services.　　　　　　　　　　　　　　　(MacLeod, 2000)

This definition also strays into the territory of the 'vortal', a vertical portal, which focuses upon one industry, subject, or niche market. The increasing popularity of vortals is due to the increasing sophistication of users:

> [Users] do not automatically go to the horizontal or megaportal sites such as Yahoo! or AOL. Instead they go directly to vertical sites that meet their needs, such as stocks, sports, travel, health or women's issues. The trend is towards narrower sites reaching a vertical market.
>
> 　　　　　　　　　　　　　　　　　　　　　　　　　(Ketchell, 2000)

Vertical and horizontal markets

A brief comment on vertical and horizontal markets and their relationship to libraries may provide illumination here. Horizontal markets are those offering a standard product to a potentially wide audience – such as the daily newspaper. There is little consumer choice other than brand. The vertical market is one where the product is not standard for a wide audience but focused upon a specific group or tailor-made as a bespoke service. Libraries have traditionally been portrayed as serving exclusively horizontal markets through the provision of large repositories of books and reading matter. Libraries have actually always served the vertical market as well: there has always been selection for the local community or a specialist readership, and libraries have always provided bespoke reference enquiry services, to name just two mechanisms. This move from being valued for both the breadth of the service and for the depth and personalization of the service is discussed in more detail later in this chapter and also in Chapter 9 'Digital librarians: new roles for the Information Age'.

Size is important

The unifying defining themes of what makes a successful portal are size and content. Whether it is a portal, vortal or a subject gateway, the more resources available that are key to the end-user's need, the better the product may be perceived. The move towards vertical markets by portal providers like internet.com does not mean fewer resources from the user perspective. internet.com acts as a hub for over 144 related sites, which is very small compared with Yahoo!, but from the user perspective it *feels* comprehensive, while still being focused on their needs. Internet.com provides a network of 250 e-mail newsletters, 136 online discussion forums, and 78 moderated e-mail discussion lists (Pack, 2001b), which is a considerable added-value component. In reward, internet.com regularly receives more than three million unique visitors and has 1500 advertisers providing revenue. A further example, as mentioned in Chapter 3 'Developing collections in the digital world', is the *American Journalism Review Newslink* vortal (**http://ajr.newslink.org/news.html**), claiming links to over 18,000 resources such as newspapers, magazines, broadcasters and news services worldwide.

The portal as a community tool

Portals are generally valued according to two components: diversity of content and community. Who the portal serves is as important as the range of content provided.

Content to address specific communities

There are a number of portal models, which each address their own communities and diversity of content in different ways. Ketchell (2000) suggests three models:

- corporate portals with broad, diverse content, targeted to a narrow community
- commercial portals offering narrow content for diverse communities
- publishing portals for large, diverse communities, often containing little content customization.

Corporate portals

The way a portal is valued will depend upon which community is addressed and what type of content they can use there. A corporate portal with information upon internal policies, documents reporting progress on work, proformas to claim travel expenses and the latest information upon the new product range has a very narrow targeted audience (often with restricted access rights) and is unlikely to be valued outside that community. The corporate portal is, however, generally also the business platform from which various chargeable services or products are offered. The library and its organization of corporate information resources may be providing the backbone of content and managed corporate memory for these services.

Commercial portals

The commercial portals such as provided by CORBIS (**www.corbis.com/**), is trying to reach the widest possible diverse audience with the narrowest amount of content, thereby optimizing available information assets for the highest return. The audience may be extremely diverse and not easily defined by age, sex, country or economic demographic, although cultural factors will probably distinguish between groups. Such sites tend towards a certain blandness in their attempt to please a diverse community and will trade heavily upon the uniqueness of the content to attract users back. They will tend to repackage and customize this core of unique content to satisfy multiple access modes by their diverse audience. Libraries may have a lesser role in this environment owing to the lack of commercially viable content. However, the development of digital libraries within national libraries, museums and other cultural institutions means that there are digital products of valued assets that are competitive with commercial content in some narrow sectors.

Publishing portals

The publishing portal will generally aggregate large volumes of external resources, with control over the resource content being secondary to access provision. The levels of content customization will therefore be lower, and the focus shifts to providing varied modes and personalization at the point of access. Ketchell (2000) feels that 'the information gateways of most academic libraries resemble primarily publishing portals' and it seems clear that library portals in other sectors will similarly resemble publishing portals. These publishing portals are the most like information gateways (described in Chapter 5 'Resource discovery, description and use'), although it is likely there will be multiple channels and gateways to feed specific communities. From the library perspective, the community and its needs will drive and define the extent of the portal more than the content.

Forced Migration Online (**www.forcedmigration.org/**), developed by the Refugee Studies Centre in Oxford, is an example of a publishing portal. It provides access to information relating to refugees and forced migrants, comprising a searchable catalogue of web resources, a digital library of documents and journals, research guides that are country and subject specific, and a news resource. DIEPER, in its aspiration to develop a European virtual library of digitized journals (d-journals), provides a different mode of publishing portal (**http://gdz.sub. uni-goettingen.de/dieper/**). Planned services include a search engine for articles, a licensing server to control access to remote archives, and a register that records all d-journals and digitization initiatives within Europe.

The importance of content

The focus so far has been upon communities. However, the scope, depth, veracity and quality of content is also vital in the building of valued portal products. When selecting resources for portals 'great content is the main criteria' (Pack, 2001b, 67). The content must also enhance the user's information experience:

> Content must make it easy for the portal visitor to make decisions. If content is difficult to ascertain, the user is likely to abandon the site and get help/product. . . . Ask yourself if your content is guiding the thought process. Is enough provided? (Frappaolo, 2001, 41)

The previous chapters have detailed the way in which new models of collection and content development are moving. These movements are important to developers of portal services, as there must be sufficient content that is of a high quality to attract use and reuse. In addition to the collection building issues already identified in earlier chapters, the following should be borne in mind when developing content for portals.

Convenience

How close to the user can you deliver the content from the portal and is this appropriate to the user base? Delivering documents directly to the desktop is usually considered an advantage over requiring the user to visit the library, especially in distance access environments. In some portals, however, the documents identified may sometimes only be accessed with subscription or at end-user direct cost, which makes them far more inconvenient than a visit to the library. Another consideration might be whether the content can interact with other resources through a seamless interface, which might become a selection issue based on user convenience. Considering the user's needs and convenience is key to gaining reuse of the portal resources and can be achieved through 'streamlining the delivery of resources . . . aligning product development with specific user groups . . . and marketing focused on tangible products' (Guenther, 2000, 38).

Quality assurance and trust

The user must be confident that the resources connected from the portal are reliable and have been verifiably assured. Trust in both the resources and the delivery mechanism is an intangible but vital benefit to be conferred on the user. Trust is the most important feature to develop and one that libraries tend to take for granted. This is expressed thus by the director of Xerox's Palo Alto Research Center, John Seely Brown, when looking at the difference between the web and a library:

> On the Web, most information does not have an institutional warranty behind it, which really means you have to exercise much more judgement. For example, if you want to borrow a piece of code or use a fact, you'll have to assess the believability of the information. If you find something in a library, you do not have to think very hard about its believability. If you find it on the Web, you have to think pretty hard.
>
> (Fisher, 1999)

Through understanding the user's needs from profiling their use of resources, the service provider can focus resource and development effort more efficiently in the quest to delight the user. Quality assurance is an iterative process that continues throughout and should therefore continually inform the content development lifecycle. See Chapter 2 'Why digitize?'.

Community

There are so many means of gaining information and resources that data can become ubiquitous and may even become devalued in the eyes of the user. Portals can offer the feeling of community, and if the user can suggest and partake in content development then there will be a higher level of satisfaction in the service. This community might be no more than the contact with other like-minded persons grouped around and enriching the content provided (as often seen in science communities who have been proactive in portal content development: **www.thescientificworld. com**). In reaction to users' perceptions then, 'the things that are wrapped around content are becoming more and more valuable as content itself is becoming less and less valuable' (Pack, 2001a, 39).

Delivery chain

The delivery chain has also changed and will affect what resources can be made available and whom those resources are intended to attract. Halm (1999, 303) identifies a change in actors in the delivery chain, and contemplates who will survive:

Old delivery chain: publisher => library => patrons
New delivery chain: publisher / aggregator => off-site patrons via www with library intermediating as licensee & patron authenticator => library => on-site patrons for print resources and in-house use of electronic resources.

It is clear that the library could become viewed as an unnecessary actor in the equation highlighted by Halm. Others see commercial providers using content 'as a condiment' to the real commercial purpose of the site and as a 'useful magnet to attract users and demonstrate respectability' (Arnold, 2001, 44). Sayeed Choudhury, Director of the Digital Knowledge Centre at Johns Hopkins University, stated during a lecture at Oxford University in September 2000 that e-publishing and commercial portals may well be the Trojan horses of the digital era. By getting libraries to show users commercial digital products, and by linking to digital resources, the commercial agencies are gaining full information on users' needs and their usage patterns, while at the same time building brand awareness. The time may shortly come when they find the economic model that allows them to approach the user directly and remove the library from the information chain altogether. This trend is already illustrated by services such as Questia (**www.questia.com/**), who claim to offer over 35,000 books and journal articles online direct to the user with services such as 'how Questia compiles your bibliography for you'.

Branding and marketing in the portal arena

The concept of branding and marketing is a subject often resisted by librarians as too commercial and not intellectually important enough to be considered as an integral part of service provision. For a portal though, strong branding is a pre-requisite to constant use. Veen (2001, 77) makes it clear that the market has room for sites that meet niche information goals and those that provide back-up, as aids to finding information in new subject domains:

User tests have shown that most Web users will have a primary source of information for subjects they care about, and a secondary source for things with which they aren't as familiar. Ask a basketball fan the score to the last New York Knicks game, and he'll go to ESPN.com. Ask him the country code for dialling Estonia, and he'll likely start at Yahoo.

The aim for any provider of portal-type services is to be the first source for information in the domain the user really cares about. Within discrete organizations (such as companies or education establishments) this can be achieved through building a community of information use via the portal focused on that community. In open and competitive user domains, building communities is usually only achievable by self-reference: people join or use the community because the product offered refers back to a predisposed preference. The essence of branding is to help prospective users identify quickly and accurately with the self-referencing elements that will make them use one resource above the others that might be available. Newspapers use it every day to sell their newspaper, which generally will contain much the same news as their competitors. Publishers like Dorling Kindersley have built strong brands to become synonymous with quality children's reference books, and thus the consumer's question isn't whose brand of children's reference book to buy, but which Dorling Kindersley title is needed. This is the power of strong branding.

The process of building a brand and marketing the service can generally be condensed into four basic stages:

- *Analyse the service offered.* What is the purpose and goal of the service (its mission statement in management parlance), and why should anyone use the specific service on offer?
- *Define value for the potential audience.* By defining the audience, and finding out what they value, and then highlighting the resonance with the values offered through the service, then strong brand awareness is delivered. For example, Forced Migration Online has a strong and obvious set of values around refugee issues, and this will confer an instant community to the portal. Assuming the portal delivers appropriate information services, then the brand is strongly self-referential. In branding terms, as pioneered by advertising giants

such as David Ogilvie (of Ogilvie and Mather who delivered the classic 'Hathaway Man' and other ground-breaking advertising campaigns), a brand is a memorable promise made visible.

- *Have a market position.* In other words, do not try to be all things to all users and do not try to build a new Yahoo with limited resources. Use the brand's context and relationship with its competition to build a strong identity. What does the service offer that is unique or exceptionally well done? What are the key market issues: size of audience, geographic location, subject specialism, methods of delivery, types of resources on offer?

- *Repeat consistently and persistently the message.* The key to branding is to have something worth procuring and to then place this product in front of the key users. The objective is to be noticed and to be remembered. However, branding is not about blanket recognition, but about attracting the most appropriate user for the resource and thus the right type of information transaction for the services offered.

Branding is about bucking the tendency to compete on price alone in ever more crowded information marketplaces, but to create a sense of lasting value in the minds of users.

Some example projects

The following brief examples will show that delivering information and delighting the customer is more than just meeting a user needs analysis. It is about delivering *information desire*: the axis point between library-assessed user needs analysis, what the user internally thinks they might want, and what services they will truly value and trust. These examples illustrate the way that several portals have addressed their user communities. The focus of the studies is health-oriented portals from across the world. Health information is a large growth area among digital information resources and tends to be highly valued by its user base. Trust is a fundamental issue in information desire in the health arena in particular, where wrong information has the most serious consequences. Here the simple user-needs analysis for information on health issues is clear. How those needs are met and the types and extent of the information needed are not so clear cut and in the digital world, value and desire are as important.

Horizontal portal: AfricaOnline

Three Kenyans studying at MIT and Harvard University in the USA founded this internet company (**www.africaonline.com**) in the early 1990s. It is the largest internet service provider in the continent outside of South Africa. This portal clearly reflects the user community it is serving, with health just one of the many areas covered in a horizontal model. As the CEO, Ayisi Makatiani, states, 'In Europe and the US, you can choose a niche and sell that niche. In Africa you have to be more of a portfolio company and choose three or four niches that complement each other' (Robinson, 2001). This is why this organization also delivers cheaper internet access in a continent where access is the biggest obstacle to widespread internet use. In Africa (excluding South Africa), a mere one person in 270 uses the internet, as compared with one in between three and five in Europe or the USA (Robinson, 2001).

As viewed in autumn 2001, this is clearly a portal in the early days of development, but is already providing focused and useful links to authoritative information resources on health. There is a circular logic to the use of digital resources that AfricaOnline addresses well – why expend scarce resources accessing the internet if the information is not worth the cost of accessing it? In AfricaOnline, the value is primarily in the access to the internet through low cost mechanisms for clients with an identifiable desire for access. The portal then becomes a simple and trusted first staging post with reliable and relevant links to the wider internet.

Commercial portals: PlanetaVida and Ezyhealth

These two portals are designed for different regions of the world but serve a very similar purpose. They are both primarily commercial sites focused upon health information, for South America in the case of PlanetaVida (**www.planetavida.com**) and for Singapore in that of Ezyhealth (**www.ezyhealth.com**). PlanetaVida appears to be completely driven by advertising revenue and associated products, while Ezyhealth is a corporate company where the portal is an outreach marketing tool for its health IT products and services, with some advertising added. Thus in both cases the portals are motivated to achieve high volumes of traffic and reuse by their users.

The emphasis is towards lifestyle health issues, and therefore the portals are visually attractive, with large amounts of choices and information, but neither site links to many resources external to its own content. The intent is clearly to retain the user within the bespoke environment for as long as possible. The information is presented as if it has high authority and yet, while there is no apparent evidence of any false information, there is no evidence either that authoritative, independent resources are used to compile information. This will always remain the largest risk to the user of commercial sites. The recognition that these sites receive for their information content is based more on the fact they serve a specific community, supporting local language needs, brand awareness and marketing, than on any typical or recognizable information strategy. The user who primarily uses the internet as a consumer will value these sites, as they provide information, products and 'infotainment' in equal measure. The users of these sites will probably also value the way the subject content is narrowly focused upon meeting their specific cultural or regional group needs. Whether these sites deliver the golden egg of consumer trust is something to measure over time and whether libraries would choose to link to them from within their health subject gateways is doubtful.

Government portals: HealthInsite

The Health*Insite* portal (**www.healthinsite.gov.au/index.cfm**) provides a wide range of detailed information, packaged for easy access via areas relating to different conditions and diseases. There is a wealth of reliable and up-to-date information in this attractive portal and the subjects range from serious conditions, such as cancer, through to lifestyle issues. That this is a government initiative is clear from the branding, and the focus upon Australian issues is apparent. Trust and veracity are obviously important to the users of this site; the portal projects this through a functional design with the emphasis at all times on depth of content and accuracy. As a national government-sponsored information resource, it has a stated purpose:

In line with the Government's strategy of delivering services via the Internet by 2001, Health*Insite* was conceived to bridge the gap between the increasing potential for consumers to access health information via the Internet, and the absence of quality control of web information.

(**www.healthinsite.gov.au/about.cfm**)

It is thus clear that this portal has an important role in national government policy and service provision. There is the option to personalize access and to save important articles and points of access for ease of reuse. This portal is completely user-centred, and covers a range of subjects with a focus on Australian issues, promoted in a reliable way. It has delivered information desire through being a reliable source, by providing news to help ensure that users return for further updates, and by allowing personalization of access and content. Its user base is self-selecting by nature of this being the definitive source of government information on health issues for Australians. It will most likely be linked to a wide variety of library subject gateways.

Library and publishing portals

There are a large number of important subject portals to health-related information provided by libraries. These include, for instance, Welch Library Online at Johns Hopkins University (**www.welch.jhu.edu/**) and the US National Library of Medicine Gateway (**http://gateway.nlm.nih.gov/gw/Cmd**). This latter allows users to search in multiple retrieval systems, including MEDLINE/PubMed and several other key databases, and users can also order documents, see clinical alerts and gain information on clinical trials, among other information services.

Another important online resource, identified by Booth and Walton (2000, 155) as 'a unique test-bed for the use of such libraries in a professional setting' is the UK National electronic Library for Health (NeLH) (**www.nelh.nhs.uk/**). As Booth further explains, the NeLH is intended to offer innovative, in-depth services and a sense of community information building aimed mainly at health professionals, but with significant appeal to the general user as well.

A single Knowledge and Know-How Platform will underpin the NeLH, a series of linked databases interrogated by a single search engine via a world wide web interface. Virtual branch libraries (VBLs) will provide special collections that organize and display information in a way most appropriate to the VBL user. Local LIS managers are seen as central to the development and delivery of the NeLH's aims and objectives.

The combination of headline news, 'document of the week', knowledge base resources (such as access to the Cochrane Library or the Research Findings Register), links to professional portals and to resource centres, all leads to the feeling of a portal front-end for a sophisticated hybrid library, delivering quality services. When viewed in 2001, this remained a pilot website, but appears to be striving to meet the challenges of building community- and user-centred resources that will delight the user and deliver information desire.

Promiscuous use of portals

The use of portals will generally be promiscuous. The user may want a readable resource for a lifestyle issue in one access, while not concerned overly whether the facts are fully verifiable. In their next access, they may require a verifiably accurate resource on an issue such as breast cancer. This is in the nature of information desire. Inherent within this is the risk that the user will continue to refer to the infotainment resource because it is a recognizable brand, or just happens to be foremost in their internet bookmark list, when they should switch to a more reliable resource. This is why the concept of information desire should be important to portal developers in libraries of all types. It will not be enough to satisfy pure information needs; it is essential that the portal is broad enough, through content branding, personalization and other mechanisms, to deliver what the user really wants and will also value enough to return to view repeatedly. There is more to the digital library or portal for access than content, especially when users are so promiscuous. As Guenther says, 'consumers want to feel as though they are being taken care of, that someone is looking out for their interests and needs' and 'convenience is one of the most important ingredients of a digital library' (Guenther, 2000).

Personalization

This underlying theme of the community served by portals comes most to the fore with the issue of personalization. Often referred to as the 'MyLibrary' trend in portals, with examples such as 'My Netscape' or 'My BBC', this is the trend towards services that appear to allow the user to customize or personalize their interaction with the portal interface, the retrieval engine or the content. This is a direct response to the sense of information overload and frustration that users frequently report when accessing massed digital resources. As far back as 1945 Vannevar Bush (1945) identified the need to deal with the sheer size of information avaliable as he saw it and suggested the 'MemEx', described in Chapter 1 'Digital futures in current contexts', a tool to enable the user to note, bookmark and organize information in the fashion that made the most sense to them. The problem is not new, but users' tolerance of massed information with low relevancy has never been lower, given the difficulties outlined here and in Chapter 1 of providing targeted access amidst the information chaos. Personalized information environments (PIE) or personalized portals are therefore becoming increasingly popular tools to stem the tide of information washing over the typical internet user.

However personalized these feel to the user, there is still massive aggregation of functionality and choice in the options offered. Therefore, these services are still based on knowing what the community of users might want, and on the ability to deliver a more focused service for them. French and Viles (1999) identify four conceptual requirements for personalization in information environments:

- customizability
- efficient and effective search
- controlled sharability
- privacy and security.

Users want to be able to customize their view of the information universe and arrange the results of searches and resources according to their personal requirements. This can be most ably assisted by effective search facilities, so that the environment can dynamically alter its context as resources and points of access are changed. Users may want to work alone or share their personalized environments with others, and so being able to share is essential. However, once you share something digitally, it opens the opportunity for abuse and thus highlights the need for security and access control.

Middleware

Libraries can sometimes best serve their user community through implementing technology known as 'middleware' to interface and integrate between the monolithic digital library, the various external portal products, the internal network, resources, services and applications. A middleware integrator is a thin-layer database that enables the library to describe content once and to act as an interface within the library portal or to be selected by users as part of their personalized information environment. Issues relating to the extent of interoperability and the availability of descriptive metadata always become limiting factors in the implementation of these middleware integrators. The aim is to enable variable levels of granularity in search and access according to the target user community. This sort of database service can also integrate resources into a user's workflow, such as a legal digital library resource linked within an electronic client legal record for law practitioners.

Why libraries should personalize: experiences at MyLibrary@NCState and HeadLine

Surveys have identified the personalization/customization trend as among the foremost technology trend for libraries: 'library users who use the Web expect customization, interactivity and customer support' (LITA, 1999). Lakos and Gray (2000, 169) state clearly the library's role:

> Customizable pages are available from many sources on the Web, but a library portal allows that customization to build upon the expertise offered by the library, both in the form of the underlying database built by librarians and in the form of greater accessibility of those librarians.
>
> (Lakos and Gray, 2000, 169)

MyLibrary@NCState

MyLibrary@NCState is a user-driven, customizable information service and portal hosted by the NCSU Libraries. It facilitates a model to provide enhanced access to local and remote sets of data and information, while enabling users to control exactly how much information is displayed at any given time. Librarians use the same tools as their users to click links and buttons and fill in forms to design content delivery, which is seen as a critical advance, for 'librarians are free to concentrate on content' (Lakos and Gray, 2000, 172) instead of having to focus on the details of the technology to deliver useful services. Both librarians and users are presented with a common view on the information, which assists in the sense of community building. Morgan and Reade (2000, 195) see other benefits as well in library and resource management terms:

> The very fact of this service's existence and use enables librarians to study the preferences of subscribers, to scan the overall user population for marketing opportunities, and moreover, to make collections management decisions.

HeadLine personal information environment

HeadLine is a hybrid library project in the UK led by the London School of Economics with the London Business School and the University of Hertfordshire as partners. Within its hybrid library model, it uses a PIE to provide a single interface to both print and electronic resources and service. It is a typical PIE implementation with users able to restrict display to the information relevant to their needs, customize their own PIE pages and build their own collections of resources, which they can share with others if they wish. HeadLine sees this personalization paradigm as a useful model for the hybrid library:

> What library users really want is their own personal library, containing all the resources they need and none of the resources that they don't need. Like hybrid libraries, portals are organized, mediated, and configurable, and they provide access to a wide range of materials.
>
> (Gambles, 2001)

176

Conclusion

The means of providing access to resources will be critical to the success of any digital library implementation and this will continue to be a vibrant and fast-moving area of technology advancement. Because of this, the data architectures and underlying system designs have to be separable from the display and access mechanisms to enable less painful transitions between technology implementations. The portal is clearly a tool that libraries can utilize to demonstrate their value and benefits to their communities as long as personalization is incorporated as a central tool. The MyLibrary@NCState is an example of an application layer for presentation, but the ultimate aim should be to provide additional services and, in so doing, 'aid in reasserting the authority of the library in a time of competitive but not necessarily equivalent information sources' (Morgan and Reade, 2000, 197).

8

Preservation

The term 'preservation' is an umbrella under which most librarians and archivists cluster all of the policies and options for action, including conservation treatments. It has long been the responsibility of librarians and archivists – and the clerks and scribes who went before them – to assemble and organize documentation of human activity in places where it can be protected and used.   (Conway, 1999)

Introduction

The digitization of valued original materials is often undertaken with the dual goals of both improved access and enhanced preservation (Kenney, 1996, 3). However, the preservation is often secondary, preserving only by reducing the physical access to the original. The digital version is generally not considered to be a primary preservation resource. Important as the preservation of originals through digitization is, these originals are unlikely to be at such immediate risk as the data and digital resources themselves, with 'born-digital' data being in the highest risk category. This chapter will cover all these topics, starting with a discussion of the scale of the digital preservation problem, then examining some key issues in preservation in the analogue world for libraries and archives, which offer concepts and models that need to be considered and adopted in the digital world. We then address the numerous issues attendant upon digital data preservation, and evaluate some international, national and institutional initiatives for the preservation of digital data.

Throughout this chapter, we differentiate between data preservation (which is about ensuring full access and continued usability of data and digital information), and preservation through digitization (which allows for greater physical security of physical analogue originals). Strategically it becomes self-evident that to reduce the stress upon the valued original, the data created must last as long as possible. Thus processes and intentions for preservation must be decided early in the digital lifecycle (see Chapter 2 'Why digitize?') to ensure that repeating the digitization directly from the original is reduced or hopefully eradicated – though we will show below that costs of digital data storage can mean that it may sometimes be cheaper to return to the originals.

This chapter will discuss the following issues:

- the scale of the digital preservation problem
- preserving the written heritage
- preservation through surrogacy
- authenticity of digital data
- surrogate versus original
- digital surrogacy: is it a preservation alternative?
- why data needs preservation
- how digital data is to be preserved
- methods of preservation of digital materials
- strategic issues in refreshing and reformatting data
- new approaches to migration
- data archaeology
- preservation metadata
- rights management
- national and international initiatives in digital preservation.

The scale of the digital preservation problem

Digital data is being produced on a massive scale by individuals and institutions both large and small: commercial, educational, private and domestic. Some of this data is created from analogue originals for a variety of reasons, some in order that it can be printed in conventional form, some of it is born, lives and dies in only digital form, and it is the potential death of this digital data, especially that which is only ever digital, that concerns us here. The scale of digital production is so large (and growing exponentially year by year) because of the change in writing and printing technologies brought about by word-processing and computer typesetting, and because of the availability of digital cameras and scanners which can convert analogue to digital in both leisure and production environments. This massive rise in the availability of digital data is often compared to the huge growth in volume of written material in the 15th century, when printing presses replaced scriptoria, as we saw in Chapter 1 'Digital futures in current contexts'. Initially, digital files were produced for the production of written, printed and visual documents only as a means to an end: they were part of the process rather than a product. But soon process became product as means of disseminating digital data became cheaply and widely available (floppy disks, CD-ROMs). With the widescale adoption of the internet and the rise of the world wide web over the last ten years, the world has been overwhelmed by digital information.

The many advantages of digital data were apparent from the beginning, and this has led to large programmes of retrospective conversion of traditional materials into digital format to support a wide range of uses (see Chapter 2 'Why digitize?'). Digital documents seemed easy to store, back-up and restore, but, as we are now realizing, this was only a short-term benefit (try to find a file a year later on the hard drive, among 500 others, when you have forgotten what it was called).

Knowledge and knowledge loss

The Gutenberg printing revolution led Europe out of the Dark Ages of the loss of knowledge of the learning of the ancient Greeks and Romans; the digital revolution may land us in an age even darker if urgent action is not taken. In particular need of attention is the ever-changing nature of information available on the internet, through e-mail and the world wide web. Details preserved in private communications, by accident or design, reveal much of the past: the writings of Roman soldiers in Britain on the Vindolanda tablets, the letters of Charles Dickens, the papers of statesmen like Jefferson or Mountbatten, offer many personal, literary and political insights unavailable in more public documents. The telegraph and telephone eroded epistolary communications, and the rise of e-mail and text messaging has meant that communication through writing is popular again, but with the disadvantage that either the written products will be deleted or destroyed, or that we will be tempted to keep so much that the problems of data organization and the expense of handling them render them virtually useless (Gleick, 2000, 249–65).

Materials published on the web may derive from professional sources such as publishers or libraries, with analogues elsewhere, which will continue to be available even after the digital versions disappear from view, but what of other kinds of digital documents? In the past, ephemera such as playbills, advertisements, menus, theatre tickets, broadsheets, etc. have survived, albeit sometimes rather haphazardly, and are now collected, stored, conserved and valued as vital witnesses to political, economic, social and private aspects of the past. Today, these artefacts appear on the web for a matter of days, to disappear in the twinkling of an eye, the flash of a pixel. There are, too, many government documents, records and other official papers that only ever have a digital form: what is to be done about these? We have a warning from recent history of the possible dangers here: tapes of many seminal radio and television programmes were destroyed after broadcasting, and many live broadcasts were never taped, resulting in serious gaps in the history of the performing arts of the 20th century. In the digital world, the experiences of solving the Year 2000 problem have demonstrated that avoiding data loss is extremely expensive, and it becomes more expensive if it is tackled later rather than sooner, given the exponential rise in the amount of data.

Preserving the written heritage

Culture, any culture . . . depends on the quality of its record of knowledge.
                                                                    (Waters, 1997, 39)

One of the key functions of libraries, and in particular of archives, is the preservation of written culture for the long term, which generally means conserving physical artefacts using techniques most appropriate to the conservators of the time, and making these artefacts available to readers for long-term access, as well as preservation reformatting of the content of important items felt to be most at risk of further deterioration. As

Waters points out, any society depends on the quality of its knowledge of its own past, and a falsification of that past, whether deliberate or accidental, damages the society. The Soviet Union is a prime example of a society which rewrote its history regularly to reflect the prevailing political mores, destroying valuable evidence along the way (Preserving digital information, 1996, 1). This practice is satirized by George Orwell in *Nineteen Eighty-Four*. Lack of care in preserving our digital past and present will certainly ensure that we will have an impoverished digital future.

While there is, naturally, no purpose in conserving documents without ensuring access, these two aims are not always mutually achievable: conservation means that access often has to be restricted in the case of rare or fragile objects: ancient manuscripts, fragile historic newspapers, brittle books. Access *always* results in a degradation of the original object; however minimal this may seem in any one interaction between user and object, the cumulative effects over decades or even centuries can be disastrous. Librarians have to constantly balance these two opposing needs as best they can. In the past, best was sometimes not good enough – some early techniques for enhancing documents so that scholars could better read them proved highly destructive to the originals, such as the application of reagents like gallic acid or sulphydrate of ammonia. These on initial application would bring up faded readings, but would leave stains, or even eventually produce holes, on the manuscript.

Libraries, archives and preservation responsibility

In archives, of course, the prime reason for acquiring material is its preservation for continued access, but this does not mean that everything available that *might* be preserved will be acquired, or that everything that is acquired will be preserved for ever. Archives operate strict retention and disposal policies, which are inevitable given restrictions on space and budgets. The UK Public Record Office, for instance, accepts no more than 5% of the government records offered for deposit, and even so this occupies 2 km of shelf space every year. (**www.pro.gov.uk/ recordsmanagement/selection/default.htm**). In entering upon any debates about preservation of the historic documentary record, it must be stressed that preservation has in the past often been an accidental process. As Ross points out, 'the survival of the historic record has always been subject to natural and man-made forces' (1993, 10). Indeed, many documents have survived more through the serendipity of their original formats (because they were written on durable animal skins, for instance) and through benign neglect, than through active conservation policies and practices. It is worth noting that animal skin is probably the most durable documentary preservation medium that has ever existed. So well recognized are its qualities that the documentary records of the British Parliament that are published in Hansard are output to one copy printed on vellum for preservation purposes at a cost of some £30,000 per year.

Many libraries of the world, even the smallest, hold rare or unique resources that require preservation and conservation. For some libraries (such as the major national copyright libraries in countries where legal deposit exists) preservation for the long term of large documentary collections is a key concern, with huge economic implications. And almost all libraries have to think about preservation in both the analogue and the digital worlds. Even if they do not themselves preserve materials, they need to be sure that some institutions are doing so in order to direct their users to them. In archives, the majority of holdings are candidates for preservation, even if policy decisions dictate that not everything is preserved. As well as having institutional policies for preservation and conservation, there also need to be national and possibly international initiatives for collaborative work for preservation in both the analogue and the digital worlds.

Preservation through surrogacy

> On preservation and conservation . . . information technology so far has had only marginal effects. (Mannerheim, 2000)

With the advent of photographic techniques for copying documents, conservation of the originals became easier. Documents could be, and were, reproduced as facsimiles in books or on microfilm and these were offered to the readers as a substitute for the originals, thus preserving the originals from further damage. The documentary heritage has always been at risk of damage or destruction through natural or human forces:

fire, flood, warfare or neglect. In the last 150 years, a new danger has threatened: the ' "slow fires" of acidic paper' (Kenney, 1996, 2), which has necessitated the large-scale microfilming of millions of pages of documents over many decades in order that the content is not lost. Many digital reformatting initiatives grew out of earlier microfilming projects, lighting the '"fast fires" of digital obsolescence' (Kenney, 1996, 2).

Substitution of originals with other objects that simulate their content does, of course, pose its own problems: when is a facsimile a satisfactory surrogate for the object itself? This depends on both the needs of the reader and the quality of the reproduction, and is not an easy question to answer. The relationship between any original object and a reproduction of it is problematic, and is a question that has exercised theorists and practitioners of artefactual disciplines for many years. In his seminal essay 'The work of art in an age of mechanical reproduction', Benjamin states that:

> Even the most perfect reproduction . . . is lacking in one element: its presence in time and space. . . . This unique existence of the work . . . determined the history to which it was subject throughout its time of existence.
> (Benjamin, 1992, 214)

The authenticity of surrogates and their acceptability to readers are of major concern, but so too is the preservation and conservation of these surrogates themselves. One great advantage of mechanically produced surrogates is the possibility of preservation through multiplication of the numbers of copies. In the analogue world this itself results in some degradation through re-copying; in the digital world every copy is theoretically an exact copy of its precursor, even after many generations of copying. The crucial questions to ask in the debate about the preservation of originals by the use of surrogates is: what is it that we are preserving and for whom? Are we preserving the objects themselves or the information that they contain? With certain unique, intrinsically valuable and highly significant works, for example the Book of Kells, the Beowulf manuscript, the object itself is as important as what it says. With more ephemeral materials such as newspapers or government documents, while there may be key issues or volumes where it is worth preserving the originals, in general it is probably the content, and the physical arrangement of that content, that needs to be preserved, rather than the objects themselves, though these are matters of much controversy.

Authenticity of digital data

Authenticity of digital documents must be distinguished from authentication as generally defined in the digital world. MacKenzie defines 'authenticity' of a documentary source as 'reliability over time' (2000, 59) while 'authentication' is a term usually used for the process of validating who is allowed access to digital data, and what they might be permitted to do with it. As Rothenberg has pointed out, 'whenever informational entities are used, and for whatever purpose, their suitability relies on their authenticity' and goes on to remark, 'the technological issues surrounding the preservation of digital information entities interact with authenticity in novel and profound ways' (Rothenberg, 2000a, 1). This is a key and crucial issue in the preservation of digital data, as validating its authenticity is so much more problematic than in the analogue world. It is frighteningly easy to change a digital document, leaving no trace, no ghostly palimpsest to tell us what was there before. If we alter the words on a written document, generally we can decipher the original and the changes become part of the cultural accretion of meaning gained by the document. A digital document always appears pristine, despite changes made by accident or design, and this means that if two readers are discussing a work, they may not always know that they are using the same version, or if there has been some hidden change. One major consequence of this is that digital data may not be legally valid, and an analogue version may need to be stored for legislative purposes.

As Cullen says, 'The problems of preserving digital objects have received more attention than questions of authentication. . . .But why preserve what is not authentic?' (2000, 3). Users of libraries and archives have, in the past, relied on curators to validate the authenticity of the resources on offer; curators are trained to know what they have and what its status is, and they rely on a broad professional network in the production and care of the documentary heritage. They purchase materials from reputable sources, have access to experts who can be called upon for second opinions, and they have bodies of meta-information (catalogues, bibliographies, etc.) regarding the provenance and history of rarer works. Forgery or misidentification is not unknown, but the former is a painstaking and difficult process. There are, too, physical character- istics of originals that can reveal information about the age, provenance or history of an object. And falsification is actually much more difficult then actually creating the object in the first place. There is a wonderful example of this in the Kipling short story 'Dayspring mishandled', writ- ten in 1928. A character forges a 15th-century copy of a supposedly lost work by Chaucer, found bound into the covers of an old Bible. The forger has to create 15th-century inks, purchase vellum from the period and even grind his own flour with a millstone to make paste – as well as composing the 'lost' poetry fragment in the first place. How much eas- ier this is in the age of digital data. As Bearman and Trant point out of forgery in the digital world, 'the underlying technology makes purpose- ful fakery easier and more tempting' (1998, 3).

How to authenticate digital documents

Digital authentication is difficult, and it is a problem that will increase over time as digital documents are preserved for the long term. Security of digital archives is of course of paramount importance, but it is not a topic that we propose to tackle here. Version control is also problematic, as very slightly different digital versions of the same exemplar could be circulating without being discovered, unless the changes are fully docu- mented throughout the life of the resource. Digital dissemination is almost unthinkably rapid, as people who have circulated a private e-mail to a public discussion list have sometimes found to their embarrassment. Some accepted system of authenticity validation needs to exist in the dig- ital world, but this is difficult to establish and to enforce for all potential uses and purposes. Markers that can be tracked can be added to the dig- ital object (watermarks, digital signatures), but hackers are never very far behind such developments, and they can be expensive to maintain. Responsible agencies producing digital documents are likely to use meta- data structures, collection records, or unique document identifiers that can be checked, but again these could be subject to abuse. Librarians and archivists are going to have to face questions of digital authenticity more often than they have faced the same issues in the analogue world, and the solutions are likely to be more diverse. As Bearman and Trant state, 'to determine which methods are suited for what purpose, it is critical that we better understand the functional requirements for authenticity on the part of creators and potential users of digital resources' (1998, 8).

Surrogate versus original

Can surrogates ever truly replace or faithfully represent the original? There is a rather extreme example of features in an original that would be impossible to preserve (at least with any current technologies) in a recently published work, *The social life of information* (Brown and Duguid, 2000, 173–4). One of the authors reports an experience when researching in an archive of 19th-century letters in the USA. Dust from the letters was causing him to have allergic reactions; he covered his nose with a handkerchief and continued working, wishing that someone had digitized the letters so that he could read them on a clean computer screen. He became aware that the person next to him was behaving very oddly – he would pick up each letter in his box, scrutinize it and then slowly sniff it all over. Unable to work out the reason for this strange behaviour, the author finally leaned over and asked his neighbour what he was doing. He replied that he was a medical historian and was trying to detect traces of vinegar, which was sprinkled on letters in cholera outbreaks, as he felt that he might be able to correlate the journeys of the letters with the spread of the cholera. For this scholar, there could be no substitute for the physical object.

The notion of representation of an original by a surrogate is always problematic and in some sense it is always a falsification, for instance, photographs of buildings or sculptures, transcriptions or editions of texts are interpretations as much as they are representations. Creating surrogates can never replicate or preserve *everything* about an original object, but creating no surrogates could mean that *everything* is lost in the case of fragile or compromised originals: brittle books printed on acid-based paper, older newspapers, ancient and medieval books and manuscripts, crumbling sculptures, ruined buildings, photographs on glass plates, explosive nitrate film stock.

Case Study: The great newspaper debate

Fidelity of surrogates to originals, and the fate of those originals, can and do become matters of grave public concern. In the second half of 2000, for instance, there was mounting controversy in Britain and the USA about the jettisoning by major libraries of some of their historic newspaper collections. These collections were all preserved on microfilm, but the disposal of originals caused an outcry in the press. Major libraries such as the Library of Congress in the USA and the British Library in the UK have been microfilming newspapers for many decades in order to preserve the historical record rather then the objects, but the critics of the disposal policy advanced many arguments for the retention of the paper copies. As a society, we are wedded to objects rather than surrogates, even if this causes expensive problems, and some of the objections to the disposal were romantic rather than rational.

The main protagonist in this debate was the American novelist, Nicholson Baker, who wrote an impassioned article in the *New Yorker* in July 2000. Baker accuses the major public libraries of a massive deception about the state of historic newspaper collections: he suggests that their claims that these newspapers are deteriorating so fast as to be almost beyond preservation are not true, and that they have been microfilming these collections for cynical reasons: 'librarians have misled us: for more than fifty years, they have disparaged paper's residual strength, while remaining as "blind as lovers" (as Allen Veaner, former editor of *Microform Review*, once wrote) to the failings and infirmities of film' (Baker, 2000, 55; see also Baker, 2001). It is not the microfilming that is so objectionable to Baker, but the disposal of the originals.

As Cox points out in his critique of Baker's piece, 'there are never any easy answers [in the preservation of information] and, at best, solutions may bring as many additional problems with them as what they are supposedly resolving' (2000). In a debate about this matter in the *Times Literary Supplement*, Pearson remarks 'critics are happy to ignore the realities of choice over the use of resources which any major library must face' (2000), and he goes on to suggest that large-scale digitization programmes might provide the answer. While this would not solve the original versus surrogate debate, the presentation of newspapers in digital form, especially if this is enhanced by indexing (preferably using indexes generated automatically) is a great advance on microfilming, and with good digital archiving, could preserve them for the long term. See Chapter 2 'Why digitize?' for some case studies on the digitization of newspapers.

Digital surrogacy: is it a preservation alternative?

The example given above of the microfilming and consequent possible destruction of newspapers begs the question, could digital surrogacy replace tried and tested analogue methods? Is digital preservation well-enough understood and sufficiently robust for it to replace photographic techniques? Microfilm is predicted to last 500 years; other photographic materials, especially colour film, are perhaps less durable, but they have been in existence long enough for there to be some knowledge of deterioration rates. The costs of storage are known and can be predicted into the future, and the surrogates generally do not require costly and time-consuming processes to be carried out on them every few years, as is the case with digital objects. Many librarians and archivists are still cautious about the digital medium as a preservation alternative, feeling that there has not been enough research into the long-term issues, and in particular costs, around the archiving of digital information for indefinite periods. Few librarians would de-accession originals and put all their trust in digital storage without perhaps having also a film surrogate as an insurance policy.

Another issue that must be addressed is the common view that digitization should only ever happen once, and then the digital image be preserved for posterity. Careful analysis of the relative costs of storing digital and analogue surrogates may, in some cases, reveal that it could be more cost-effective to rescan originals than to store archive-quality digital files. The determining factor may be the age and condition of the original itself: if digitization is undertaken as a rescue strategy, then it is probably advisable to produce archive-quality files and accept the attendant costs. If, however, it is carried out to provide access to images from media that are in good condition and are relatively stable, then capturing access-quality files and rescanning later if needed could prove more cost-effective.

In cases where owners of digital objects must pay ongoing repository (storage) costs, the scan-once, store-forever approach might prove to be more expensive in some cases than rescanning materials at designated intervals. Current costs for digital repository services in the Harvard University Library, for example, are $20.50 per GB per year. For digital image collections, preservation services are higher for uncompressed formats than for colour images with compression (see the Harvard DRS Policy Guide, Rev: 21 May 2001, **http://hul.harvard.edu/ois/systems/ drs/policyguide.html**). Choices about file size at the time of digitization, therefore, reverberate throughout the lifecycle of the image in the repository. When a manager has scanning and storage prices in hand, cost-benefit comparisons can easily be made during project planning (Chapman, 2001).

Why data needs preservation

The nature of data

Data is at risk because it is recorded on a transient medium, in a specified file format, and it needs a transient coding scheme (a programming language) to interpret it. As we explain in more detail in Chapter 1 'Digital futures in current contexts', the basic unit of data, the 'bit' (BInary digiT), is represented by one of only two states: '1' or '0', linked together in a 'bit stream' consisting of many millions of bits or electrical impulses. The kind of digital data that concerns us here is complex, and meaning derived from data can depend as much on how individual data objects are linked as on what those objects are. Of course, written documents are also highly complex objects, but their structure does not need to be comprehended for their preservation, only for their interpretation. Over time, knowledge of how to interpret documents can be lost, but this can usually be re-created, as their textual and physical characteristics are explicit. Their decipherment generally needs only human faculties. Meanings re-created in modern contexts will necessarily differ from 'original' meanings, but this is generally the case in the interpretation of the past, even when the language and contexts have come down to us in an unbroken line: the past is always interpreted through our own historical moment. As we discussed in Chapter 3 'Developing collections in the digital world', digital documents differ from analogue, too, in that they are not inextricably bound to their 'containers', and therefore preserving them is not necessarily a matter of preserving containers as it is in the analogue world. As Rothenberg points out, with physical documents 'saving the physical carriers saves all those attributes of the original that it is possible to save' (2000b, 16). With digital data, a machine needs to be interposed between it and its human interpreter, which adds another layer of complication.

Data impermanence

Digital data is in danger, not because it is inherently fragile or flawed, but because there is a continually accelerating rate of replication, adaptation and redundancy of hardware, software and data formats and standards which may mean that the bit stream may not be readable, interpretable or usable long into the future. All data is stored as a code and therefore requires an element of decoding before it is recognizable and usable in a computing environment, even if open data standards are used. For most people, the bit stream for the word-processing document used to write this book would be totally unintelligible without the suitable computer applications, software and operating system environments to interpret and repackage the data into a readable form. We take this automatic decoding for granted until we try to read a word-processing file from ten years ago and find that none of our current systems or software have any idea what the bit stream means without significant coaching or expert help. The longer the data is left unattended, its data coding unrecorded, systems will become obsolete and the expertise to recognize and decode that specific type of bit stream will become unavailable. Data could be lost forever, irrecoverable without effort that will probably not be cost-effective. There is a direct analogy with the decipherment of ancient scripts where the knowledge of the language used and the system of coding of the written scripts is lost and must be re-created from scraps of knowledge, intuition, research and other language fragments that may be stems of the ancient script. The linguistic bridges to the past built upon the decipherment of hieroglyphics or Linear B are very highly valued for the historical information we now have about those societies and cultures of up to 3000 years ago. These decipherments were often life works for the people who succeeded and were preceded by centuries of hard-worked failure. In the case of Linear A, the battle continues (see Singh, 1999). As described by Maurice Pope (1975),

> Decipherments are by far the most glamorous achievements of scholarship. There is a touch of magic about unknown writing, especially when it comes from the remote past, and a corresponding glory is bound to attach itself to the person who first solves its mystery.
>
> (Pope, 1975)

The challenge for our digital future is to not perpetuate the scenario of data loss and poor records that has dogged our progress over the last 25 years. Otherwise, in just 50 years from now the human record of the early 21st century may be unreadable, and its decipherment an expensive and intellectually challenging feat way beyond the achievements of the great codebreakers of the 20th.

The complexity of digital data

The complexity of digital data will not be apparent to the readers and users of the future if the creators of the present have not made it explicit. An innovative, multimedia CD-ROM derives as much of its meaning from links between digital objects as from the informational content of those objects themselves. Complex digital objects, too, need complex programs to run them, and these programs are constantly in flux, with new versions appearing frequently. If the CD-ROM has been produced by a publisher with today's market in mind rather than tomorrow's users, then documentation of the links and the methods used to create them might not be a priority: the objective is sales, not preservation. After all, some publishers may not even want the products preserved for too long, as they will want to produce new versions, updates, etc. which they can sell again and again. The library that purchases, delivers, then tries to preserve that CD-ROM could have a very expensive task, especially as in order to maintain market advantage, many publishers have very different interfaces, encoding schemes and media structures. Librarians can be faced with thousands of products in hundreds of formats: a difficult and expensive enough situation for providing access to them, a disastrous one for their preservation.

How is digital data to be preserved?

There are two key issues for data preservation, which surprisingly have little to do with preserving the original bit stream:

* preserving the physical media on which the bit stream is recorded
* preserving the means of interpreting, reading and utilizing the bit stream.

Given that the bit stream is merely a very long series of binary codes, the preservation of the physical media should maintain its integrity over time. However, being able to read, use or interpret that bit stream may become increasingly difficult as systems evolve, adapt and eventually become redundant, so presenting a fog through which the bit stream is unusable.

Why the urgency?

Digital data does not have a long enough natural lifetime for us to wait for better media to come along. The life of data written even to optical media, such as CD-ROM or DVD, may be measured in years rather than decades, though the writing to gold-layered optical disk appears to provide a solution to the longer-term storage of data with reduced risk from the media. Even then finding machinery to read the bit stream might become tricky within a few years, very hard after a decade and require some very serious computer archaeology after 15 to 20 years. As yet, data storage has not found its stability equivalent of paper or microfilm, but the evolution of the technology may be around the next corner. The storage of data started with punched cards only some 50 years ago and has transitioned through paper tape, magnetic tape, to magnetic disk, optical disk and portable memory such as flash memory cards to the present day. It is now extremely difficult to find card or tape readers if old archives of the originals come to light.

Data is bad at self-preservation

Unlike many analogue originals such as paper or paintings, data is very bad at self-preservation. Active measures must be taken at its birth to ensure that it survives longer into the future: this is known as the 'reten-tion intention' and is essential to data preservation. Data preservation cannot and must not be left to chance. At particular risk is the category of data which is 'born-digital' – that is, which has no analogue originals. A great deal of data is being produced in this category, much of which it is necessary to preserve: government documents, e-mails, electronic journals, dictionaries and encyclopaedias, computer games, and, proba-bly the most ephemeral category, websites. While it is of course neces-sary to propose strategies for dealing with all categories of digital data, it is not feasible to propose that all digital data should be preserved for the long term.

Selection of data for preservation

In any format, analogue or digital, data is selected for long-term preser-vation because it is felt to have some enduring value. For why preserve something that has no value? But whose values are taken into account, and how can they be known? Historians of the future will rely on what is preserved from today, but their needs will be different from those of present historians, and their research paths will be partly prescribed by the data that is available. Given that it is not possible to preserve every-thing, it is a complex matter to decide what should be preserved. Even the world's major copyright libraries, which are offered copies of every published product of their nation, do not accept everything, though most of what is offered is stored somewhere. It is a vital strategic deci-sion to have selection and retention policies for digital data, just as it is for analogue, and the decisions should be made on the value of the con-tent, not the ease of preservation. It will take complex teams of data orig-inators, librarians, archivists, historians and others concerned with the documentary heritage to decide upon robust selection and retention policies, and these are strategic issues of national and international importance.

Jones and Beagrie have recently produced a decision tree on the selec-tion of digital resources for long-term retention (Jones and Beagrie, 2001, 96–100), which examines the issues in great detail. The first ques-tion posed is 'Is there an institutional policy and guidelines for the selec-tion of digital materials for long-term preservation?' Several surveys have found that while many institutions feel that they *should* have such a policy, very few have produced and implemented one. See for instance the survey carried out by Lievesley and Jones for the British Library (Lievesley and Jones, 1998). International and national guidelines that could be adopted and adapted for local circumstances are urgently needed.

Methods of preservation of digital materials

As is clear from the discussions above, the paradox of digital materials is that they are fundamentally simple, being made up of only two electrical states, but those states can be configured into patterns so complex using programming techniques that a limitless number of different documents and other artefacts can be represented. As we discuss in Chapter 1 'Digital futures in current contexts', digital data derived from different sources differs greatly in the amount of storage needed. Electronic text, even with complex encoding, is compact; still images can be very space hungry, with digital cameras now available that can capture files of 300Mb or more from visually rich objects; sound and video, especially if captured at high quality, take orders of magnitude more storage than images or text; satellite images or complex maps created with GIS systems can be even larger. While file sizes can be reduced to some degree by compression of the data, the compression techniques that offer the greatest economies have the disadvantage that this comes at the price of loss of information. There are some lossless compression algorithms, but these do not produce a significant reduction in file size.

There is also a great variety of media on which digital materials can be stored, from punched cards and tapes which represent the patterns as a series of holes, to the wide range of electronic recording materials: floppy disks, hard drives, tapes, CD-ROMs, DVDs, etc. The methods of digital preservation or digital archiving we propose to discuss here are:

- technology preservation
- refreshing
- migration and reformatting
- emulation
- data archaeology
- output to analogue media.

Technology preservation

Technology preservation is the maintenance of the hardware and software platforms that support a digital resource, and if adopted as a preservation strategy would need to be accompanied by a regular cycle of media refreshing. It is relatively impractical and financially unfeasible, given the large number of computers and programs that would need to be managed over a long period of time: 'any collection manager in charge of a large collection of digital resources who relied solely on this strategy would very soon end up with a museum of ageing and incompatible computer hardware' (Feeney, 1999, 42). One can imagine a library reading room littered with PCs with every version of Windows and Macintoshes running nine generations of operating system; that is to name just two current platforms. For certain rare and important resources, perhaps the technology could be preserved for a time, until a better long-term solution could be found, but this is an approach clearly fraught with difficulty.

Refreshing

Digital storage media have short lives, the length of which can be estimated but which is ultimately unknown. Data therefore has to be moved periodically to new media to ensure its longevity. Sometimes this involves a change of medium: CD-ROMs will be copied on to hard disks in a digital data store, floppy disks may be copied on to CD-ROMs; at other times refreshing may take place because a particular substrate has become unstable, and the files need to be copied to a newer, more stable version of the same medium. Refreshing copies the bit stream exactly as it is, it makes no changes to the underlying data. It is a process that needs to be carried out whatever other preservation strategies are adopted. It is technically relatively straightforward, with low risk of loss if performed and documented properly.

Migration and reformatting

Migration involves change in the configuration of the underlying data, without change in its intellectual content. This is necessary when hardware and software changes mean that the data can no longer be accessed unless it is migrated to the newer machines and programs. Migration will generally involve some reformatting, which begs the question of whether the data still conveys the same content information as it did before it was migrated. The simpler the data structures, the more likely it is that the content will be preserved. With complexly linked artefacts such as websites, it is difficult to see how they can be preserved without loss unless complex (and costly) documentation is produced that annotates the structures. If libraries and archives have to cope with a plethora of digital formats, one approach to their sustainability over the long term is to convert the digital objects into standard formats when they are first accessioned. This involves assessment of the object and extracting its data formats and inner structure, and conversion of the structures into the institution's own models. This is expensive initially, but could prove cost-effective over the long term, making migration easier and faster. The costs here are front loaded; with other preservation strategies they come later in the lifecycle.

Strategic issues in refreshing and reformatting data

Migration, reformatting and refreshing of data are processes that may need to be carried out many times over the lifetime of digital objects identified as sufficiently significant for long-term preservation. Instability or obsolescence of media means that data will need to be moved regularly and changes in software and hardware platforms will dictate constant reformatting. Refreshing and migration cycles will not necessarily coincide, which means that documentation and management of the digital archives will be complex.

The main disadvantage of a reformatting approach to digital preservation is that *all* data must be converted in each reformatting cycle, whether there is any indication that particular resources will be accessed in the future or not. Missing a cycle could mean that the data is unreadable in subsequent cycles. This relates closely to the just-in-case model of library acquisition discussed in Chapter 3 'Developing collections in the digital world'. Reformatting is costly and labour-intensive and is likely to stretch the resources of all libraries, large and small, which could compromise decisions about effort to be apportioned for other activities, digital and non-digital.

During refreshing and migration, too, time and care needs to be spent in validating data to ensure that there has been no corruption. The (relatively straightforward) process of copying the bit stream from one medium to another can sometimes be problematic, and even slight corruption can be cumulative, resulting soon in irrecoverable data. Reformatting *ipso facto* involves the loss of the original digital object, given that the premise upon which it is based is that the original is not preservable. Lorie (2001) says of migration:

> It is the most obvious, business-as-usual, method. When a new system is installed, it coexists with the old one for some time, and all files are copied from one system to the other. If some file formats are not supported by the new system, the files are converted to new formats and applications are changed accordingly. However, for long-term preservation of rarely accessed documents, conversion becomes an unnecessary burden. Another drawback of conversion is that the file is actually changed repeatedly – and the cumulative effect that such successive conversions may have on the document is hard to predict.

Migration is also time-critical and needs to be carried out as soon as new formats are defined and before the current format is obsolete. If a generation is missed, the data may already be difficult to recover; if more generations are missed, it could be completely lost. Migration cycles need to be relatively frequent – few digital originals will survive more than five to seven years without some attention.

New approaches to migration

The CAMiLEON (Creating Creative Archiving at Michigan and Leeds: Emulating the Old on the New) project has recently suggested some more complex approaches to data migration that might solve some of the problems outlined above. Wheatley (2000) points out that the term migration actually encapsulates a number of different techniques that might be useful for different data formats, and he discusses the relative merits of these. They range from a minimalist approach suitable for, say, a word-processed document, which could be stripped of formatting and retained as a string of ASCII characters (though this would only work if no special fonts or symbols had been used), to much more complex re-creations of richly interlinked and interactive objects like computer games or multimedia objects. Migrations, he suggests, can be carried out through a mix of automatic and manual conversions, with processes requiring significant human interventions always being more costly. There will almost always be some degree of loss in migration. Some of this is likely to be minimal, especially with less complex text files or data-base records. Though Wheatley points out that 'nothing of the original environment in which the object was created is preserved', this is often of antiquarian interest that may be only of concern to software histori-ans. For the everyday user of a migrated electronic text in a library, it would have little significance. Pursuing a goal of absolute fidelity to orig-inals can be a counter-cultural anachronism that does not reflect what happens in the analogue world. The ordinary reader of Shakespeare, for instance, does not usually access the text through the 16th-century ver-sions, but through modern editions. It is the specialist who obtains full value from the originals, and it will be a specialist who will want to view 1970s electronic text via a long-dead word-processing package.

The UK-based CEDARS project has proposed that a migration on request approach might be a useful and cost-effective solution to the dig-ital preservation problem. Objects would be retained in their original form, along with a migration tool written for a current platform. As plat-forms become obsolete, the migration tool would be rewritten for new platforms. Wheatley lists a number of advantages to this, which seem to solve some of the problems we discuss above. In particular, objects are only migrated as they are needed, and the migration is only ever one stage from the original bitstream, which reduces the risk of error from successive migrations.

Migration is a strategy that is likely to be most effective with data objects that are not overly complex or interactive, or that have been orig-inally created with their long-term survival prospects firmly in mind. Tak-ing the lifecycle approach outlined in Chapter 2 'Why digitize?' is likely to yield migratable resources, but there exists much valuable data that has not been created according to these principles.

Emulation

The more complex a digital object is, the more loss there will be in its migration to new formats and generations of hardware and software. This has led some researchers to suggest that for such resources emulation might be a better technique. 'Without emulation it is unclear how interactive digital objects could be preserved in a useful way' (Holdsworth and Wheatley, 2000; see also 2001). Emulation is the process of re-creation of the hardware and software environment required to access a resource. It would be theoretically possible to emulate either the hardware or the software: software could be re-engineered in the future if sufficient metadata about it could be stored, or the software and operating systems that created the digital object could be stored with it, and the hardware platform to run them could be emulated in the future. Russell is of the opinion that 'although emulation as an approach for preservation has been viewed with some scepticism, it is gaining support because it offers potentially a solution for the very long term' (1999, 8). She argues that this is a long-term solution because the technical environment is only emulated when it is needed, rather than being preserved along with the data. This means that costs occur at a later stage than if data is constantly reformatted.

Clearly, emulation has promise, but has not yet been fully tested as a preservation strategy; as Rothenberg avers, 'neither has any other approach' (Rothenberg, 2000b, 1).

Data archaeology

Sometimes it may be necessary to rescue a digital resource that has not been migrated but contains vital information, or to which some unforeseen disaster has occurred. Occasionally data is discovered on old disks or tapes that have been accidentally preserved and data archaeology has successfully rescued it. A wide range of techniques can be employed for this, with varying degrees of success. Data archaeology has also been proposed as a preservation strategy. In this model, data would be refreshed regularly, but no migration would be performed, and no programs would be preserved to be emulated at a later stage. Instead, data archaeologists of the future would be left to puzzle out the data structures and connections in order to reaccess the information. This is an extreme form of just-in-time rescue which has the virtue of being low-cost, but which is highly risky. The argument for it is that better techniques are likely to be available in the future to recover data, and if the resources are felt to be of sufficient value, methods would be developed. This is analogous to present recovery and interpretation methods of historians and archaeologists, and has the virtue that it would be for them to decide what has value to their society, rather than current content creators and managers making decisions about the future that could easily be misguided.

Ross and Gow carried out a useful study in 1999 on the state of the art in digital archaeology and found that records could be recovered from quite severe damage or long obsolescence. There are similarities between data archaeology and emulation, and indeed emulation is a technique proposed as one method of recovery of lost materials. However, data archaeology is probably a strategy of last resort for valuable data and programs.

Recovery of records after German reunification

An important application of data archaeology is described by Wettengel (1998). After German reunification at the beginning of the 1990s, archivists were faced with vast amounts of paper records and digital files from East German government agencies that had been closed down. Wettengel makes the important point that organizations creating data are not necessarily the best custodians of it. He reports that 'many data files were no longer legible, and data documentation was at best incomplete, and in most cases missing' (266). Many of the data-creating agencies were privatized after reunification and, while the information was supposed to be in the public domain, companies charged inordinate fees for preservation activities. Large numbers of records were stored on media that were deteriorating fast, but the worst problem was that the hardware and software used to create the files was obsolete, rendering them inaccessible. Much data was recovered, but the worst problem was the lack of documentation, and in some cases former workers in the data-creating agencies had to be hired in as consultants to interpret some of the data and encoding standards. However, a substantial amount of data was recovered, and the main lesson to be learnt is that good documentation is vital to the recovery process.

Output to analogue media

For many years an integral part of the conservation of fragile materials was the creation of a high-quality surrogate during repair, restoration or rebinding. This might have been produced using photography, but more likely microfilming or even high-quality photocopying would have been employed to provide a surrogate that would satisfy the access needs for the majority of users and would thus help to preserve the original. Now that valued originals are being captured in digital form, does there still also need to be an analogue surrogate of the item? Is the production of an analogue version of the data file an appropriate preservation strategy?

In any digitization project, consideration must be given to the question of whether to microfilm before the digital imaging is done. This provides a preservation copy in an analogue format and circumvents some of the concerns over the longevity of the digital files. However, there are plenty of features in an original that microfilm cannot capture but digitization can, and so the digital file is a valuable primary surrogate in its own right. For access purposes, high-quality prints and also large-sized screens for viewing might satisfy most users' needs. The printing company Oce Limited even has technology that can print out full-colour images straight on to vellum, thus re-creating the experience of a manuscript as accurately as is feasible. However, these address only the preservation of the original analogue or the provision of analogue surrogates for access. To consider using analogue output as a preservation mechanism for digital files the options are fairly limited to 'Computer Output to Microfilm' or 'COM'.

The COM process involves printing the digital data file directly on to microfilm, so that each page of data becomes a separate frame in the film. The COM approach is thus most successful for large volumes of straightforward alphanumeric text or for bitonal images. It is not really suitable for greyscale or colour images, as too much information is lost in the process to consider it for preservation purposes.

The Cornell project showed that computer output microfilm created from 600 dpi 1-bit images scanned from brittle books can meet or exceed national microfilm standards for image quality and permanence.

(Chapman, Conway and Kenney, 1999)

The COM process is also limited in useful application to linear text-based resources such as books, journals, catalogues or collections of individual images such as engineering drawings. Other digital products are likely to be rendered almost meaningless in analogue form (websites, games, interactive fiction, etc.) unless what is stored is the underlying code, plus supporting documentation, from which they can be re-created. This is probably an unrealistic expectation.

Preservation metadata

> If digital information objects that are currently being created are to have a chance of surviving migrations through successive generations of computer hardware and software, or removal to entirely new delivery systems, they will need to have metadata that enables them to exist independently of the system that is currently being used to store and retrieve them.
>
> (Gilliland-Swetland, 2000, 10)

Whatever strategies or techniques are adopted to preserve digital data, they will only be successful if the data is fully documented throughout its lifecycle. The importance of this has been shown in the case of the East German files discussed above. This is a strategic issue for data creators and curators, and one that has long-term organizational, managerial, practical and economic consequences. As a resource moves through its cycle, responsibility for its documentation will pass to different agencies and individuals who will have different needs and sometimes divergent views. As Lagoze and Payette suggest, 'preservation metadata does not exist in isolation . . . it can be thought of as the union of all metadata that pertains to the continued discovery, use and integrity of an object' and 'all types of metadata have the potential to affect long-term preservation' (2000, 96). We have dealt with metadata in detail in Chapter 5 'Resource discovery, description and use', and much of what is discussed there is of relevance to the preservation of digital objects. It must also be remembered that the metadata itself is a digital resource that must be preserved, so it must be created with consideration for its own long-term survival.

A number of bodies and projects are currently grappling with the issues of preservation metadata and publishing detailed recommendations as to its implementation. The CEDARS project (**www.leeds.ac.uk/cedars/**) has produced a specification for preservation metadata that is required to support meaningful access to the archived digital content and includes descriptive, administrative, technical and legal information. CEDARS is closely following the reference model for an Open Archival Information System (OAIS) in its metadata schema, and has implemented the schema in XML. The Networked European Deposit Library (NEDLIB) is also using the OAIS reference model (Lupovici and Masanès, 2000). See Chapter 6 'Developing and designing systems for sharing digital resources' for a fuller discussion of the OAIS model.

The PANDORA (Preserving and Accessing Networked Documentary Resources of Australia) project at the National Library of Australia has developed a logical data model which integrates all the metadata for digital objects into a consistent view. (**www.nla.gov/pandora/ldmv2.html**). The highest-level entities in this model are:

- identification
- selection and negotiation
- capture
- preservation
- rights management and access control.

Within this, the proposed metadata system has 25 top-level elements, some of which are repeatable and some of which have detailed sub-elements (**www.nla.gov.au/preserve/pmeta.html**).

CEDARS recommendations are detailed, and their schema proposes more than 50 metadata elements. The Research Libraries Group (RLG) Working Group on Preservation Issues of Metadata proposes 15 metadata elements in their recommendations for preservation metadata. Other groups – the British Library, the Library of Congress, Harvard University, Cornell University and many more – are defining complex metadata systems for the preservation of digital data. Clearly this is an issue of long-term, global, strategic importance.

Rights management

Issues of intellectual property rights and copyright will need to be considered when preserving digital materials for long-term access, and it may be necessary to obtain permission from the rights holders for any reformatting. Given that laws, customs and practices differ from country to country, we offer no particular examples here, but merely warn that this will be an issue that librarians must consider when preserving, reformatting or even emulating data. As Day (1999) points out:

> Solving rights management issues will be vital in any digital preservation programme. Typically, custodial organizations do not have physical custody of digital objects created or made available by other stakeholders (e.g. authors or publishers). Instead they will negotiate rights to this information for a specific period of time. Permissions to preserve digital information objects will also need to be negotiated with rights holders and any such agreement may, or may not, permit end user access. A digital archive will have to collect and store any relevant rights management information which could be stored as part of the descriptive metadata.

National and international initiatives in digital preservation

The costs of digital preservation are high. The costs of not preserving our digital heritage will be even higher in terms of lost data and lost history, and there is no time to waste in putting strategies and practices in place to preserve key materials. Many individual projects and institutions are working hard on this problem, and there are also national and international initiatives collaborating to find long-term solutions. The Australian PADI project (Preserving Access to Digital Information) at the National Library of Australia has useful pointers to a number of these at **www.nla.gov.au/padi/topics/18.html** and indeed has an abundance of up-to-date information on all aspects of digital preservation.

At particular risk, as we have discussed earlier, is the plethora of data that is born digital. The LOCKSS project (Lots Of Copies Keep Stuff Safe) (**http://lockss.stanford.edu/**) is run from Stanford University and is conducting a worldwide trial with more than 40 libraries and 30 publishers. LOCKSS is addressing the long-term preservation for access of electronic journal publications. It is 'a tool designed for libraries to use to ensure their community's continued access to web-published scientific journals. LOCKSS allows libraries to take custody of the material to which they subscribe, in the same way they do for paper, and to preserve it' (Reich and Rosenthal, 2001). LOCKSS is not an archive, but a set of tools for maintaining user access to the journals, even if the publishers no longer supply them. LOCKSS is a distributed project and if it proves successful, could provide models for the long-term preservation and access of other digital materials.

The most ephemeral content is that residing on websites around the world, and there are a number of national initiatives established to archive the websites of particular countries. The National Library of Australia archives 'snapshots' of a whole range of websites, public, private, serious and light-hearted, including those of the 2000 Sydney Olympics. Key sites are archived every few months, and there are no guarantees that external links will continue to work (**http://pandora.nla.gov.au/**). In the USA, the Library of Congress has been awarded $100 million to develop a national programme for the preservation of digital materials, in particular that which is only ever digital (**www.loc.gov/**). Also, in the USA, the General Printing Office (**www.access.gpo.gov/**) is archiving defunct government websites, and in January 2001 was expecting an increase in demand as Clinton government agencies were replaced under the Bush regime. Future historians will:

> thank government workers who paid attention to archiving web sites. After all, saving the content will allow Internet researchers to compare politicians' past promises with their current votes, track reports on health care and social security, or even reread the Starr report – all without leaving their computers. (Bowman, 2001b)

In Europe, national libraries in Denmark, Sweden, Finland and the UK are grappling with the issues around preserving ephemeral information on the web.

There are also a number of initiatives to establish national and international partnerships to solve digital preservation problems. In the UK, the Joint Information Systems Committee (JISC), the National Preservation Office (NPO), the British Library and other leading UK organizations are establishing a Digital Preservation Coalition, together with international organizations such as RLG and OCLC. This has been set up to deal urgently with digital preservation issues in the UK within an international context (**www.jisc.ac.uk/dner/preservation/**).

Conclusion

The preservation of the written heritage in whatever format it is being produced is of crucial significance to civilized society. Given that it is so important, and that there are many strategic factors and costs that need to be established and predicted for the long term, it is an area where there are many uncertainties. Issues are hotly debated (sometimes in a wide public arena, as described above in the context of the disposal of newspapers) and different strategies have passionate adherents or opponents. The current key topic in the digital preservation community is the use of emulation.

Rothenberg (2000b) proposes a number of possible approaches to future emulation of obsolete programs, all of which rely on the emulation of the original hardware in software because re-creating the applications and operating systems is likely to be more difficult than emulating hardware. This would then enable the original software to be run, thereby permitting access to the preserved digital objects. In order to do this, the original programs would need to be preserved, as well as the digital objects. Rothenberg suggests that these should be encapsulated with all information needed for their future use. Full hardware specifications would also need to be kept in order that the architecture could be re-created. If we assume that these objects may be needed only many decades or even centuries after their creation, some method of high-level, simple description will need to be devised to tell human operators what they have and how to begin accessing it. It is likely that some kind of human-readable records would have to be kept, perhaps attached to the physical container of the objects. Or, given that this data will need regular refreshing, a simple high-level file could be checked and migrated to the new storage media, with the underlying complex objects ported without change.

It would, of course, be redundant to store complete software and operating systems, and hardware specifications, with every data object.

Central repositories of these would need to be maintained, and the metadata of the data objects could specify or point to the appropriate stored platforms. Rothenberg is firmly of the opinion that emulation is the *only* answer to the long-term survival of digital content: a position that has come under some criticism. See Bearman, 1999, and Granger, 2000.

The CAMiLEON project takes a different approach to that suggested by Rothenberg, and suggests that emulators need to be produced sooner rather than later, and certainly while there is still the possibility to run the original program and to seek information from individuals who had experience of it. Holdsworth and Wheatley (2000; 2001) propose the development of an 'abstract emulation interface' that will then evolve over time to keep pace with technical evolution. Experiments carried out by CAMiLEON suggest that emulation is a viable option in digital preservation, but that 'emulating a platform for which you do not have any examples of the original source text may be particularly arduous'. CAMiLEON's experience of emulating an operating system have led them to believe that they would not have succeeded if they had been taking the Rothenberg route of preservation of data, programs and specifications.

IBM are taking yet another approach, which they claim is designed to overcome the two main problems of emulation as they perceive them: that the saving of the original program to archive data could be excessive and that extracting the data from the programs at a later date could be very difficult (Lorie, 2001). They insist upon a clear distinction between data and programs, and are currently developing a Universal Virtual Computer (UVC) which will a) allow data to be archived and accessed on future systems and b) emulate future computers when archived programs need to be accessed. 'For archiving data, the UVC provides a means for writing methods that interpret the archived data stream. For archiving a program behaviour, the UVC provides a means to specify the functioning of the original computer' (Lorie, 2001). The results of these trials will be of great interest as this could be a more cost-effective approach than others which have been proposed.

Such debates are surely healthy, as there is no clear consensus on the way forward in digital preservation. It therefore behoves the library community to participate fully in these debates and to begin to formulate institutional strategies for preserving humanity's digital capital.

9

Digital librarians: new roles for the Information Age

The ends of information, after all, are human ends. The logic of information must ultimately be the logic of humanity . . . it is people, in their communities, organizations, and institutions, who ultimately decide what it means and why it matters. (Brown and Duguid, 2000, 18)

Digital libraries require digital librarians. Computers are certainly essential . . . but people are required to put it all together and make it work. (Hastings and Tennant, 1996)

Introduction

Throughout this book the most important element in developing the digital library has been implicit: the librarian. This chapter brings librarians to the forefront and discusses the various new roles and skills now required of them and the new challenges they face. Acceleration of technological change is accompanied by reductions in funding and in the numbers of professional staff employed. Lack of recognition of the unique skills of librarians is also a crucial issue as there is an underlying assumption that librarians are no longer needed and libraries are dull and replaceable. As Brophy (2001, xv) suggests:

The public image of librarians remains poor and distinctly old-fashioned, while technologists lay claim to so-called digital libraries that will apparently replace place-based libraries with a few simple key-strokes.

There are some who view the future of libraries, and consequently of librarians, as determined by technology, and who therefore predict a diminished role for both in the digital future. This is likely to be as true as the predictions of the 'paper-less office' in the 1980s or 'home working' of the 1990s were:

> But 'all-digital, all the time' is an article of faith. It may ultimately come to pass, but like the various apocalyptic prophesies which run wild at a time like ours, it simply isn't supported by the current facts. Ethnographic studies of actual workplaces reveal the diverse mix of materials, digital and otherwise, commonly in use and offer no suggestion that this diversity is diminishing. (Levy, 2000)

Technological determinism has been discredited recently, as writers and thinkers acknowledge the significance of the cultural, social, political, philosophical and natural forces that will certainly shape the future. So while this chapter will discuss the technological impacts upon libraries, the authors are well aware that this is but a small part of the complete picture and all solutions offered will be partial. Brophy points out, in his insightful work on the library in the 21st century, that much of 'our understanding of the foundations of librarianship is based on myth: libraries have never given access to anything more than a small proportion of the world's information. Perhaps their continued inability to do so will not after all mean that they are doomed to irrelevance' (Brophy, 2001, 13).

Rather than gloomily predicting the end of libraries, we need rather to rise to the challenges identified by Borgman in rethinking libraries in the digital age (2000, 208). These challenges are how to:

- maintain visibility while being part of a well-functioning information infrastructure
- manage collections as they become more hybrid and distributed
- preserve physical and digital materials
- take advantage of the blurring boundaries between information institutions and information professions.

This chapter will discuss the following issues:

- the current state of libraries and the changing nature of information
- what librarianship is in the digital future
- buildings or bytes: how librarians are not defined by the library infra-structure
- new roles in the digital era
- key skills for digital librarians
- training and education
- organization cultures and management styles
- the need to be prepared for change, flexible in all things and ready for competition.

The current state of libraries: shifting sand and contrasts

Libraries have seen a series of changes over the past decade with the move-ment of information resources and funding opportunities from the physi-cal to the electronic. Programmes and improved funding for technology-based projects, such as seen in the UK's eLib programme, have had a marked effect. In a growing number of libraries, there is now an atti-tude that user demands will be met through digital media and electronic dissemination as much as through paper-based media. Universities are investing in providing improved teaching and distance-learning resources via digital media. Other institutions, including the British Library and the Library of Congress, are developing large technical infrastructures. The public library sector in the UK and elsewhere is also making the shift towards digital service and resource provision, a change characterized in India as moving from 'brick and mortar' to 'click and conquer' (Sadagopan, 2000). Government ministers predict that by 2002 more than 80% of UK public libraries will be online (Howarth, 2000). In other areas of the world the 'digital divide', as described in Chapter 1 'Digital futures in current contexts', is a significant factor in library development. The implementation of infrastructure and improvement of access to the digital world is seen as hugely important for regions such as Africa, which lacks overall investment in social economic growth (Shibanda, 2001, 2), and Latin America, where development has been limited by the relatively lower economic status of the library (Rodríguez, 2001, 2). The development of technical infrastructure and access to digital resources within libraries is a vital trend for success in the future. Libraries have always been about information management and although the format of the information changes, the library will still be the best place to manage it.

These achievements have to be set against a background trend of decreasing numbers of professional librarians. In the UK, for instance, the number has dropped in public libraries by 13% over the 1994–9 period and the number of points of service has at the same time reduced by 6% (Maynard, 2000). Yet, libraries and librarians still strive to serve their communities effectively despite this continuing erosion. As Brophy (2001, 12) points out:

> Libraries are their own worst enemies. While the competition hots up they find themselves closing branches and reducing opening hours. Grandiose claims to be 'the people's universities' are simply not borne out by the facts.

The contrast becomes even starker when we consider that, in the same period in the UK, there has been a 21% increase in the number of book titles published each year and that journal prices have increased by a massive 55% (Maynard, 2000). From the librarian's perspective, there are fewer professionals, less funding in real terms, a huge acceleration in resource and information availability (at a price), plus a higher demand for information from the potential user base.

The other side of this particular coin is the user perspective. Information users are no longer solely reliant upon physical storehouses of information to satisfy their desire for information. Nor are users so dependent upon the intermediary skills of a librarian to answer reference enquiries and search for information, or so they might believe. The addition of electronic resources and easy access from home and office may seem, from the user perspective, to degrade the need for library professionals. A librarian who acts as a custodian and friendly guide can no longer meet the needs of users. Cronin (1998, 7) suggests that the:

> Consequences of disintermediation may well be progressive deprofessionalization of the traditional roles and functions performed by librarians. A less extreme scenario posits that disintermediation will trigger a process of remediation, as the intermediary community creates new value-added roles.

User desires are a powerful driving force in our newly wired world and we suggest that users will require librarians to become expert facilitators, resource providers, fundraisers, creators and distributors focused upon meeting their specific community needs, and providing the expertise to guide users through the ever burgeoning mass of electronic resources. As Biddiscombe (1996, 5) predicted,

> One certainty is that there is no option than to accept that change is inevitable. It is not possible to remain as we are; it will be necessary for everyone to re-examine traditional methods and systems in the light of end-user needs and demands.

What is librarianship in the digital future?

There are technical, social, legal and economic environmental factors that form an increasingly complex set of boundaries to the area in which libraries operate. In a world supposedly of 'libraries without walls', these complex boundary areas could become as impenetrable to the library user as the traditional brick and mortar library is reputed to be. How many times have users found the information resource he or she wanted is locked behind legal or economic walls, and how much more impenetrable may these be in the digital world? When will social factors be accounted for in the equal, open and untrammelled access to information in the digital world – a fundamental goal of librarianship?

The great library thinker, S. R. Ranganathan, has something to tell us about librarianship in this modern era, with his profoundly simple and durable Ranganathan's Laws (1931):

1 Books are for use.
2 Every reader his book.
3 Every book its reader.
4 Save the time of the reader.
5 The Library is a growing organism.

In the information age there is still no better theory of the library, or the role of librarians, than these five simple principles based upon linking people, libraries and the information they use. Crawford and Gorman

(1995) offered 'Five New Laws of Library Science' in the hope of reinterpreting Ranganathan for today's libraries and their likely future:

1 Libraries serve humanity.
2 Respect all forms by which knowledge is communicated.
3 Use technology intelligently to enhance service.
4 Protect free access to knowledge.
5 Honor the past and create the future.

However, these do not stand on their own or encompass the whole of library and information science in the way achieved by Ranganathan's Laws and thus they are a useful adjunct for our current social contexts, and nothing more, to Ranganathan's fundamental concepts. As Kuny and Cleveland point out 'technology will not substantially alter the business of librarians – connecting people with information' (1998, 107). Open access to information lies at the heart of the modern library according to Kuny and Cleveland (1998, 112), and this is a principle above all others that should be preserved. But these visionaries also look deep into the future where the value in the library is not defined by the collection, but by the librarian. They perceive a time when the librarian's role will be significantly different and based around knowledge and services and not around collections:

> These digital librarians/knowledge workers, who are imbued with an ethic of equitable access, would function as well-trained intermediaries in an heterogeneous information environment. The knowledge that 'digital librarians' bring to this information environment would make sense of a multiplicity of digital and paper-based collections and resources, provide access to a network of key contacts, identify cost effective strategies for information retrieval, and assist users in the publication and creation of new information.   (Kuny and Cleveland, 1998, 112)

In their vision of the future there is a change of direction, with the focus of attention shifted from developing digital libraries to developing digital librarians. They state very clearly where they feel the priorities lie:

> The time has come to invest in people and not in technology. Central to the vision of the new digital library is a digital librarian/knowledge worker who cares about people.   (Kuny and Cleveland, 1998, 113)

To invest in technology over people is extremely tempting to strategists, governments, funding agencies and senior managers who are driven by some fundamental prerequisites as defined in the 'law of disruption' by Downes and Mui. This states that 'social, political and economic systems change incrementally, but technology changes exponentially' (Downes and Mui, 1998). In other words, we will spend more on technology in the hope that society and institutions will eventually catch up with the changes brought about through technology, rather than allowing social and economic need to drive technological development. The challenge for librarians is to not expend so much effort in 'catching up' with technology and spend more time in adjusting and taming it for society's information needs.

> We teachers and librarians need to forget the novelty of our computers. . . . Know what the computers can do and what can be done with them. Then ask yourself what human qualities you want to preserve into the 21st century. . . . We are being changed by the machine. And we are being changed radically. But let us not be changed absolutely. Let us help one another to draw just a few crucial lines in the sand.
>
>   (Lienhard, 1997)

As Jonscher (2000, 274) points out,

> Fifty years of computer technology will not substitute as easily as technology enthusiasts would have us think for the natural processes of interaction between people and other people, and between people and their surroundings.

Buildings or bytes: librarians are not defined by the library infrastructure

The traditional library placed in buildings with large collections remains of great importance, but maybe that importance is based more on the valued services and skilled librarians it houses than the rows of shelves filled with books and journals. As Appiah warmly notes, 'the library I never go to is already one of the most important places in my life' (Appiah, 1997).

So, although Borgman might state that 'libraries serve as gathering points for communities, bringing together people, information resources in physical forms, access to information in electronic forms, and professionals to assist people in their information-related activities' (2000, 182), we have to consider that the service the user most values may not be within the actual walls of the building.

Perhaps we can throw off what may amount to the golden shackles of Carnegie's inheritance – the buildings as the focus of what makes a library. What defines a library is that librarians work there, collecting together information and resources of interest to a distinct community, whether scholarly, public, corporate, government or special interest. Librarians should redefine the profession, not in terms of the collections we hold, but in terms of the skills, abilities and value we bring to our communities. Libraries are not just Carnegie buildings or places of moral worth (Brophy, 2001, 26) but are indeed the focal point of valued community information in partnership with the stewardship provided by librarians. Just as no one would willingly seek to be defined by the technical infrastructure that is used to deliver information services, then librarians must not remain in any way defined by the physical infrastructure of the library building.

It is very easy to forget that librarians begot libraries and not the other way around. The press coverage in the UK for various building closures by library managers with a fresh vision of public service is generally negative, even when those closures are matched by new buildings in more user centred locations (Benjamin, 2001). *The Guardian* reports in the same article that the UK House of Commons Culture Select Committee recently concluded that 'some library campaigns have achieved their immediate goals in preventing closure. However, if the effect of this achievement delays the development of improved library services, then this committee fears the victories may prove Pyrrhic' (Benjamin, 2001). It is librarians who are evolving past the specific environment of the library storehouse into a new breed with wider skill bases and fresh visions of the future. Great librarians will build great library services and collect great resources, whether in buildings or bytes. The time has come for us not to be defined by infrastructure.

New roles in the digital era

Libraries should always be the best place to manage information. In the digital Information Age librarians are going to have to foreground their information management roles in relation to their physical custodial roles and some of the newer digitally oriented activities are suggested below. Many of these will seem very familiar, but there are subtle differences from the traditional roles and specifically they go beyond the role Megill (1997, 51) suggests librarians sometimes inhabit:

> In their traditional role, however, librarians often do not organize information – they simply collect and organize containers of information and put them together with others related to similar subjects.

There will certainly be a subtle shift in emphasis and McDonald illustrates this in his speculation about the person specification for the post of a digital librarian:

> We require a professional who has the skills and experience to turn our vision for a digital library into a reality. You should be imaginative and thrive on taking risks and change; you must be independent and flexible; you will read constantly and experiment endlessly; and you should love learning and be self-teaching. You will have an understanding of the potentials and pitfalls of communications and information technology to achieve the digital library. Above all you must have an understanding of the human factors involved. (McDonald, 2000, 8)

This illustrates that skill and strategic perspectives will define the new librarian's roles more than strict job descriptions. Tom Wilson in an interview for the *Library Association Record* stated that:

> However, ICT is now so ubiquitous that the idea of an 'information profession' is fast disappearing, as everyone discovers a need for information skills. That need will grow and coming generations will be better prepared

> to satisfy that need. The 'information professional' will look, I suspect, a lot like the librarian of the immediate post-war period, but operating in an electronic environment – the organizer of resources, indexer of sites, 'reference librarian' and so on. As the role of the amateur webmaster is taken on by professionals, the opportunities (or need) for the information professional to be an amateur IT specialist will diminish and the field will return to its roots. (Hyams, 2001, 428)

We suggest some of the additional roles that librarians are likely to inhabit.

Knowledge mediator

The librarian, in this role, is extending the information sources beyond the catalogue, through the digital library, to provide insights into the existing body of knowledge and to guide users to the most relevant resources (Kuny and Cleveland, 1998; Owen and Wiercx, 1996). In the context of the digital library this role can be summarized through the following functions:

* resource discovery
* resource provision
* resource delivery.

These have many parallels with traditional library 'technical service' roles and the activities described at length earlier in this book in Chapters 1 'Digital futures in current contexts', 3 'Developing collections in the digital world' and 5 'Resource discovery, description and use'.

Information architect

As defined by Veen (2001, 78) an information architect is:

> 1. the individual who organizes the patterns inherent in data, making the complex clear; 2. a person who creates the structure or map of information, which allows others to find their personal paths to knowledge.

The information architect is concerned with the way that content is structured for use. Should certain information elements or choices be associated with other elements to aid the user or will this hinder their progress? They will have an intimate knowledge of how resources are used, how the elements fit together and the patterns of use, relationships and decisions users make or should make at any given point in the information resource. These must be presented and organized in such a way as to enhance and at times direct the use of the resources. Librarians have always been about connecting information and people together, and this role is a new one that librarians could profitably enter if they can adopt all the internet, technical, computing and architectural knowledge required.

Hybrid librarian

The hybrid library seeks to bring a range of information resources and technologies together in the context of an existing library structure. It is a pragmatic response to the current mixed resource base present in most libraries and, as a concept, looks set to continue for the immediate future at least. The hybrid librarian's role will be to explore and provide further integration of services and systems using whatever is the most appropriate resource, whether print or technology based, to achieve the user's information desire. This is closely related to the slightly more specialist role of the knowledge mediator suggested above, but is firmly rooted in services based around traditional place-based library collections, while adding new resources to those offered the user. This undoubtedly will be among the most important roles for librarians to take up and champion into the immediate future.

Knowledge preserver

As a set of skills and strategies, preservation of digital objects is discussed in detail in Chapter 8 'Preservation'. There will be a growing role for the librarian to take forward policies and strategies to ensure digital preservation is successful. Libraries are often the bastions of our corporate and cultural memory, and the need for an extended role in the digital era has never been clearer as the risks to the cultural memory is emphasized by recent events:

The burning of the national library in Sarajevo was not just the loss of a fine building and a unique collection: it symbolized a decline into barbarism. A library makes a statement about the value that a society places on knowledge and learning, and thus on truth.

(Brophy, 2001, xv)

Therefore, librarians may find they are ever more valued for the digital preservation role they can forge for themselves. Within this role the librarian will be defining new strategies for retention, conservation and preservation in this highly complex hybrid of physical and digital information spaces. The librarian has a unique set of skills and interests that are applicable to this growing area of activity.

Key skills for digital librarians

There are plenty of skills that librarians will need to master to enable them to deal with the requirements of digital libraries. They break down into three main areas of expertise:

- management skills
- technical skills
- subject skills.

These skills will be interwoven and overlapping. Metadata creation requires far more subject skills than scanning photographs to digital images, but this latter probably needs more technical capabilities. Management skills will be essential in all circumstances and will interact with the other skill sets most intimately.

There is a skills shortage for staffing digital library and digitization projects at present (McDonald, 2000, 8; Tanner, 2001). People with the requisite mix of project experience and technical ability are in short supply, and it will take time before there are enough projects and programmes completed to deliver experienced people into the wider workforce. This is a worrying reflection of a wider trend in some library sectors, especially the UK public library sector. A study reported in the *Library Association Record* identifies a 'lack of high-quality managers' and difficulties retaining skilled staff (Public libraries, 2001, 260). The solution appears to be training, and the report also identifies ICT training as the top of librarians' wish list. Training is an investment that should be made early and with frequency to reap the maximum benefits. Unfortunately the management roles that librarians now fill, for instance, project management and fundraising, are not covered in sufficient depth by our formal education process.

> The technology is complex and librarians have not developed the skills to understand it, exploit it or create it. Those few who do have such skills find they have a very marketable commodity and can make a much better living elsewhere. (Brophy, 2001, 11)

We do not discuss subject skills in any detail, as they are implicit to a notion of librarianship, and they do not change radically when the information container becomes digital rather than analogue: indeed the focus upon content rather than container in the digital resource means that subject skills are as valuable as they ever were. We will, however, discuss technical and management skills in a little more detail.

Technical skills

The technical skills required are probably better understood and defined in the literature than the managerial skills. As identified by Tennant (1999), the key skills for the new millennium are:

- imaging technologies – the means of capturing images from physical objects
- OCR – the means of converting imaged text into machine-readable text
- markup languages – the means of adding metadata or structuring digital content
- cataloguing and metadata – identifying the resources for future access
- indexing and database technology – building search systems or supporting finding aids
- user interface design – the creative function of enhancing user interactions with data
- programming – basic understanding of programming techniques

and some languages, such as Perl
- web technology – being well versed in every aspect of the primary delivery medium of digital libraries
- project management – the means of achieving goals and objectives within set limitations of time, money and other resources.

Most of these are skills based in technology, but project management cannot be excluded from any list of key skills whether technology based or not. These technical skills are not all required for every job and no individual should expect to be highly skilled and experienced in all of them. What is essential is that there is at least a familiarity with all these skills and what they encompass. It will be much easier for people to manage or work in a digital library environment if there is a general understanding of the foundation technologies that underpin it, and how these relate and interact with each other. In this way there is a better team understanding and also less time spent constantly translating 'tech-speak' into 'library-speak' and vice versa.

Management skills

The managerial skills required now are developing from resource management, which librarians tend to understand very well, into the more flexible, competitive regions of project management, systems implementation and fundraising. Whatever the size of library, there will be technology to implement in our newly wired world and the management of this process has become a key skill for librarians to master. As the size of the organization grows, the likelihood is that such implementations, whether for digital library infrastructure or digitization initiatives, will be larger, more complex, include more partners and thus require formal project planning and management. Further, the growth in competition for resources in the form of funding has meant that meeting obligations on time and to budget is critical, not just for the task in hand but for future funding prospects as well. Recent UK research showed that in the period 1997–2000 'only 32% of archives, 3% of libraries and 30% of museums had *not* submitted bids for projects worth over £10,000' (Parker et al., 2001, 2). The competition is real and fundraising is an activity to which all librarians will have to become accustomed.

Managing projects and resources

Management is often characterized as 'getting results through people' and this remains a vital aspect of any library manager's role. Resource management in the form of controlling ever dwindling budgets for staffing, purchase of information resources and buildings maintenance is an art at which librarians are often highly skilled, and they can often gain the maximum service provision from the minimum investment. But as more information technology is added to the library, and money comes in the form of short-term funded projects, then the librarian has to implement management strategies that are simultaneously more flexible and more stringent. The goals and objectives have to be more clearly articulated and delineated to achieve successful and noticeable completion of the project, but the way that resources are utilized and assigned has to be more flexible than has possibly been the case previously. Project management is a relatively new practice, even though projects have obviously been with us for many centuries. It grew out of the resource strictures of World Wars 1 and 2 and in part was due to the need to achieve goals with far fewer people available. Lock defines project management as 'achieving project goals with the resources available' (1997, 3) and the resources are time, space, money, materials, technology, information and people.

Key to this project approach to implementing either large-scale technical solutions or running small content-creation projects is a clear vision, and good organization and risk management skills (Tanner, 2000). To develop the vision for the project and its planning, it is necessary to be able to perceive how all the elements of the proposed project fit together.

> Effective leadership will permit the articulation of a clear vision and mission for the organization, its staff and its publics. Such effective leadership and strategic management are not always evident and some organizations are characterized by an unfocused, uncoordinated and chaotic approach . . . perhaps reflected in success rates.
>
> (Parker et al., 2001, 2)

Library managers also fear that because they do not understand the in-depth technical details of digital libraries, digitization, or metadata schemes, or are not a subject specialist, this will constrain their capacity to plan effectively. It is not essential to be a technical expert in all the areas encompassed by the development, but it is very important to appreciate the interactions between project elements and their potential impact upon the wider organization and goals (Tanner, 2001). A holistic overview of the whole lifecycle of the technical development will be important to ensure that the objectives, aims, available resources, and the deliverables are complementary and achievable (see Chapters 1 and 2 'Digital futures in current contexts' and 'Why digitize?').

Fundraising

Large proportions of digital library or digitization programmes get started through some initial short-term funding. The competition for this initial funding has increased as, for many public organizations, this is 'the only viable means by which to develop and improve services, given existing deficiencies in core funding' (Parker et al., 2001, 2). Getting that initial funding is hard and requires a lot of effort and focus. Kenney and Rieger (2000, 135), Deegan (2001) and others feel that all funding should be viewed as the first step on the route to developing a sustainable service. These findings, along with the research from the Information Management Research Institute (Parker et al., 2001), suggest the following strategic issues relating to fundraising:

- Fundraising should be part of the strategic management function and an organization-wide activity. Fundraising should not happen in isolation.
- Understanding the vision, aims and objectives for the project and how it will enhance the organization's objectives will enhance fundraising success.
- Good planning and co-operation are essential within the organization. All stakeholders must be involved early to gain their commitment and to share the vision of the desired final product.
- Services need to select suitable projects for fundraising that meet their needs and match the collections and infrastructure available, rather than trying to skew the vision to meet available funding.
- Partnerships and wide co-operation between organizations are very

important factors in success.

* Publicity and promotion is required to disseminate results and to create a sense of a successful track record which will aid the finding of new potential partners and further fundraising efforts.

Training and education

In developing skills for managing, creating and providing services in the digital environment, training and education will become ever more important. There will be increased need for educational organizations to inform students of the new realities and the new skills that they will need in the digital environment. These will not just be technical skills but will include project, fundraising and management skills oriented towards developing technologically based services.

Education

Spink and Cool identify through their research that digital library 'education is behind in funding and practice' (1999). They also reveal that in the USA several universities have restructured courses to emphasize digital information and electronic resources. This has been matched in other countries (Carpenter, 1999), but is not enough to enable future librarians to address effectively the fundamental shift in society's attitude to, and use of, digital information. To enable this will mean further restructuring and the fusion of aspects of library and information science with aspects of the computer science curriculum. 'The development of a "digital libraries" track for information and computer science students that focuses on the technical and human aspects of the web and digital libraries seems inevitable' (Spink and Cool, 1999). Prime, however, feels this may be the wrong direction and she is wary of these 'quasi-computer scientists' who are 'neither librarians or computer scientists, neither fish nor fowl' (Prime, 2000). In Prime's estimation (2000):

Librarians have always been about organizing information so that you can retrieve it again. It is not organizing information just to store it. Others do that.

There is clearly much that computer scientists can learn from librarianship in terms of human interaction with the data, but librarians should not be averse to learning from other disciplines as well. Spink and Cool suggest the following as core curriculum components for digital library education:

- theoretical and historical foundations
- technical infrastructure of the digital library
- knowledge organization in digital libraries
- collection development and maintenance
- information access and utilization of digital libraries
- social, economic and policy issues – including copyright, for instance
- professional issues – including management of digital libraries.

Training

Even more important than initial education will be ongoing training to establish, develop and foster key skills. We feel it will be essential to develop a large number of transferable skills that are not limited to specific job roles or tasks in hand, but developed using a more holistic approach. As research has suggested, there is a need for more money to be spent on training and for the focus to shift from function to goal orientation.

> Staff training inputs are usually very related to job specification or done on a need-to-know basis, and not undertaken as part of an across-the-board strategy. There is a real need to look more strategically at long term needs, rather than the functions. (Carpenter, 1999, 47)

Training is definitely a viable solution for lack of suitable skills, as this will reap immediate benefits in terms of increased productivity and raised confidence. Paul Conway, in his final report on Yale University's Project Open Book (**www.library.yale.edu/preservation/pobweb.htm**), is reported as documenting the significant impact of training and practice on processing costs: 'extensive analysis showed that the "practice effect" improved productivity 44% for scanning and 50% for indexing' (Kenney and Rieger, 2000, 159). McDonald also identifies that many 'successful digital librarians are often self-starters who have picked up relevant skills through experience and on-the-job training rather than through any formal ICT qualifications' (2000, 8). There is a need to move away from the ad hoc means of achieving success in digital libraries and digitization projects described by McDonald, and to formalize better training provision for all library personnel, especially enhancing non-professional experience.

Strategically focused, well-funded, extensive and repeated in-depth training is now an essential element of library management success. Training is the only feasible way to encourage the positive attitudes in library personnel towards technology and information that will then lead to the digital services being fully valued and accepted by the user base. Both professional and non-professional personnel will have an everyday influence upon the user's experience of the technologies in place within a library context. If the people in the service cannot effectively guide the user, help them optimize their time in using library resources or perceive the benefit in using the service, then those users will seek services elsewhere. As stated earlier the time is ripe to invest in people rather than in technology alone.

> A partial holistic approach – based on identifiable skills among staff – would need to stress interpersonal skills and flexibility in post and job specifications.
> (Carpenter, 1999, 48)

In response to the skill shortages, managers will have to look for aptitude and lateral experience to find suitable staff where experience might otherwise be lacking. This may not seem ideal, but librarians have a large amount of transferable skill that could be useful. The way that transferable skills are recognized by both the individual and the employer is important to enable mobilization of the most essential resources – talent and ability. As expressed by Susan K. Martin in a review of her 40-year library career, there is no such thing as a single set of skills that will stay unchanged throughout:

> Over the decades I have been thoroughly immersed in data processing, helped to set standards, and gradually have become an administrator, focusing on issues that I never conceived of being interested in, such as paper acidity or manuscript preservation.
> (Martin, 2001, vii)

Organizational cultures and management styles

Change can only be achieved within organizational and management structures or styles, which have sometimes proven to be barriers to progress, as found by Carpenter (1999, 6):

> There is an overall understanding that digital and electronic library development will lead to new management styles and changes in organization, but these changes, and the problems connected with them, are usually underestimated.

Libraries are large and complex organizations, based upon functional units that interact to provide a hopefully unified end-user service. It is unlikely that structures that have been in place for decades, if not centuries, will be easily or quickly changed – but that change has never been needed so urgently as within this highly accelerated world of digital resources and services.

> Since the origin of the modern organization emerged in the late 1700s with Adam Smith, it is not surprising that at the end of the 20th century organization principles need to be rethought. As organizations grew in size, a hierarchical structure based on functional units containing specialized operations developed with management and employees focusing attention and communication almost exclusively within their own organization segment . . . communication and interaction among staff evolved with a vertical orientation. . . . There are many examples in libraries that reflect these principles for organizing work.   (Creth, 1996)

Library management culture tends to focus on functions and processes rather than goals and results. There is a need to think outside of the fixed boundaries of the functional entities and hierarchies seen in most libraries to focus on the core goals and achieve them through the innovative use of the large skills base resident, but largely not optimized, in the majority of library staff.

Creth also predicts that such changes will inevitably make some individuals uncomfortable as the lines of responsibility, authority and communication both overlap and blur. The larger the organizational structure, the longer and more painful the deconstruction and rebuild-

ing. There will be a need for constant clear communication of both success and failure, of the progress towards the goals and the results of
change. This enhances the opportunities for all involved to feel comfortable yet responsible, and to have ownership for both the problems and
successes, in order that the team will be able to feel proud of their
achievements.

Managers also need to work hard at empowering the right people
throughout the organization. Leadership is not just a management function. It is something that all individuals do within the organization at one
time or another as they influence the actions of colleagues. But leadership without empowerment would be a frustrating experience for individuals trying to build digital libraries or digital resources. As Boddy and
Patton point out 'anyone who wants to get something done needs to
exercise leadership. If management expects people to use their initiative
to get things done rather than wait to be told what to do, they will need
effective leaders at all levels' (1998, 160).

Prepared for change, flexible in all things and ready for competition

Librarians will need to be ready for competition and prepared to find
new ways to make their skills and services distinct from those offered by
the competition from media companies, publishers, internet companies,
intermediary service providers and also from technologists parking on
traditional library territory with technical names for old-fashioned
library ideas. As Prime suggests, librarians will have to 'name it to own
it' (Prime, 2000). She gives the example of two Compaq researchers who
gave a paper 'about "a new linguistic approach to the construction of
terminological feedback for use in an interactive query refinement". In
other words, the "reference interview"' (Prime, 2000). Also 'we talk of
descriptive cataloguing, they have metadata'. Librarians will have to
address this issue and maintain visibility while being part of a successful
information infrastructure. In the wired world, the danger of librarians
becoming marginalized by cheap, shallow but pretty information products is a real one.

The competition, at least in some of its forms, is cheap: the whole world wide web is just a local phone call away. What is more, web content looks great even if in the end much of it is disappointing. In the glamour stakes, libraries haven't yet reached the starting gate.

(Brophy, 2001, 12)

To return to Borgman (2000, 194), whose challenges we enumerate at the beginning of this chapter:

Libraries risk being victims of their own success. The more ubiquitous their presence in their organizations and communities, the less apparent their role may be. The more services that are provided electronically, and the less need to visit a physical place, the less their users may be aware of who provides those services.

Librarians will have to remain flexible in management and service provision and to think constantly 'outside the box' to prevent them becoming invisible. Hopefully, the issues raised throughout this book will help to lead librarians towards the more promising land as envisioned by McDonald (2000, 9):

A full understanding of the human, cultural and organizational factors will assist library managers in grasping the nettle and developing effective, high-quality electronic services. In this way libraries, and the digital librarians who manage them, can retain their justifiable position at centre stage of the Information Society and the New Learning Age.

Conclusion

Librarians find themselves expected to manage increasingly technical projects to achieve their goals of delivering valuable information to their ever-growing user base. It is a challenge that must be matched with practical skills and the vision to implement these in a controlled and manageable fashion. The key is good project planning and risk management for success in a project based in information technology. The range of skills needed is expanding and there is a shortage of experienced staff for digital library and digitization projects. Employers will need to nurture talent and transferable skills to ensure that skills are developed in a supportive environment with sufficient training opportunities made available in a holistic way.

Digital futures . . .

I could foretell the future with some accuracy, a thing quite possible, after all, when one is informed on a fair number of the elements which make up the present.   (Yourcenar, 1986, 76)

Trying to predict the future is a mug's game. But increasingly it's a game we all have to play because the world is changing so fast and we need to have some sort of idea of what the future's actually going to be like because we are going to live there, probably next week.

(Adams, 1999)

Introduction

Throughout this book we have examined the strategic issues in realizing a digital future for libraries and librarians, and in order to do so have so far taken a logical path from the creation and collection of digital content through to its delivery and management for the long term. We now look at what is on the near horizon for libraries and librarians.

As we suggested in Chapter 1 'Digital futures in current contexts', trying to see the future in the realm of technology is likely to lead to some risibly erroneous predictions, but unless the future can be imagined, it cannot be brought about. As Einstein famously said 'Imagination is more important than knowledge, for knowledge is limited while imagination embraces the entire world'. All inventions and developments begin with the question 'What if the world were different?' and from answering that question comes the march of human progress. The examples we cite at the beginning of Chapter 1 were famously proved to be wrong, though at the time they probably seemed to be reasonable statements. Predicting the future is a hit-and-miss affair: who could have conceived how very accurate Vannevar Bush and his contemporaries would be in describing that which we now know as the world wide web? Ted Nelson's description of his Xanadu project (also referred to in Chapter 1), linking all the books in all the world, seemed incredible in the 1970s, but those of us in the digital library field are now working hard to make it a reality. Writing a conventional book on digital technologies has made us realize just how fast the future is racing towards us: over the time we have been writing, many revisions and updates have been necessary to statements made just weeks before. We may be well informed but are we any wiser about where all this is leading? As DeGranopre points out, 'we as a society have a great capacity to develop digital and other related technologies, but this capacity seems inversely related to our capacity to envision the future that these technologies will usher in' (2001, 164). Will the coming digitopia (DeGranopre's word) be a glimpse of heaven or a vision of hell? And what does the future hold for libraries and librarians?

Some new developments

In the months that this book has been in gestation, a number of new developments have appeared that may be important for the digital future of libraries and cultural organizations. There are organizational and intellectual changes, as well as technical, and some are so fresh that their effects cannot possibly be known. New storage media, for instance, have been developed which could increase capacity exponentially: Keele High Density have announced a development in solid state memory capacity of 10.8 terabytes for a production cost of less that $50 (**www.cmruk.com/cmrKHD.html**). This may be good news for digital preservation as it could enable libraries to store digital resources for the long term much more cheaply than has hitherto been thought. However, it could also have a negative influence upon information glut. Data abhors a vacuum, so more extensive and cheaper data storage capability could just mean more material to manage. As we have suggested throughout this book, management and other human factors are always likely to be the most costly part of any library process.

New technology is leading to new information spaces and the place of the library remains unclear in this developing environment. Will the library regularly provide information services via mobile telephones or directly to people's personal data devices? To assess the demand for mobile internet access it is instructive to examine the situation in Japan where mobile telephone use is pervasive and thus may be an early indicator for Western usage. In 2001, 50% of the users who access the internet also do so by mobile telephone (Maamria, 2001). The growth of mobile telephone access linked to the development of wireless networks and the potential increase in bandwidth means that information access from anywhere and at anytime could become ubiquitous and deeply ingrained. The constraining factors will be bandwidth and the portability of screen technology. Until screens become as easy to read and portable as paper, then this type of access will always be constrained – but developments such as 'E-ink' and 'electric paper', described in Chapter 3 'Developing collections in the digital world', are leading the way towards viewing mechanisms that one day will be as portable and versatile as paper.

The growth in digital interactive television (including WebTV) seems to suggest even greater accessibility to information resources via the medium available in most living rooms. The UK Department of Health is spending £4.7 million on four pilot interactive services to enable access to large banks of health information via the television (Gunter, 2001, 558). The use of a familiar delivery medium and the large audience television attracts suggests this will be a popular mechanism for information access. Can libraries take advantage of this and other media to provide equitable access to the digital datastream for their users? It is certainly something libraries will need to consider as information providers 'choose the most suitable digital platform for a particular audience or specific message' (Gunter, 2001, 559). There are some interesting developments in libraries which take advantage of these advances. In chapter 2 'Why digitize?' we discussed the personalized digital workspaces being developed for users at the Bibliothèque nationale de France. At the University of Kentucky, The William T. Young Library has installed a wireless modem system, and users may checkout laptop computers and access the internet and local resources, together with generic computing applications, from anywhere in the library (see **www.kcl.ac. uk/humanities/cch/malibu/reports/projuky.htm** for more details of this). The library at Vassar College, which reopened after major refurbishment in May 2001, has developed 'e-carrels' for students to use. This is a revolutionary approach to library architecture and digital resources, and is described as 'an active networked portfolio, workspace and repository of intellectual activities and connections for each student' – a true hybrid library environment (**http://mediacloisters.vassar.edu/flash/**).

The down side of many of the new developments is that we now live in an age of what has been designated as 'continuous partial attention', where there are so many interactions and devices competing for our attention that we can give only a small part to each (Friedman, 2001). This is predicted to worsen over the next five years, for:

> By 2005 we will see a convergence of wireless technology, fiber optics, software applications and next-generation Internet switches, IP version 6, that will permit anything with electricity to have a web address and run off the Internet . . . This Evernet will allow us all to be online all the time from everywhere. People will boast: 'I have 25 web addresses in my house! How many do you have?'
> (Friedman, 2001)

The information explosion revisited

The burgeoning mass of information now available everywhere, and the pervasive nature of information technology, are among the complex social forces that are making modern life ever more rushed and pressured. From the beginnings of human society, individuals, corporations, and nations have perceived the personal, financial, and political advantages of exchanging information ever more rapidly (and usually discreetly). Information is power, and control of the means to inform allows one to secure maximum advantage from it. Broadcast technologies were developed to inform the many by the few, interactive technologies to connect more directly. Current information and communication technologies are a mixture of both.

The development of all communications technology is predicated on the need to communicate faster, further or more durably with those separated by space or time. So African drums, runners and riders, smoke signals, semaphore and many forms of ground transport like the railways were aimed at transporting that most valuable of commodities, information, that little bit faster, that little bit further. The book developed so that the preservation of information over time was not reliant on the human memory, but could be recorded more durably. Cultural memory relies upon the durability of some medium upon which it can be inscribed for future generations. The paradox of the digital world is that the durability of cultural memory is made problematic by the impermanence of the medium, as we have shown throughout this book.

The roots of the current communications revolution were firmly established during the 19th century and life and culture were transformed then as much as they are being transformed now by new technologies. The telegraph was the first communications technology to enable complex messages to be delivered faster than they could be carried by the fastest means of physical transport (at that period, the railways). From one relay point to the next messages were, for all intents and purposes, instantaneous, and even in the world of the internet, you don't get much faster than that. In the 1870s, messages could be conveyed on the telegraph to Bombay and back within four minutes, which caused the *Daily Telegraph* newspaper to pronounce 'Time itself is telegraphed out of existence' (Standage, 1998). Gorman offers some interesting and salutary comparisons between the information revolutions in libraries happening at the end of the 20th century and those which occurred in the last quarter of the 19th century, and points out that the rhetorical statements used then 'could be and are used by pundits and sages today concerning the cyberfuture' (2000, 5). In predicting the digital future he urges caution lest we lose the traditional values of librarianship, something we wholeheartedly endorse.

There are many problems inherent in the increasing desire for speed. As the production of information gets faster, the total volume increases, and therefore the speed at which it can be processed decreases – another paradox. Sifting through the mass takes ever longer. So there is no smooth transition from initial complexity to eventual simplicity and stability, as we would like to believe, but an ever faster dance to keep up with the pace. The result is shrinking attention spans, and an ever greater need for the stimulation that speed brings, along with which goes a feeling that however much we read or sift, the mountain of the unread and the unsifted is even larger.

> When a smorgasbord of information and entertainment lies at the touch of a finger, how long can we concentrate on any one train of thought? Can we allow ourselves the time to reflect, or resolve an emotional conflict? Both the speed of the net, and the wealth of information it offers, militates against certain thought processes. We become good at multitasking and skim-reading, but less good at the kind of reflection and contemplation which is essential for true originality and emotional wisdom. The biggest danger of the net is its urgency; can we ringfence the internal space and silence essential for having something original and wise to communicate?
>
> (Bunting, 2001, 46)

It is our belief that in this world of speed and continuous momentum, libraries and librarians can come into their own to create some order and some important signposts. As Kuny and Cleveland (1998, 112) suggest:

> One important consequence of the information revolution is that the costs of organizing information are beginning to match the costs of producing the information. . . . In this view, it is the context not the content that will be locus for value.

They also point out (1998, 112) quoting Dyson, that:

> . . . value shifts from the transformation of bits rather than bits themselves, to services, to the selection of content, to the presence of other people, and to the assurance of authenticity – reliable information about sources of bits and their future flows.

In the digital world, librarians are finding innovative ways to add value to bits to help users create knowledge out of information, just as they have always added value to information in the non-digital world.

Legality and ownership in the digital future

The difficulties faced by libraries entering the digital future are more likely to be concerned with ownership, permissions and access to digital resources as opposed to purely technical issues. It becomes ever easier for users to find, search and obtain key library resources, and consequently there is nervousness on the part of producers and suppliers of digital content about how to ensure that payments are made, rights respected and unauthorized copying disabled. Piracy in the digital world is frighteningly easy, as suppliers of software, videos and music have found. Apple, for instance, reported in 2000 that the costs of software piracy to the industry are 'numbing' and that the situation is worsening, especially in Europe. Billions of dollars of revenue are lost each year (**http://maccentral.macworld.com/news/0011/16.piracy.shtml**). Naturally, publishers are nervous that similar losses will be incurred through misuse and exploitation of digital materials. Libraries and cultural institutions, too, fear that if they make digital versions of their unique or rare holdings too easily available, revenue will be lost and illegal copies will flood the world. The consequence of these fears, whether well-founded or not, will be even tighter restrictions on the use of digital content. In the music business, apprehension that downloading digital music over the web using software like Napster (**www.napster.com/**) could destroy the industry has led to large legal battles which could result in draconian new laws to prevent copying and distribution, and more encryption of content. This could have serious impact on all institutions that provide or use digital materials.

Libraries are well-used to dealing with copyright and copyright restrictions in the analogue world, but some of the mechanisms that allow the use of in-copyright materials are likely to weaken in the digital world because of the fears of exploitation. Fair use and fair dealing, which allow use of materials under restricted circumstances that do not harm the rights of the copyright owner, are under threat from new laws and directives in the USA and Europe, in particular in relation to digital copying. In this case, use of the digital version is more restricted than use of the print. In the case of some e-books, technical restrictions are applied to the digital files, which mean that a title can be read by only one person at a time, and libraries which 'loan' e-books are having to check the books in and out in much the same way as in the print world.

As we have stressed throughout, among the many advantages of digital data are sharability, instant exchange and the power to multiply and copy with ease and with no degradation of quality. But this has led to misuse by users and restrictions on use by owners, both of which are likely to impede rather than advance the digital future. It is difficult to see in this complex environment of abuse, changing legality and increasing restriction, who is being protected by what and whose interests are being served. In particular, preserving digital information in a world where laws and mechanisms exist to prevent sharing and copying will be a great challenge. These matters need urgent attention if the promise held out of equitable access for all is to be fulfilled. Libraries, especially public libraries, have been at the forefront of the provision of information and knowledge to the wider public at low or no cost, and they need to fight hard to retain those rights in the digital future.

Bridging the digital divide

In Chapter 1 'Digital futures in current contexts' we suggest that the divide between rich and poor, between developed and developing countries is likely to be widened in digital contexts, but there are some creative solutions now emerging which might mitigate some of the negative impacts of information technology. In India, for instance, only 2% of the population have access to PCs, but despite this many will soon be able to send and receive e-mail through the Indian post office. The post office has set up more than 200 e-post centres in five states linked to more than 5000 distribution centres. Under the new scheme, the offices are wired up to computers and the internet, and individuals are provided with e-mail accounts. The local postman will then distribute mail received on the internet in the name of account holders (**http://news.bbc.co.uk/hi/ english/world/south_asia/newsid_1489000/1489470.stm**). There is a similar scheme in Bangladesh that is bringing telephony to remote rural villages promoted by the Grameen Bank, which lends money to local women to enable them to rent and operate mobile phones to be used by the entire village. Since its launch four years ago, this scheme has placed 950 pay phones in as many villages, providing telephone access to more than 65,000 people. The target for the next year is 30,000 villages. (**www.wfsnews.org/freeread1.html**). In Africa, telecentres are being established to enable the rural poor to connect to the internet, and all over the world internet cafés are providing relatively low-cost connection – though this is mostly confined to cities. Such creative and collaborative approaches to resources could transform information and communications in remote, developing areas and offer new opportunities for education and for library services. Where creating a physical infrastructure would be difficult and costly, the start-up costs of delivering virtual library services and digital information resources may be an attractive alternative.

The digital divide will not just be about access but also about the resources available at each access. From January 2002, publishers of '1,000 leading medical and scientific journals will offer electronic subscriptions at "free or deeply-reduced" rates to institutions in the developing world' in an initiative backed by the World Health Organization (**www.who.int/inf-pr-2001/en/pr2001-32.html**). The delivery of these journals is mutually beneficial in that it costs the publishers virtually nothing to make these journals available in digital format for the three years initially agreed but they gain significant market knowledge and customer loyalty. The developing nations gain access to an information resource they were very unlikely to have been able to afford previously.

Conclusion

There are some findings described in this book that are fundamental to our understanding of how libraries and librarians will develop in the digital future. Not least of these is the historical precedence that demonstrates the willingness of librarians to embrace new technologies to mechanize routine processes, improve services and to enhance user access to information resources. Libraries have co-operated to develop unified modes of information and service provision that are a model of economic and intellectual efficiency. For the hybrid libraries of the future the resources created, retained and managed will be from both the analogue and digital realms (and in some libraries the analogue will remain pre-eminent for decades or even centuries to come). For librarians the skills and abilities required to manage these resources will be more diverse as described in Chapter 9 'Digital librarians: new roles for the Information Age'. It is clear that librarians have the potential to be at the heart of society's digital future, but only by making radical and determined efforts to carve a place for themselves.

The future of the digital library is assured and we should like to reiterate some principles we consider essential to their healthy and sustainable development. The principles mentioned in Chapter 1 'Digital futures in current contexts' distinguish a digital library from other types of digital collections:

1 A digital library is a managed collection of digital objects.
2 The digital objects are created or collected according to principles of collection development.
3 The digital objects are made available in a cohesive manner, supported by services necessary to allow users to retrieve and exploit the resources just as they would any other library materials.
4 The digital objects are treated as long-term stable resources and appropriate processes are applied to them to ensure their quality and survivability.

Sustainable development is best guaranteed through demonstrating added value and services that are embraced and appreciated by the community served by each library. The development cost of technology is high but the services possible in the digital arena are exciting and groundbreaking. However, the principles listed above should enable those considering such innovative technical developments to keep in mind what makes libraries special: linking information to people, managing collections, providing cohesiveness of provision and service, sustainability, preservation, authenticity and quality.

Physical collections have been amassed over centuries and will not and should not be easily displaced by digital formats. These resources bear witness to the wisdom and cultural heritage of the world and must not be allowed to fall into disuse or dissolution, overwhelmed by a digital onslaught. Conversely, digital content created now and future 'born-digital' content is more fragile and short-lived by its very nature than the physical resources it may threaten. Creating and preserving fixity is one of the areas identified in this book as an essential role for librarians. We have shown that fixity can be delivered in a number of ways: resource description, finding aids, persistent identifiers, authentication and digital preservation. It is digital preservation that stands out as the most pressing and important issue facing librarians in this digital world. This single subject alone encompasses all the strategic management issues that librarians will be faced within the digital domain. The need for policy frameworks to ensure the continuity of data once created and stored are vital. Having the means to use the data into the future, preserving the information context of the original data and managing the rights to allow the user access are important and remain very difficult to resolve. Digital preservation is the cutting edge of digital librarianship and information management technology. The future librarian's role will be to find and promote islands of simplicity, and create secure harbours of stability, trust and authenticity, in this fluid world of information turmoil.

Bibliography

In this bibliography, we include only works that we have cited in the text. There are many useful guides to further reading in the field of digital libraries and digitization generally. Borgman (2000) has an excellent bibliography, and we also recommend perusal of the archives of *D-Lib Magazine* at **www.dlib.org** and *RLG DigiNews* at **www.rlg.org**. The National Library of Australia maintains a useful bibliography at **www.nla.gov.au/padi/format/bib.html**.

All URLs were checked at the beginning of November 2001.

Adachi, J. et al. (1999) Academic digital library and contents in Japan, *Literary and Linguistic Computing,* **14** (1), 131–45.

Adams, D. (1999) How to stop worrying and learn to love the Internet, *The Sunday Times* (29 August), available at **www.douglasadams.com/dna/19990901-00-a.html**

Adams, D. (1999) Predicting the Future, H2G2 Entry ID: A216433, available at **www.bbc.co.uk/h2g2/guide/A216433**

Alexander, M. and Prescott, A. (1998) The Initiatives for Access programme: an overview. In Carpenter, L., Shaw, S. and Prescott, A. (eds) *Towards the digital library*, The British Library.

Anderson, M. (1999) A tool for building digital libraries, *D-Lib Magazine,* **5** (2), available at **www.dlib.org/dlib/february99/02journalreview.html**

Appiah, A. (1997) Realizing the virtual library. In Dowler, L. (ed.) *Gateways to knowledge: the role of academic libraries in teaching, learning and research,* MIT Press.

Arms, W. (1995) Key concepts in the architecture of the digital library, *D-Lib Magazine*, (July), available at
www.dlib.org/dlib/July95/07arms.html

Arms, W. (1997) An architecture for information in digital libraries, *D-Lib Magazine*, (February), available at
www.dlib.org/dlib/february97/cnri/02arms1.html

Arms, W. (2000) *Digital libraries*, MIT Press.

Arnold, S. E. (2001) Arnold on pricing: disturbing trends ahead, *EContent*, **24** (1), 42–6.

Baker, N. (2000) Deadline: the author's desperate bid to save America's past, *The New Yorker* (24 July), 42–61.

Baker, N. (2001) *Double fold: libraries and the assault on paper*, Random House Trade.

Beagrie, N. (2000) Economy: some models for sustaining innovative content-based services. In Cranfield, V. (ed.), *Digitising journals: conference on future strategies for European libraries, Copenhagen, Denmark*, Danish National Library Authority.

Bearman, D. (1999) Reality and chimeras in the preservation of electronic records, *D-Lib Magazine,* **5** (4), available at
www.dlib.org/dlib/april99/bearman/04bearman.html

Bearman, D. and Trant, J. (1998) Authenticity of digital resources: towards a statement of requirements in the research process, *D-Lib Magazine* (June), 1–12, available at
www.dlib.org/dlib/june98/06bearman.html

Benjamin, A. (2001) Read alert, *The Guardian* (13 June), available at
www.guardian.co.uk/Archive/

Benjamin, W. (1992) The work of art in an age of mechanical reproduction. In *Illuminations*, Fontana Press.

Berners-Lee, T. (1999) *Weaving the web*, Orion Business Books.

Biddiscombe, R. (1996) *The end-user revolution*, Library Association Publishing.

Bide & Associates (2000) *Standards for electronic publishing: an overview*, The Hague, Koninklijke Bibliotheek.

Blagdon, J. (1998) Overview: managing the just-in-time library. in Day, J. and Hansen, T. (eds) *Managing the electronic library*, Bowker-Saur.

Block, M. (2001) Go where it is, part II, *Ex Libris,* available at
www.marylaine.com/exlibris/xlib95.html

Boddy, D. and Paton, R. (1998) *Management: an introduction*, Prentice Hall.

Bogen, M. et al. (2001) Requirements and architectures for administration and maintenance of digital object libraries. In *Museums and the web 2001*, Seattle, WA, available at
www.archimuse.com/mw2001/papers/bogen/bogen.html

Booth, A. and Walton, G. (eds) (2000) *Managing knowledge in health services*, Library Association Publishing.

Borgman, C. L. (2000) *From Gutenberg to the global information infrastructure: access to information in the networked world*, MIT Press.

Bowman, L. M. (2001a) Disappearing ink: e-book self-destructs, *cnet News.com* (8 August), available at
http://news.cnet.com/news/0-1005-200-6815857.html

Bowman, L. M. (2001b) Bush camp takes charge of Whitehouse.gov in transition, *cnet News.com* (9 January), available at
http://news.cnet.com/news/0-1005-201-4421306-0.html

Braude, R. M. (1999) Virtual or actual: the term library is enough. In *Bulletin of the Medical Librarians Association*, **87** (1), 85–7.

Braukmann, J. R. and Pedras, M. J. (1990) Preparing students for living in a technological society: a problem-solving approach to teaching, *Journal of Technology Education*, **1** (2), available at
http://scholar.lib.vt.edu/ejournals/JTE/v1n2/html/braukman.html

Bray, T. (1997) *Beyond HTML: XML and automated web processing*, available at
http://developer.netscape.com/viewsource/bray_xml.html

Brophy, P. (2001) *The library in the twenty-first century: new services for the information age*, Library Association Publishing.

Brophy, P. and Craven, J. (2001) Accessible library web sites: design for all. In *Library services for visually impaired people: a manual of best practice*, National Library for the Blind, available at
www.nlbuk.org/bpm/contents.html

Brown, J. S. and Duguid, P. (2000) *The social life of information*, Harvard Business School Press.

Buckland, M. K. (1992) Emanuel Goldberg, electronic document retrieval, and Vannevar Bush's Memex, *Journal of the American Society for Information Science*, **43** (4), 284–94.

Bunting, M. (2001) Digital futures: an agenda for a sustainable digital economy. In Wilsdon, J. and Miller, P. (eds) *Forum for the future*, available at
http://www.digitalfutures.org.uk/report.pdf

Burke, M. A. and McGuiness, C. M. (1997) An investigation of the paradigm shift from ownership to access in academic libraries, *International Journal of Electronic Library Research*, **1** (1), 3–24.

Busa, R. (1998) Concluding a life's safari from punched cards to world wide web. In Burnard, L., Deegan, M. and Short, H. (eds) *The digital demotic: a selection of papers from DRH97*, **10**, 3–12, OHC, King's College London.

Bush, V. (1945) As we may think, *Atlantic Monthly* (August), 101–8.

Caplan, P. (2000) International metadata initiatives: lessons in bibliographic control. In *Bicentennial conference on bibliographic control for the new millennium: confronting the challenges of networked resources and the web*, Library of Congress, Washington, DC, available at
http://lcweb.loc.gov/catdir/bibcontrol/caplan.html

Carpenter, J. (1999) *What makes a digital librarian? A critical analysis of the management culture needed for effective digital library development*, British Library Research and Innovation Centre, Report 174.

Castells, M. (1996) *The rise of the network society*, Blackwell.

Caterinicchia, D. (2001) Cut databases, Oracle chief says, *Federal Computer Week* (11 July), available at
www.fcw.com/fcw/articles/2001/0709/web-oracle-07-11-01.asp

Cave, M., Deegan, M. and Heinink, L. (2000) Copyright clearance in the Refugee Studies Centre digital library project, *RLG DigiNews*, **4** (5), available at
www.rlg.org/preserv/diginews/diginews4-5.html#feature1

CCSDS (2001) *Reference model for an Open Archival Information System (OAIS)*, Consultative Committee for Space Data Systems, CCSDS 650.0-R-1.2 Red Book, available at
http://ssdoo.gsfc.nasa.gov/nost/isoas/us/overview.html

CEDARS project (1999) *Metadata for digital preservation: the CEDARS project outline specification draft for public consultation*, available at
www.leeds.ac.uk/cedars/

Chapman, S.. (2001) Personal correspondence (16 August).

Chapman, S., Conway, P. and Kenney, A. R. (1999) Digital imaging and preservation microfilm: the future of the hybrid approach for the preservation of brittle books, *RLG DigiNews*, **3** (1), available at
www.thames.rlg.org/preserv/diginews/diginews3-1.html

Chartier, R. (1992) *The order of books*, translated by L. G. Cochrane, Stanford University Press.

Chaucer, G. (1988) *The Riverside Chaucer*, edited by L. D. Benson, Oxford

University Press.

Chisenga, J. (1998) A study of university libraries' home pages in sub-Saharan Africa, *Libri*, **48**, 49–57.

Conway, P. (1999) *The relevance of preservation in a digital world*, Northeast Document Conservation Centre, available at
www.nedcc.org/plam3/tleaf55.htm

Cox, A. and Ormes, S. (2001) *E-books*, Library and Information Briefings 96, available at
http://litc.sbu.ac.uk/publications/libs/libs96.pdf

Cox, R. J. (2000) The great newspaper caper: backlash in the digital age, *First Monday*, **5** (12), available at
http://firstmonday.org/issues/issue5_12/cox/index.html

Crawford, W. and Gorman, M. (1995) *Future libraries: dreams, madness, and reality*, American Library Association Editions.

Creth, S. (1996) Slouching toward the future or creating a new information environment. In *Follet Lecture Series: The electronic library*, University of Ulster, available at
www.ukoln.ac.uk/services/papers/follett/creth/paper.html

Cronin, B. (1998) Social dimensions of the digital revolution, *Journal of Information, Communication and Library Science*, **4** (4), 3–9.

Cullen, C. T. (2000) *Authentication of digital objects: lessons from a historian's research*, Authenticity in a digital environment, CLIR.

Day, M. (1999) Issues and approaches to preservation metadata. In *Joint RLG and NPO preservation conference: guidelines for digital imaging*, available at
www.rlg.org/preserv/joint/day.html

Deegan, M. (2001) Money makes the world go-around: finding further sources of funding. In *Digitisation solutions, HEDS conference*, available at
http://heds.herts.ac.uk/conf2001/heds2001_deegan.pdf

Deegan, M., King, E. and Steinvil, E. (2001) *British Library microfilmed newspapers and Oxford grey literature online*, available at
www.olivesoftware.com/bl_oxford.htm

DeGranopre, R. (2001) *Digitopia: the look of the new digital you*, AtRamdom.com.

Dempsey, L. and Weibel, S. (1996) The Warwick metadata workshop: a framework for the deployment of resource description, *D-Lib Magazine*, (July/August), available at
www.dlib.org/dlib/july96/07weibel.html

Dempsey, L. and Heery, R. (1997) *A review of metadata: a survey of current resource description formats*, available at **www.ukoln.ac.uk/metadata/desire/overview/rev_01.htm**

Denison, D. C. (2001) Web mapping is the newest phase in efforts to make the internet more navigable – and essential, *digitalMASS*, available at **http://digitalmass.boston.com/printer_f...=news/daily/04/04301/web-mapping.html**

Dillon, M. (2000) Metadata for web resources: how metadata works on the web. In *Bicentennial conference on bibliographic control for the new millennium: confronting the challenges of networked resources and the web*, Library of Congress, Washington, DC, available at **http://lcweb.loc.gov/catdir/bibcontrol/dillon.html**

Dolphin, P. (2001) Free pork pies for all?, *Library Association Record*, **103** (2), 104–5.

Dorner, D. D. (2000) The blurring of boundaries: digital information and its impact on collection management. In Gorman, G. E. (ed.) *International yearbook of library and information management: collection management*, Library Association Publishing.

Downes, L. and Mui, C. (1998) *Unleashing the killer app: digital strategies for market dominance*, Harvard Business School Press.

Drew, W. (2001) Questia: who is behind it?, *Web4Lib Discussion List*, available at **http://sunsite.berkeley.edu/Web4Lib/archive/0102/0006.html**

Dyson, E. (1997) *Release 2.0: a design for living in the digital age*, Broadway.

Ebert, R. (1998), *Yahoo! Internet Life* (September), available at **http://marylaine.com/exlibris/xlib27.html**

Elion, A. (1999) Technology focus: a window of opportunity, *Document Manager*, **7** (4), 32–4.

Feeney, M. (ed.) (1999) *Digital culture: maximising the nation's investment*, National Preservation Office.

Fisher, L. M. (1999) An interview with John Seely Brown, *Strategy and Business*, Fourth Quarter, 93–4.

Fosmire, M. and Yu, S. (2000) Free scholarly electronic journals: how good are they?, *Issues in Science and Technology Librarianship*, available at **www.library.ucsb.edu/istl/00-summer/refereed.html**

Fox, E. A. and Marchionini, G. (1998) Towards a worldwide digital library, *Communications of the ACM*, **41** (4), 29–32.

Frappaolo, C. (2001) Content is king – still, *e-doc*, **1** (6), 40–3.

French, J. C. and Viles, C. L. (1999) Personalized Information Environments: an architecture for customizable access to distributed digital libraries, *D-Lib Magazine*, **5** (6), available at
www.dlib.org/dlib/june99/french/06french.html

Frey, K. L. (1997) Business models and pricing issues in the digital domain. In Lee, S. H. (ed.) *Economics of digital information: collection, storage and delivery*, The Haworth Press.

Friedman, T. L. (2001) The wired serfs may soon rise up in Cyberland, *International Herald Tribune*, 8.

Gambles, A. (2001) The HeadLine Personal Information Environment, *D-Lib Magazine*, **7** (3), available at
www.dlib.org/dlib/march01/gambles/03gambles.html

Getz, M. (1997) Evaluating digital strategies for storing and retrieving scholarly information. In Lee, S. H. (ed.) *Economics of digital information: collection, storage and delivery*, The Haworth Press.

Gibbons, S. (2000a) Electronic ink, *The Librarian's eBook Newsletter*, **1** (1), available at
www.lib.rochester.edu/main/ebooks/newsletter1.1/vol1-e-ink.htm

Gibbons, S. (2000b) Some emerging ebook business models: netLibrary, Questia and ebrary, *Librarian's Ebook Newsletter*, **1** (2), available at
www.lib.rochester.edu/main/ebooks/newsletter1-2/vol2-business_models.htm

Gibbons, S. (2001) Ebooks: some concerns and surprises, *portal: Libraries and the Academy*, **1** (1), 71–5, available at
muse.jhu.edu/journals/portal_libraries_and_the_academy/v001/1.1gibbons.html

Gibbs, N. J. (2000) Ebooks: report on an on-going experiment, *Against the Grain*, **11** (6), 23–5, available at
www.shylibrarian.com/ebooks/articles/gibbslayer.htm

Gill, T. (2000) *Metadata and the world wide web*, Getty Research Institute, available at
www.getty.edu/research/institute/standards/intrometadata/

Gilliland-Swetland, A. (2000) *Setting the stage*, Getty Research Institute, available at
www.getty.edu/research/institute/standards/intrometadata/

Gleick, J. (2000) *Faster*, Abacus.

Gorman, M. (2000) From card catalogues to WebPACS: celebrating cataloguing in the 20th century. In *Library of Congress bicentennial conference on bibliographic control for the new millennium*, available at
http://lcweb.loc.gov/catdir/bibcontrol/gorman_paper.html

Gould, S. and Ebdon, R. (1999) *IFLA/UNESCO survey on digitisation and preservation*, IFLA Offices for UAP and International Lending, available at
www.unesco.org/webworld/mdm/survey_index_en.html

Gould, S. J. (1980) *The panda's thumb: more reflections on natural history*, W. W. Norton.

Granger, S. (2000) Emulation as a digital preservation strategy, *D-Lib Magazine*, **6** (10), available at
www.dlib.org/dlib/october00/granger/10granger.html

Greenstein, D. (2000) *Digital Library Federation draft strategy and business plan*, Digital Library Federation, available at
www.diglib.org/about/strategic.htm#archs/

Guenther, K. (2000) Designing and managing your digital library, *Computers in Libraries*, **20** (1), 34–9.

Guernsey, L. (2000) The library as the latest web venture, *New York Times on the Web* (15 June), available at
www.nytimes.com/library/tech/00/06/circuits/articles/15book.html

Gunter, B. (2001) Is TV good for you?, *Library Association Record*, **103** (9), 558–9.

Guthrie, K. (2000) Comments made during the closing panel session. In Cranfield, V. (ed.), *Digitising journals: future strategies for European libraries, Copenhagen, Denmark*, Danish National Library Authority.

Hakala, J. (1999) Uniform Resource Names, *Tietolinja News*, available at
www.lib.helsinki.fi/tietolinja/0199/urnart.html

Halm, J. V. (1999) The digital library as access management facilitator, *Information Services and Use*, **19** (4), 299–303.

Hastings, K. and Tennant, R. (1996) How to build a digital librarian, *D-Lib Magazine* (November), available at
www.dlib.org/dlib/november96/ucb/11hastings.html

Hazen, D., Horrell, J. and Merrill-Oldham, J. (1998) *Selecting research collections for digitization*, CLIR, available at
www.clir.org/pubs/reports/hazen/pub74.html

Heery, R., Powell, A. and Day, M. (1997) *Metadata*, UKOLN, The UK Office for Library and Information Networking, available at

http://agent.sbu.ac.uk/publications/libs/lib75.pdf

Hendley, T. (1998) *Comparison of methods and costs of digital preservation*, JISC/NPO studies on the preservation of electronic materials, British Library Research and Innovation Centre, Report 106.

Hill, L. L. et al. (1999) *Collection metadata solutions for digital library applications*, available at
http://citeseer.nj.nec.com/267118.html

Holdsworth, D. and Wheatley, P .(2000) *Emulation, preservation and abstraction*, available at
http://129.11.152.25/CAMiLEON/

Holdsworth, D. and Wheatley, P. (2001) Emulation, preservation and abstraction, *DigiNews*, **5** (4), available at
www.rlg.org/preserv/diginews/diginews5-4.html

Houston, A. L. and Chen, H. (2000) Electronic commerce and digital libraries. In Shaw, M., et al. (eds) *Handbook on electronic commerce*, Springer.

Howarth, A. (2000) Speech given by the Minister for the Arts at a seminar on the 'Role of the public library in delivering e-government', available at
www.davidhaynes.co.uk/alanhowarth.htm

Hyams, E. (2001) As much fun as possible, *Library Association Record*, **103** (7), 427–8.

Ince, D. (2001) *Dictionary of the Internet*, and CD-ROM bundle, Oxford University Press.

Jackson, W. (2001) *The net plumber*, available at
www.gcn.com/vol20_no2/tech-report/

Jones, M. and Beagrie, N. (2001) *Preservation management of digital materials: a handbook*, The British Library.

Jonscher, C. (2000) *Wired life*, Anchor.

Kenney, A. R. (1996) *Digital to microfilm conversion: a demonstration project 1994–96, Cornell University Library*, available at
www.cornell.library.edu/preservation/publications.html

Kenney, A. R. and Rieger, O. Y. (eds) (2000) *Moving theory into practice: digital imaging for libraries and archives*, Research Libraries Group.

Kenny, A. (1982) *The computation of style*, Pergamon Press.

Ketchell, D. S. (2000) Too many channels: making sense out of portals and personalisation, *Information Technology and Libraries*, **19** (4), 175–9.

Kilgour, F. G. (1998) *The evolution of the book*, Oxford University Press.

Klijn, E. and de Lusenet, Y. (2000) *In the picture: preservation and digitisation of European photographic collections*, The Hague: Koninklijke Bibliotheek.

Kuhn, T. (1970) *The structure of scientific revolutions*, University of Chicago Press.

Kuny, T. and Cleveland, G. (1998) The digital library: myths and challenges, *IFLA Journal,* **24** (2), 107–12.

Lagoze, C. and Payette, S. (2000) Metadata: principles, practices and challenges. In Kenney, A. R. and Rieger, O. Y. (eds) *Moving theory into practice: digital imaging for libraries and archives*, Research Libraries Group.

Lakos, A. and Gray, C. (2000) Personalized library portals as an organizational culture change agent: reflections on possibilities and challenges, *Information Technology and Libraries,* **19** (4), 169–73.

Lawrence, G. W. et al. (2000) *Risk management of digital information: a file format investigation*, Council on Library and Information Resources, available at
www.clir.org.pubs/pubs/reports/reports.html

Lawrence, S. and Giles, L. (1999) Accessibility of information on the web, *Nature,* **400,** 107–9.

Lee, S. D. (2000) *Digital imaging*, Library Association Publishing.

Lenzini, R. T. (1997) Having our cake and eating it too: combining aggregated and distributed resources. In Lee, S. H. (ed.) *Economics of digital information: collection, storage and delivery*, The Haworth Press.

Leonhardt, T. W. (2000) Electronic publications. In Gorman, G. E. (ed.) *International yearbook of library and information management: collection management*, Library Association Publishing.

Lerner, F. (1998) *The story of libraries from the invention of writing to the computer age*, Continuum.

Levy, J. (2000) Digital libraries and the problem of purpose, *D-Lib Magazine,* **6** (1), available at
www.dlib.org/dlib/january00/01levy.html

Lienhard, J. (1997) *Children, literacy and the computer*, American Libraries Association, available at
www.uh.edu/engines/alatalk.htm

Lievesley, D. and Jones, S. (1998) *An investigation into the digital preservation needs of universities and research funders: the future of unpublished research materials*, British Library Research and Innovation Centre, Report 109.

LITA (1999) Technology and library users: LITA experts identify trends to

watch, *ALA Midwinter Meeting*, available at
www.lita.org/committe/toptech/trendsmw99.htm

Lock, D. (1997) The nature and purpose of project management. In Lock, D. and Farrow, N. (eds) *The handbook of project management*, Gower.

Lorie, R. A. (2001) A project on preservation of digital data, *DigiNews,* **5** (3), available at
www.rlg.ac.uk/preserv/diginews/diginews5-3.html

Lucas, M. (2000) Demystifying metadata, *Mappa-Mundi*, available at
http://mappa.mundi.net/trip-m/metadata/

Lupovici, C. and Masanès, J. (2000) *Metadata for long-term preservation of electronic publications*, The Hague: Koninklijke Bibliotheek.

Maamria, K. (2001) Made in Japan, *Telecommunications Magazine*, (February), available at
www.telecommagazine.com/telecom/default.asp?journalicl=2&func= ARCHIVE

McDonald, A. (2000) Developing digital libraries: they won't work without people, *Refer,* **16** (2), 4–10.

MacKenzie, G. (2000) Searching for solutions: electronic records problems worldwide, *Managing Information*, (July/August), 59–65.

McKnight, C., Dillon, A. and Richardson, J. (1991) *Hypertext in context*, Cambridge University Press.

MacLeod, R. (2000) Comment: what's the difference between a gateway and a portal?, *Internet Resources Newsletter,* **70,** available at
www.hw.ac.uk/libWWW/irn/irn70/irn70.html

McPherson, M. (1997) Managing digital libraries. In *CSIRO Australia: information, management & technology conference*, available at
www.usq.edu.au/library/homepgs/mcpherso/csiro.htm

Maly, K., Nelson, M. L. and Zubair, M. (1999) Smart objects, dumb archives: a user-centric, layered digital library framework, *D-Lib Magazine,* **5** (3), available at
www.dlib.org/dlib/march99/maly/03maly.html

Mannerheim, J. (2000) The WWW and our digital heritage: the new preservation tasks of the library community. In *66th IFLA Council and General Conference,* Jerusalem, Israel, available at
www.ifla.org/IV/ifla66/66cp.htm

Martin S. K. (2001) Forty years, and we're still here, *portal: Libraries and the Academy,* **1** (2), v–viii, available at

http://muse.jhu.edu/journals/portal_libraries_and_the_academy/v001/1.2martin.html

Maynard, S. (2000) *Library and information statistics tables for the UK 2000*, Library & Information Statistics Unit, available at **www.lboro.ac.uk/departments/dils/lisu/list00/list00.html**

Megill, K. A. (1997) *The corporate memory: information management in the electronic age*, Bowker-Saur.

Mercer, L. S. (2000) Measuring the use and value of electronic journals and books, *Issues in Science and Technology Librarianship*, (Winter), available at **www.library.ucsb.edu/istl/00-winter/article1.html**

Miller, E. (1998) An introduction to the resource description framework, *D-Lib Magazine* (May), available at **www.dlib.org/dlib/may98/miller/05miller.html**

Miller, P. (2000a) Interoperability: what is it and why should I want it?, *Ariadne*, **24**, available at **www.ariadne.ac.uk/issue24/interoperability/intro.html**

Miller, P. (2000b) Collected wisdom: some cross-domain issues of collection level description, *D-Lib Magazine*, **6** (9), available at **www.dlib.org/dlib/september00/miller/09miller.html**

Miksa, F. (1989) The future of reference II: a paradigm of academic library organization, *College and Research Libraries News*, **50**, 780–90.

Morgan, K. and Reade, T. (2000) Pioneering portals: MyLibrary@NCState, *Information Technology and Libraries*, **19** (4), 191–8.

Muswazi, P. (2000) Digital library and information services in southern Africa, *Information Development*, **16**, 75–82.

Naughton, J. (1999) *A brief history of the future: the origins of the internet*, Phoenix.

Negroponte, N. (1995) *Being digital*, Coronet.

Nuttall, C. (2001) Internet map to help stop the rot, *The Standard Europe*, available at **http://europe.thestandard.com/article/**

Nyce, J. and Kahn, P. (eds) (1991) *From Memex to hypertext: Vannevar Bush and the mind's machine*, Academic Press.

Ormes, S. (2000) It's the end of the world as we know it (and I feel fine) or how I learned to stop worrying and love the e-book, *Ariadne*, **26**, available at **www.ariadne.ac.uk/issue26/e-book/**

Owen, J. S. M. and Wiercx, A. (1996) *Knowledge models for networked library services: final report*, Office of Official Publications of the European Communities, PROLIB/KMS 16905.

Pack, T. (2001a) Content unchained: the new value web, *EContent*, **24** (1), 34–8.

Pack, T. (2001b) Profile: Meckler's media methods, *EContent*, **24** (1), 66–7.

Parapadakis, G. (2000) Portal design, *e-doc magazine*, **1** (2), 53.

Parker, S. et al. (2001) *The bidding culture and local government: effects on the development of public libraries, archives and museums*, School of Information Studies, University of Northumbria, available at
http://is.unn.ac.uk/imri/

Parry, D. (1998) *Virtually new: creating the digital collection*, Library and Information Commission.

Passant, N. (1995) *The realisation of Repro 2000*, 3M UK plc.

Pearson, D. (2000) Letter, *Times Literary Supplement* (8 September).

Pinfield, S. et al. (1998) Realising the hybrid library, *The New Review of Information Networking*, **4**, 3–22.

Pitti, D. V. (1999) Encoded Archival Description: an introduction and overview, *D-Lib Magazine*, **5** (11), 1–9, available at
www.dlib.org/dlib/november99/11pitti.html

Pope, M. (1975) *The story of decipherment*, Thames and Hudson.

Powell, A. (1999) *Metadata collection level description*, available at
www.ukoln.ac.uk/metadata/cld/simple/

Powell, A., Heaney, M. and Dempsey, L. (2000) RSLP collection description, *D-Lib Magazine*, **6** (9), available at
www.dlib.org/dlib/september00/powell/09powell.html

Preserving digital information: report of the task force on archiving digital information (1996) The Commission on Preservation and Access and The Research Libraries Group.

Price, D. J. (1961) *Science since Babylon*, Yale University Press.

Prime, E. (2000) The spider, the fly and the internet, *EContent*, **23** (3), available at
www.ecmag.net/Magazine/articlelist.html

Public libraries: good managers missing – report on Recruit, Retain and Lead: the public library workforce study, Department of Information Studies, University of Sheffield (2001) *Library Association Record*, **105** (3), 260.

Puglia, S. (1999) The costs of digital imaging projects, *RLG DigiNews*, **3** (5), available at
www.rlg.ac.uk/preserv/diginews/diginews3-5.html

Ranganathan, S. R. (1931) *Five laws of library science*, Madras Library Association.

Rayward, W. B. (1994) Visions of Xanadu: Paul Otlet (1868–1944) and hypertext, *Journal of the American Society for Information Science*, **45** (4), 235–50.

Reich, V. and Rosenthal, D. S. H. (2001) LOCKSS: a permanent web publishing and access system, *D-Lib Magazine*, **7** (6), available at
www.dlib.org/dlib/june01/reich/06reich.html

Rennie, J. (1997) Civilizing the internet, *Scientific American*, **276** (3), 6.

Robins, J. (1999) Sell first, print later, *The Independent* (19 October), 13.

Robinson, P. (ed.) (1996) *Chaucer: The Wife of Bath's prologue on CD-ROM*, Cambridge University Press.

Robinson, S. (2001) Wiring Africa's new frontiers: patience helped turn an online mailing list into an Internet portal, *Time Magazine*, available at
www.time.com/time/europe/af/magazine/1,9868,99037,00.html

Rodríguez, A. (2001) The digital divide: the view from Latin America and the Caribbean. In *67th IFLA Council and General Conference*, available at
www.ifla.org/IV/ifla67/papers/111-114e.pdf/

Ross, S. (1993) Historians, machine-readable information, and the past's future. In Ross, S. and Higgs, E. (eds) *Electronic information resources and historians: European perspectives*, Max-Planck-Institut für Geschichte.

Ross, S. and Gow, A. (1999) *Digital archaeology: rescuing neglected and damaged data resources*, A JISC/NPO study within the Electronic Libraries (eLib) Programme on the preservation of electronic materials.

Rothenberg, J. (2000a) Preserving authentic digital information. In *Authenticity in a digital environment*, available at
www.clir.org/pubs/reports/pub92/rothenberg.html

Rothenberg, J. (2000b) *Using emulation to preserve digital documents*, The Hague, Koninklijke Bibliotheek.

Rowley, J. (2000) Portal power, *Managing Information*, **7** (1), 62, 64.

Rumsey, S. (2001) Exam papers on-line, *Ariadne*, **26,** available at
www.ariadne.ac.uk/issue26/exam-papers/

Rusbridge, C. (1998) Towards the hybrid library, *D-Lib Magazine* (July/August), available at
www.dlib.org/dlib/july98/rusbridge/07rusbridge.html

Russell, K. (1999) *Digital preservation: ensuring access to digital materials into the future*, Leeds: CEDARS Project, available at
www.leeds.ac.uk/cedars/Chapter.htm

Sadagopan, S. (2000) Librarians in the dot.com era, *SRELS Journal of Information Management*, **37** (1), 1–4.

St Pierre, M. and LaPlant, William P. Jr (1998) *Issues in crosswalking content metadata standards*, National Information Standards Organization (NISO), available at
www.niso.org/crsswalk.html

Schummer, J. (1999) Coping with the growth of chemical knowledge: challenges for chemistry documentation, education, and working chemists, *Educación Química*, **10** (2), available at
www.uni-karlsruhe.de/~ed01/Jslit/eduquim.htm

Seaman, D. (1999) Digital libraries in the new millennium: partners, publishers, potentials and pitfalls. In *3rd IFIP/ICCC conference on electronic publishing*, available at
www5.hk-r.se/elpub99.nsf/

Shaughnessy, T. W. (1997) Digital information and the library: planning and policy issues, *Journal of Library Administration*, **24** (4), 3–14.

Shibanda, G. G. (2001) Skills and competencies for digital information management in Africa. In *67th IFLA Council and General Conference*, available at
www.ifla.org/IV/ifla67/papers/009–143e.pdf/

Singh, S. (1999) *The code book: the science of secrecy from Ancient Egypt to quantum cryptography*, Fourth Estate.

Sosteric, M. (1998) At the speed of thought: pursuing non–commercial alternatives to scholarly communication, *ARL Newsletter*, (200), available at
www.arl.org/newsltr/200/sosteric.html

Spink, A. and Cool, C. (1999) Education for digital libraries, *D–Lib Magazine*, **5** (5), available at
www.dlib.org/dlib/may99/05spink.html

Standage, T. (1998) *The Victorian internet*, Weidenfeld & Nicolson.

Sullivan, D. (2001) WebTop Search Rage Study, *The Search Engine Report*, available at
http://searchenginewatch.com/sereport/01/02/02– searchrage.html

Swade, D. (2000) *The cogwheel brain*, Little, Brown and Company.

Tallim, P. and Zeeman, J. C. (1995) *Electronic Data Interchange: an overview of*

EDI standards for libraries, IFLANET, UDT Series on Data Communication Technologies and Standards for Libraries, available at
www.ifla.org/VI/5/reports/rep4/rep4.htm

Tammaro, A. M. (2000) Document delivery as an alternative to subscription. In Connoly, P. and Reidy, D. (eds) *The digital library: challenges and solutions for the new millennium*, IFLA.

Tanner, S. (1995) *Rolls-Royce and Associates EDM – 5 years on!*, 3M UK plc.

Tanner, S. (2000) Project management. In *Planning and implementing a digitisation project, HEDS conference*, available at
http://heds.herts.ac.uk/conf/st.pdf

Tanner, S. (2001) Planning your digitisation project: technologies and skills. In *JUGL conference*, available at
http://heds.herts.ac.uk/resources/papers/Planning_HEDS_JUGL.pdf

Tanner, S. and Lomax, J. (1999) Digitisation: how much does it really cost?, *DRH99*, King's College London, available at
http://heds.herts.ac.uk/resources/costing.html

Taylor, D. J. (2001) Curse of the teenage cybergeeks: review of Michael Lewis, The Future Just Happened, *Sunday Times Culture* (15 July), 34–5.

Tennant, R. (1999) Skills for the new millennium, *The Library Journal Digital*, (January), available at
www.libraryjournal.com/

Trippe, B. (2001) Content management technology: a booming market, *EContent*, **24** (1), 22–7.

Veen, J. (2001) *The art and science of web design*, New Riders.

Venters, C. C. and Cooper, M. (1999) *A review of content-based image retrieval*, University of Manchester, available at
www.jtap.ac.uk/reports/htm/jtap-054.html

Waters, D. J. (ed.) (1997) *Digital archiving: the report of the CPA/RLG Task Force*, Preservation and digitization: principles, practices and policies, National Preservation Office.

Wendler, R. (2000) Why are there so many catalogues and what can we do about it? In *Descriptive metadata*, Tufts University, available at
www.tufts.edu/tccs/at/digital-library/RobinW.ppt

Werf-Davelaar, T. van der (1999) Long-term preservation of electronic publications – the NEDLIB project, *D-Lib Magazine*, **5** (9), available at
www.dlib.org/dlib/september99/vanderwerf/09vanderwerf.html

Wettengel, M. (1998) German unification and electronic records. In Higgs, E. (ed.) *History and electronic artefacts*, Clarendon Press.

Wheatley, P. (2000) Migration: a CAMiLEON discussion paper, available at **http://129.11.152.25/CAMiLEON**

Whitfield, S. (1998) A database for cataloguing Chinese and Central Asian manuscripts: the International Dunhuang Project. In Carpenter, L., Shaw, S. and Prescott, A. (eds) *Towards the digital library*, The British Library.

Whitfield, S. (1999) The International Dunhuang Project: addressing the problem of access and conservation of a scattered manuscript collection. In *DRH99*, King's College London, available at **www.kcl.ac.uk/humanities/cch/drhahc/drh/abst20.htm**

Wilson, M. (2000) Understanding the needs of tomorrow's library user: rethinking library services for the new age, *Australasian Public Libraries and Information Services*, **13** (2), 81–6.

Wolf, G. (1995) The curse of Xanadu, *Wired*, (June), available at **www.wired.com/wired/archive/3.06/xanadu_pr.html**

Woodley, M. (2000) *Crosswalks: the path to universal access?*, The Getty Research Institute, available at **www.getty.edu/research/institute/standards/intrometadata/2_articles/woodley/**

Yoder, S. M. (2000) Sustainability through integration case study. In Kenney, A. R. and Rieger, O. Y. (eds) *Moving theory into practice: digital imaging for libraries and archives*, Research Libraries Group.

Yourcenar, M. (1986) *Memoirs of Hadrian*, Penguin Books.

Zweig, R. W. (1998) Lessons from the Palestine Post project, *Literary and Linguistic Computing*, **13** (2), 89–96.

Glossary

The *Dictionary of the Internet* from Oxford University Press (2001) is also recommended for terms not contained in this glossary.

AACR	Anglo-American Cataloguing Rules
ACDP	Australian Co-operative Digitisation Project
AHDS	Arts and Humanities Data Service
ALA	American Library Association
ASCII	American Standard Code for Information Interchange
Bandwidth	The amount of data that may be transmitted through networks in a fixed amount of time, usually expressed in bits or bytes per second (bps)
Bath Profile	An international Z39.50 specification for library applications and resource description
BICI	Book Item and Component Identifier standard
bit depth	The number of bits per pixel in a digital image. For instance, 1-bit is black and white and 8-bit is 256 shades of grey
BLCMP	Birmingham Libraries Co-operative Mechanisation Project
Bluetooth	A wireless communications protocol providing short-range wireless links between electronic devices

Boolean	Boolean searches are made from logic operators to construct more complex searches in a database. There are three logical Boolean operators: AND, OR and NOT
born digital	A resource which has been created in a digital format without being analogue at any intermediary stage
CAMiLEON	Creating Creative Archiving at Michigan and Leeds: Emulating the Old and the New
CCSDS	Consultative Committee for Space Data Systems
CEDARS	CURL Exemplars in Digital ARchiveS
COM	Computer Output to Microfilm
compression	The translation of data to a more compact form for storage or transmission
crosswalk	A specification for mapping one metadata standard to another
DAISY	Digital Audio-based Information System
DCMI	Dublin Core Metadata Initiative
DDC	Dewey Decimal Classification
DIEPER	DIgitized European PERiodicals
Digitization	The process of converting an analogue original into any digital format
d-journal	A journal initially available only in paper format that has been digitized
DOI	Digital Object Identifier
DTD	Document Type Definition
Dublin Core	A metadata element set that consists of 15 descriptive data elements
DVD	Digital Versatile Disk also known as Digital Video Disk
EAD	Encoded Archival Description
EDI	Electronic Data Interchange
EdNA	Education Network Australia
e-journal	A journal available in electronic format that is born digital.
eLib	UK Electronic Libraries Programme
expert system	An artificial intelligence computer application

	that uses a knowledge base of human expertise to aid in solving problems
GIS	Geographic Information System
GML	Generalized Markup Language
GUI	Graphical User Interface
harvesting	Gathering, indexing and accessing internet information using an automated system
HEDS	Higher Education Digitisation Service
HTML	Hypertext Markup Language
HTTP	Hypertext Transfer Protocol
HUMI	HUmanities Media Interface
HURIDOCS	Human Rights Information and Documentation Systems International
hypertext	A nonlinear system of information browsing and retrieval that contains associative links to other related content and documents
ICAAP	International Consortium for Alternative Academic Publication
ICONCLASS	A system of letters and numbers used to classify the iconography of works of art
ICT	Information Communications Technology
I-mode	An open international standard for applications that use wireless communication, e.g. internet access from a mobile phone
information gateway	see subject gateway
interoperability	The capability of divergent systems to exchange data, usually through a mediating system
intranet	An internet-style network belonging to an organization, usually a corporation, accessible only by the organization's members, employees, or others with authorization
IP	Internet Protocol
ISAD(G)	International Council of Archivists standard for describing archival structures
ISBN	International Standard Book Number
ISO	International Organization for Standardization
ISP	Internet Service Provider

ISSN	International Standard Serial Number
JAVA	A high-level programming language developed by Sun Microsystems that is frequently used to add functionality to websites
JIDI	JISC Image Digitization Initiative
JISC	Joint Information Systems Committee
JSTOR	Journal Storage – The Scholarly Journal Archive
KDEM	Kurzweil Data Entry Machine
LCSH	Library of Congress Subject Headings
LOCKSS	Lots Of Copies Keeps Stuff Safe, a digital preservation initiative
MARC	MAchine-Readable Cataloguing record. A standard way to represent bibliographic information in library management systems
MEDLINE	A medical database
MeSH	Medical Subject Headings
metasearch engine	A search engine which invokes a number of other search engines in order to give better retrieval from large and complex information spaces such as the web
metacrawler	A type of metasearch engine which searches and indexes the web without human intervention
metadata	Structured data about a digital resource
metadata schema	An application or formal definition of the elements and rules for implementing a metadata standard
micro payment	A process supported by Micro Payment Transfer Protocol to facilitate very small payments for services received via the internet
middleware	Software that mediates between an application program and a network
MIRACLE	Music Information Resources Assisted Computer Library Exchange
MODELS	MOving to Distributed Environments for Library Services
Mosaic	A free internet browser originally produced

	by the National Center for Supercomputing Applications (NCSA)
NACSIS-ELS	Electronic Library Service of the Japanese National Center for Science Information Systems
NEDLIB	Networked European Deposit Library
NeLH	UK National electronic Library for Health
NIJL	National Institute for Japanese Literature
NISO	National Information Standards Organization
NOF	New Opportunities Fund
NORDINFO	Nordic Council for Scientific Information
NPO	National Preservation Office
NSF	National Science Foundation
NZDL	New Zealand Digital Library
OAI	Open Archives Initiative
OAIS	Open Archival Information System
OCLC	Online Computer Library Center
OCR	Optical Character Recognition. A software process that interprets the textual portion of digital images and converts it to formatted or unformatted digital text
OED	Oxford English Dictionary
OPAC	Online Public Access Catalogue
OTA	Oxford Text Archive
PADI	Preserving Access to Digital Information
PANDORA	Preserving and Accessing Networked Documentary Resources of Australia
PDA	Personal Digital Assistant. A handheld device that combines computing, telephone/fax, and networking features
PDF	Adobe Portable Document Format. A popular file format for digital documents
PERL	Practical Extraction and Report Language. A programming language that has become one of the most popular languages for writing programs invoked within websites
PIE	Personalized Information Environment

pixel	The smallest of the picture elements that make up an electronic image; pixels are located in a grid array in which each pixel has its own location and only one value of brightness or colour
portal	An entry point to the internet that offers value-added services such as directories, searching, news, and links to related websites
PubMed	A medical database
PURL	Persistent Uniform Resource Locator
RDF	Resource Description Framework
rekeying	The process of keyboard entry for textual content to convert texts into a digital format
resolution	Number of pixels (in both height and width) making up a digital image. The higher the resolution of an image, the greater its visual definition and density
RLG	Research Libraries Group
RSLP	Research Support Libraries Programme
scanning	The process of digital capture to an image format
search engine	A program that searches across documents or the internet for specified keywords and returns a list of locations where the keywords were found
SEPIA	Safeguarding European Photographic Images for Access
SGML	Standard Generalized Markup Language
SICI	Serial Item and Contribution Indentifier standard
SPARC	Scholarly Publishing and Academic Resources Coalition
STM	science, technology and medicine
subject gateway	An internet portal that provides access to selected and catalogued resources in a specific subject category or set of categories
tagging	The process of adding markup elements to convert plain text into, e.g. SGML, HTML or XML

TEI	Text Encoding Initiative
TIFF	Tagged Image File Format. A widely used file format for digital images
UKOLN	UK Office of Library and Information Networking
UNICODE	A 16-bit character coding system, intended to cover all the world's written languages
URL	Uniform Resource Location
URN	Uniform Resource Names
UVC	Universal Virtual Computer
VBL	Virtual Branch Library
vortal	A vertical portal focused upon one subject or niche market
W3C	World Wide Web Consortium
WAP	An open international standard for applications that use wireless communication, e.g. internet access from a mobile phone
WebTV	The technology that enables access to the web via a television
world wide web	A graphical client-server information system that uses the internet to access computers containing hypertext (HTML or XML) documents. Not all internet servers are part of the world wide web
XML	eXtensible Markup Language. A markup language written in SGML, designed especially for web documents
XSL	eXtensible Stylesheet Language. A style sheet system for use with XML
Z39.50	An information retrieval protocol for library applications. A standard intended to enable the user of one system to search and retrieve data from another system using local search and retrieval commands
Z39.56-1996	SICI code creation standard

266

Index